VERBAL IMAGINATION

VERBAL IMAGINATION

Coleridge and the Language of Modern Criticism

A. C. Goodson

New York   Oxford
OXFORD UNIVERSITY PRESS
1988

Oxford University Press

Oxford New York Toronto
Delhi Bombay Calcutta Madras Karachi
Petaling Jaya Singapore Hong Kong Tokyo
Nairobi Dar es Salaam Cape Town
Melbourne Auckland

and associated companies in
Berlin Ibadan

Copyright © 1988 by Oxford University Press, Inc.

Published by Oxford University Press, Inc.
200 Madison Avenue, New York, New York 10016

Oxford is a registered trademark of Oxford University Press

Library of Congress Cataloging-in-Publication Data
Goodson, A. C. (Alfred Clement), 1946–
Verbal imagination.
Bibliography: p.
Includes index.
1. Coleridge, Samuel Taylor, 1772–1834 — Knowledge — Language
and languages. 2. Coleridge, Samuel Taylor, 1772–1834 — Knowledge —
Literature. 3. Coleridge, Samuel Taylor, 1772–1834 — Influence.
4. Criticism — Great Britain — History. 5. English philology —
Study and teaching (Higher) — England — Cambridge
(Cambridgeshire) — History. I. Title.
PR4487.L33G66 1988   821'.7   87-31456
ISBN 0-19-505450-4

1 2 3 4 5 6 7 8 9

Printed in the United States of America
on acid-free paper

For Judith

οὐκ ἔστ᾽ ἐραστὴς ὅστις οὐκ ἀεὶ φιλεῖ.

Euripides, *Troades*

Contents

III   Coleridge's Poetics of Response

Abbreviations of Citations to Standard Texts

N.B.: Works cited occasionally, as indicated in notes, are not included in this list.

AR   *Aids to Reflection,* 2nd. ed. (London, 1825).

BL   *Biographia Literaria*, ed. J. Shawcross, 2 vols. (Oxford: Oxford University Press, 1907; rpt. 1971).

CC   *Collected Works of Samuel Taylor Coleridge*, gen. ed. Kathleen Coburn (Princeton: Princeton University Press, 1969–).

Individual volumes cited by number as follows:

CC 1   *Lectures 1795 on Politics and Religion*, ed. Lewis Patton and Peter Mann, 1971.

CC 2   *The Watchman*, ed. Lewis Patton, 1970.

CC 4   *The Friend*, ed. Barbara E. Rooke, 2 vols, 1969.

CC 10   *On the Constitution of Church and State*, ed. John Colmer, 1976.

CC 13   *Logic*, ed. J. R. de J. Jackson, 1981.

CL   *Collected Letters of Samuel Taylor Coleridge*, ed. Earl Leslie Griggs, 6 vols. (Oxford: Clarendon Press, 1956–71).

CN   *The Notebooks of Samuel Taylor Coleridge*, ed. Kathleen Coburn, 3 vols. (Princeton: Princeton University Press, 1957–).

CPW   *The Complete Poetical Works of Samuel Taylor Coleridge*, ed. Ernest H. Coleridge, 2 vols. (Oxford: Clarendon Press, 1912).

CSC   *Coleridge on the Seventeenth Century*, ed. R. F. Brinkley (Durham, N.C.: Duke University Press, 1955).

LBP   Coleridge and Wordsworth, *Lyrical Ballads 1798*, ed. W. J. B. Owen (Oxford: Oxford University Press, 1967; 2nd. ed. rpt. 1971). The "Preface" is cited from the text of this edition.

LR *Literary Remains of Samuel Taylor Coleridge*, ed. H. N. Coleridge (London: William Pickering, 1836–39).

PL *The Philosophical Lectures of Samuel Taylor Coleridge*, ed. Kathleen Coburn (London: Pilot Press, 1949).

SC *Coleridge's Shakespearean Criticism*, ed. Thomas M. Raysor, 2 vols. (Cambridge, Mass.: Harvard University Press, 1930).

TT *Table Talk and Omniana of Samuel Taylor Coleridge*, ed. T. Ashe (London: George Bell, 1884).

Introduction

Coleridge is the Ancient Mariner of English critical tradition, an ancestral voice inspiring allegiance from generation to generation while exciting Johnsonian scepticism and triple-thinking. His importance as cultural arbiter was recognized in an early essay by Mill, and it has been confirmed in our own time and condition by Raymond Williams. While their enlarged understanding has gone mostly unremarked by Coleridge's modern adherents, influential opinion since Leavis has discounted his defense of poetry along with his metaphysical aspiration, abandoning the example of his responsive reading. Scholarship has been catching up with this imposing archive in the meantime, but to limited effect among professional readers. Its dispersion, and the occasional nature of the notebooks and marginalia in particular, make his critical achievement difficult to command and assess. The transmission of his understanding by I. A. Richards counts among the deeper causes of his diminished authority. Coleridge's situation in the culture of criticism is a focal one, and should compel attention at a time when critical values are under stress everywhere. It is not only that his latter-day reception is symptomatic. The quality of his commitment remains worth considering for what it offers modern reading.

I have tried in this book to approach Coleridge's idea of poetry as both a monument and a living resource. By drawing him into a reflection on the formation of modern criticism, I wanted to bring his way of reading to bear on current mediations of his position: on Cambridge English and its institutional inheritors. For it is through this dominant critical idiom that he is known to most readers now. Richards established the new school on Coleridgean foundations, shaping a sense of his master's achievement that is widely accepted and often presumed on by readers hostile to the romantic legacy. They have been with us since Richards's time, and Frank Lentricchia's broadside, in *After the New Criticism*, against everything associated with Coleridge's name shows how influential they have become. An effective reply to so peremptory a challenge must of course recur to the archive. But it should also take account of the process by which a metaphysical critic was constructed from the bits and pieces of an ambitious philosophical aspiration. The metaphysical critic came to grief in the first volume of the *Biographia*, but the effort has encouraged continuance despite his afterthoughts and a critical testament evincing a less cloistered response to literature.

Confronting the Coleridge we know with a more expansive figure means qualifying the basically idealist version of his poetics promoted by Richards—not because it is entirely wrong but because it is partial and often misleading. Despite a considerable secondary literature on Coleridge's dissenting attitude and his engagement in the scientific and political culture of the 1790s, his formulae for imagination remain the standard version of his position—as if they encompassed his horizon. Recent studies have complicated our picture of Coleridge on imagination, showing how deeply rooted his thinking was in the native element. Kant and Schelling provided him with an orientation and a terminology, certainly, but the aesthetic line of his critical reflection counts for less in his response to writing than commentators have supposed. Powerful as the German idea was to prove, his sense of imagination had a broader base and bearing. Thomas McFarland was already insisting in 1969 that what Coleridge meant by the word was consistent with what we ordinarily take it to mean. More recently he has observed, provocatively, that the critical formulation of "imagination is primarily a connective developed because of Coleridge's commitment to systematic philosophizing. It would not appear to be rewarding, accordingly, to try to make very much critically of its presence in particular poems."[1] The revision of Richards is advanced, then, yet it has only begun to yield alternative accounts of Coleridge's poetics.

Preeminent among these is a paralinguistic understanding derived from Coleridge's erratic meditation on language. Richards's real originality as a commentator lies in his recognition of the large significance of a few notes pointing to poetic values at odds with those codified by imagination. Yet he did not pursue it to this end, in part because of the limitations of the texts he had to hand, but also because a linguistic idea of the workings of imagination was his goal. His synthesis is interesting now mainly for its impact on the formation of the new criticism. It remains an essential part of the story because it shows how this speculative notion of Coleridge's poetics became the cornerstone of an institutional way of reading which remains current, sometimes in surprising places. Against this background, Coleridge has become the scapegoat for those who would liberate our responses from the prison house of language.

Coleridge's distinctive approach to language emerges in his early responses to Hartley, Tooke, and Locke. Broadly speaking, his symbolic understanding represents an effort to save language from fealty to the images of nature, to save it for thinking. The implications for poetry are striking but not very clearly developed. These are most evident in his ambivalence about the image in the poetic setting. His turn against the descriptive idiom of the poetry of sensibility is based in part on a suspicion of "distinct, clear, full made Images" which fix the reader's attention on the forms of nature at the expense of the meditative process at the heart of the exercise. His attack in the *Biographia* on Wordsworth's "matter-of-factness" lies at the end of this line. It can be seen to stem from a divergence within the "Preface" between conflicting ideas of language. For Coleridge it was always a question of "how language and the human mind act and react on each other." The countervailing emphasis on "the best objects from which the best part of language is originally derived" is what he contested forever after.

A discussion of this linguistic excursion and its poetic consequences in scholarly and critical contexts occupies the center of the book. It is introduced in Part I in the environment of Coleridge's assimilation by Cambridge English. A preliminary idea of his symbolic understanding is presented at the outset in counterpoint to Richards's derivative "science of the future," semasiology. The chronological inversion is meant to encourage readers who are interested in thinking through some of the large issues before taking the plunge into the scholarly fine print. A full exposition of Coleridge on language involves detailed textual argument, including related work in the history of ideas and the continuing romantic reception. It lies at the heart of the project and remains essential for grasping the impact of an idea of language on a way of reading. Though it starts from current research in the field, Part II presumes familiarity with the situation of poetic language in the modern institutional setting as sketched in Part I. The direction of my argument will, I think, make best sense in this established context.

The renovation of Coleridge on language undertaken by Richards and described in my opening chapter lies at the confluence of romantic and modern, of older and newer senses of literary meaning and value. It represents an effort to continue, under modern auspices, a commitment to poetry, broadly conceived, which Coleridge had himself revised for his contemporaries. With imagination as his vehicle, Richards expanded on Coleridge's recognition of the essential interiority of the poetic image. As I shall be suggesting, he went further, in response to the challenge of science, than his informant was prepared to do, consigning poetry to a sort of cognitive Xanadu: an artificial paradise of the mind. Science was the contrary term by which poetry was to be conceived and defended, as Coleridge had led the way in arguing. The linguistic criteria which Richards spun out to distinguish them divides more than two zones of discourse, however. It divides two worlds. There is no better way to grasp the significance of Coleridge's integrated understanding than to present it in conjunction with this impossible scission. And no better way, I would suggest, of pondering the premises of modern reading as it proceeds from such a division of language, and of experience.

What happened when Coleridge was subjected to this treatment is exemplified in the contentious career of F. R. Leavis. The turn against Richards, against his science of meaning, and finally against Coleridge himself appeared at the time a constructive act of resistance. Yet Leavis's insistence on "English" as the basis of the new reading depends, as commentators of various persuasions have noticed, on an untenable abstraction. It is deeply parochial and isolationist in implication. Dogmatic about language, Leavis lacked the resources to defend his own literalism. His particularist assumptions undermine his interpretations of major texts, subverting from within an exclusive and influential view of English tradition.

Reaction against Richards lay at the bottom of it, for Leavis had showed himself to be an alert respondent to the new poetics of Hopkins, Eliot, and Pound. The penetrating reflection on language which so distinguishes Coleridge's thinking about writing was missing in Leavis because it had been misconstrued by his mentor. In promoting semasiology on the basis of a supposititious understanding of Coleridge on language, Richards buried his informant's way of reading. The consequences are conspicuous in Leavis and in the institutional version of the new criticism fostered by John Crowe Ransom. William Empson's pursuit of a linguistic idea of poetic process provides a contrasting instance of English formalism in the moment of Jakobsonian structuralism. Empson followed Coleridge around Richards, not through him, challenging the central assumptions of Cambridge English on Coleridgean principles.

It is an irony of the large historical variety that Raymond Williams should have occupied rooms at Jesus College, Cambridge, where Coleridge once lodged. Their common cause has been entirely overlooked by commentators for whom Williams is counted among the Marxists, Coleridge among the born-again Tories. From such quarters they would appear to have little indeed to say to one another. In the perspective developed here both assume a different character, for Williams is surely the most original of Coleridge's modern inheritors. He represents the point at which Cambridge English recovers the direction of Coleridge's meditation on language and literature. Williams's long meditation on the common condition touches constantly on the instance of his spectral fellow lodger. The critique of culture opened by Coleridge is realized in a modern form in Williams's account of writing in society. It is a sign of general confusion that the labels should have obscured this essential relation. Williams draws on both the form and substance of Coleridge's thinking while discovering his roots in the soil of an older critical idea. The fact that the politics do not conform says something important about the politics — and about those who would insist too strenuously on them.

As prolegomena to Part II, the linguistic foundation and development of Cambridge English outlined in my opening chapters should make clear the modernity of Coleridge's sense of situation. His effort to answer preliminary questions about words and things looks forward to a later interrogation of language, though he cannot, I think, meaningfully be accounted protostructuralist, as Emerson Marks has proposed — whatever such a designation might bear. His place is with an older idea of language. If this excludes him from living interest for students of linguistics, it should not put off literary readers concerned with the formation of institutional practices. Coleridge's growing attention to language has everything to do with his revision of poetic value, as his developing meditation shows. The original interest in words as "living Things" became associated with the critique of empiricism which launched his philosophic career. As I shall be proposing, his reaction to his own early mechanist phase was drawn into his doubts about the "Preface" at first publication. Through his conviction of the primary cognitive function of language he distinguished his own understanding from Wordsworth's. And on this basis, in part, he developed his momentous reading of Wordsworth's verse in the *Biographia*. It is a thoughtful critical performance, whatever we may think of his motives, and one with important modern resonance, as I hope the discussion of Leavis will have suggested.

Rereading Coleridge thus becomes an exercise in deciphering an institutional legacy that is now largely ignored despite its persistence in current forms of critical response. An archaeological exercise insofar as it would associate Leavis with Wordsworth's literalism, for example, yet fully critical in intention insofar as it would evaluate the issues from a point of view identified with Coleridge's own. Thus, in chapter 5 the discussion of image and idea responds to Frank Kermode on literary imagism through his recourse to the romantic example. Coleridge's obscure consideration of the image is bound up, as I hope to show, with his conception of language. The contest of image and idea for poetic supremacy is a leading, if largely buried, feature of his critical thinking. His defense of "living words" against images of nature underwrites a literary agenda. Kermode's effort to enlist his sympathies for a poetry committed to a logic of images rings true to the associative discourse of "Kubla Khan" but not to its author's enduring commitments. It was perhaps on account of his advocacy of a thinking verse that Coleridge considered this production a "curiosity," devoid of "any supposed *poetic* merits" (*CPW* I, 295). Without detailing the affiliations, Kermode's defense of imagism can be said to extend the ascendent values of Cambridge English while reasserting the continuity of romantic and modern suppressed by Leavis. Such an observation, with all it implies of an institutional standard, depends on taking the long view opened by arguing from Coleridge's position.

I have tried to epitomize the conflict of image and idea discussed in chapter 5 through a close reading of "Frost at Midnight"—a reading some would call deconstructive but which I prefer to treat in the context of its author's meditation on language in the world and as it functions in verse. A paradigmatic reading, then, though true to the poem's textual history, and to its latent fears, in a way that readers have been reluctant to recognize. The attention to the conflict of image and idea is extended in Part III to a general discussion of Coleridge's verse, with particular reference to the conversation poems and the "Ancient Mariner." Hazlitt observed that "in writing verse, Coleridge is trying to subject the Muse to *transcendental* theories: in his abstract reasoning, he misses his way by strewing it with flowers."[2] Coming to the poetry with an eye on his early thinking about language and imagination underlines Coleridge's vocation as poet-critic.

The conversational verse dramatizes a heuristic intelligence under stress from within and without. It represents a search for an authentic voice in straits flanked by Milton and Wordsworth, image and idea. And it shows a poet galvanized by words, at sea in a flux of mind and matter, where sounds begin to signify. Reading these poems with Coleridge's linguistic meditation in place reveals a prescient watchfulness and the beginnings of critical commitment born of poetic doubt and failure. It opens up a vista in his critical prehistory, with Erasmus Darwin in the distance and the obsessive imagery of the "Ancient Mariner" in the foreground. Here he tried out Darwin's pictorialism to mixed effect. The fixation of the protagonist on a world of vivid images acquires fresh significance in the setting of his author's concern about the snare of natural impressions. The reading offered in chapter 7 takes the text as an act of critical dreamwork without presuming to offer a comprehensive new interpretation.

My concluding doubts about a notable recent rendition of the "Ancient Mariner" bring the argument full circle, returning to Richards and the way of reading which he promoted. Coleridge was the first, albeit inadvertent, casualty of new critical method, and he remains its prisoner of conscience. The reduction of so urgent a vision of modern experience to a handful of poems and a dozen formulaic critical passages shows how far the process has gone. A general revaluation is overdue, as Lentricchia's broadside surely indicates. Coleridge on language makes a natural beginning for such an enterprise, situated as the matter is at a critical crossroads. To be effective, this should not be a partisan operation. Many of the poems now seem more interesting than compelling, a judgment which their author anticipated in shifting weight from his poetic to his critical foot. With this dual vocation in mind, the verse remains valuable as a reflection on the condition of poetry. It is more than merely ruminative, more than a poetry of sensibility. Coleridge the meditative critic still speaks powerfully to our condition, I believe, to our institutional condition, certainly. He remains one of our exemplary readers, an enduring model of response. But only if his position is recognized in its extensive relations — as responsive in the living world of human values, of language and ideas.

No discussion of Coleridge today can proceed far without recognizing a debt to the editors of the *Collected Works*. With the publication in progress of the *Notebooks* and *Marginalia*, in particular, Coleridge's instance (to use Williams's valuable word for it) has become altogether more imposing. This book was inspired by the portrait of a penetrating and responsive reader presented there. It is silently indebted to Kathleen Coburn and her collaborators at every turn.

I am grateful to the Alexander von Humboldt-Stiftung, Bonn-Bad Godesberg, for a grant which took me to Germany to look into philosophical sources for romantic ideas of language. Professor Dr. Jochen Schmidt, of the Deutsches Seminar at Tübingen, admitted me to his Hauptseminar on Hölderlin and idealist thinking in the period while recognizing that my research led me afield of it. Professor Dr. Eugen Coseriu of the Romanisches Seminar was helpful in directing me to recent dissertations. If the traces of this exposure are not always evident in my text, its impact on the formation of the idea of expressive language developed here remains considerable.

The department of English, Michigan State University, encouraged the development of the project and sustained me through its completion. For constant support and forbearance in the face of delays I should like to thank its current chair, Victor Paananen, and especially Alan Hollingsworth, Fred Carlisle, and Sam Baskett. They will recognize how much the institutional setting contributed to the book's sense of purpose. An All-University Research Initiation Grant from the Office of Vice President for Research and Graduate Studies released me from teaching to complete work on the manuscript when the end was in sight. I am happy to recognize these obligations here.

Readers and audiences have been willing collaborators from the beginning. Roger Meiners was instrumental in guiding me through the maze of the earlier new criticism when I lost the tracks I was following. His responses to a first draft led me to work through Coleridge's affiliations in Cambridge English and establish the institutional context for the study of Coleridge on language which follows. Zachary Leader read the second chapter from an antithetical sense of Leavis's bearing on modern criticism. I have tried to answer his concerns without compromising my own. Arnold Davidson and Cathy Davidson read an intermediate draft with alert intelligence and their enthusiasm quickened the completion of the manuscript. To Albert Cook, Robert Marteau, Don Bialostosky, Irving Massey, William Johnsen, Charles McCracken, James A. Hill, Hans Kellner, Gary Handwerk, Diane Wakoski, and Evan Watkins I owe thanks for engaging the dialogue, at various times and places, which is continued here. It is a pleasure to acknowledge the contributions of all to the finished work.

Gerald Bruns was an encouraging respondent to an early version of the fourth chapter; this was published as "Coleridge on Language: A Poetic Paradigm," *Philological Quarterly*, 62 (1983), 45–68. The opening section of the fifth chapter, on "Frost at Midnight," was composed for the Conference in Modern Literature of 1979 and was published in the proceedings — in a different form and setting — as "Absence Present: The Resurrection of Language in Romantic Poetics" (Michigan State, 1981). Owen Barfield was good enough to both listen and attend to it: his thoughtful letter led me to pursue the matter. Part of the fifth chapter was composed on invitation for the Critical Theory Colloquium at the University of Michigan. I am grateful to Julie Ellison for that occasion.

Family and friends sustained me on the way, keeping the conviction alive. Michael Koppisch in particular offered constant encouragement and companionship. To Judith Stoddart, who married into the manuscript, I offer the finished work in token of a *vita nuova*. She alone perhaps will appreciate its truth to life.

I

COLERIDGEAN AFFILIATIONS IN CAMBRIDGE ENGLISH

1

I. A. Richards and the Renovation of Coleridge on Language

Language has been one of the grand passions of the modern imagination, the object of a nostalgia for roots and of a quest for secure ground in a time of general disorientation. Under constant surveillance since Bacon and Port Royal, it has been exalted as an organ of reason and damned as a source of error and confusion. The idea of language continues to exert a gravitational pull on thinking about writing and the modern condition; the names of Heidegger and Wittgenstein, Foucault and Derrida sound out the enduring power of its appeal. As compelling as they have sometimes appeared, their hypotheses count for less for literary study in the institutional setting than those of others observing the cult of language in more local and limited ways. In the English sphere it was I. A. Richards who raised the decisive questions for a generation of readers in modernism's dawn. Coleridge was his model, and with Coleridge's responsive attitude in mind he developed a method of paralinguistic reading as the basis of Cambridge English.[1]

Richards cast a long shadow, and his understanding remains a living one not just among the scholastic tribe of Coleridgeans but among educators concerned to preserve an audience for literature. He was the promoter of Coleridge on imagination for academic purpose in the wake of a war which had corroded the values of an exhausted culture.[2] Coleridge was to provide a bridge between the old world and a new one just emerging. His emphasis on imagination was made to valorize a way of reading for linguistically intensive meaning; to authorize an engagement with writing as shaped statement. Under these auspices Coleridge himself has come down to us, and under them institutional readers have been trained—and continue for the most

3

part to perform. Richards's promotion of Coleridge on imagination included a considerable thesis about Coleridge on language, linking a modern idea of mind to the practice of writing, and to ways of reading. This too has become part of a critical habit and a common terminology. Connotation and denotation, tenor and vehicle continue an approach to literature through an idea of linguistic process.

The convergence of Richards and Coleridge, language and imagination in the formative moment of Cambridge English was a remarkable event, and it remains an important one for the institutional revaluation underway everywhere now. For it is typically against an institutional idea of textuality rooted in Richards's reading at one remove or another that the inquisition is being conducted.[3] The limitations of his psychologism were recognized from the start, but his linguistic aspiration expressed something which was evidently widely felt. Empson and Leavis challenged him from inside, Ransom and Burke revised him, yet they all transmitted him, building on the meaning that was the cornerstone of his pedagogic project. Richards was the founding father of Cambridge English, though Leavis became its presiding genius and tutelary spirit. In a long perspective, the persistence of his agenda is the remarkable fact. It is only by recurring to it that we shall come to appreciate what is involved in surpassing it.

Recalling the process by which a curriculum was founded on a paralinguistic approach to reading is one way of querying the dominant values of English as a discipline today. Such an exercise would have only limited historical value, however, if it did not extend to a consideration of larger questions about criticism and critical authority in the English sphere. Richards is a linchpin in critical transmission, a bridge in his own right between literature conceived on the model of poetry and, as it is now increasingly conceived, with the novel in mind. His transitional position is important even if his practical criticism does not make a strong claim on our attention. With Coleridge and Arnold behind him, Leavis and the new criticism in the near future, he provides an indispensable point of reference for thinking about the function of criticism, and the culture of criticism, in postmodern circumstances. His position is significant in dynamic relation to Coleridge's informing example and in connection with the practice of his continuers. It is as the carrier of an idea of language that Richards remains useful for current revaluations.

Coleridge on language is one of the discoveries of modern thinking. Despite his long attention to words and their meanings, he was driven by an idea of imagination which has little or nothing to do with language. The effort to recover his peripheral vision of the function of language began with Richards, amid doubts about the vitality of poetry in a scientific world. Later studies have elaborated on the formation of Coleridge's conception against the background of a rising empiricism and in the context of his German adventure.[4] As I shall be proposing in Part II, this developing understanding has an important bearing on our grasp of Coleridge's poetics, and of romantic poetics in general. Situating such an understanding by reference to Richards and his way of reading means asking first questions first. Why should the idea of language have impinged on the activity of reading? What did it appear to offer institutional criticism in this transitional moment? For Richards was motivated by a sense of how an older idea of language might be brought to bear on reading at a time when this essential cultural means was under threat. His instinct remains interesting quite apart from the significance (and the limitations) of his transmission of Coleridge.

It is interesting, first, because it points to the language problem at the bottom of a cultural crisis. Established patterns of communication were under stress, ruptured or at least disturbed by the Great War. Diasparaction, the rending of the fabric of conventional language, was a prominent feature of the new writing.[5] The associated difficulty of understanding was integral, and the point was typically that with the center no longer holding, nothing made sense. Language itself had failed. Reading must therefore prove difficult. For students in the new English curriculum, this would mean recognizing the problematics of language, and not only in the literature of their own time.

Interesting, also, is Richards's recourse to Coleridge in the face of a general crisis of confidence. Where was he to turn for orientation in the massive language question which he took to be central to it? Even as he floundered in the shallows of various approaches in an early collaboration with C. K. Ogden (*The Meaning of Meaning*, 1923) he was drawn to Coleridge's thinking by a natural process of assimilation. For his bearings were literary despite his incipient social scientism, and Coleridge's was still the authoritative treatment of poetry for the English common reader. As Eliot had put it in 1920 in the opening words of *The Sacred Wood*, "Coleridge was perhaps the greatest of English critics, and in a sense the last." For he had taken account of the largest cultural circumstances, differentiating poetry and science while distinguishing convincingly between verse and prose within the former. He had made the case for poetry on grounds reverting to principles but also to current practices, with an eye to their continuance under changing conditions. And he had always attended to the language of verse, speculatively and effectively.[6] He is Eliot's own distant precursor, behind Arnold and Battitt, and he was the obvious model for Richards's paralinguistic exploration.

Yet Coleridge had never been recognized for enlarged linguistic intelligence. His orientation was traditional, not philological. Committed with David Hartley, his principal early informant, to the divine origin and meaning of language, he made his way with Horne Tooke to a paronomastic sense of semantics devoid of historical value. Even after freeing himself from the grip of association psychology he continued to play at Tooke's peculiar etymologic. He made no enduring contribution to linguistic knowledge, though his idea of desynonymy is an appealing one, providing machinery for the elaboration of a conception of understanding. This line of his thinking has been brought to attention by scholars concerned with some of the same questions posed by Richards in the 1920s, and Coleridge's position remains a limited one for all the effort involved.[7] It is something more than an anachronism all the same, and not only because what Richards made of it has assumed a life of its own. Coleridge on language matters archaeologically but also critically: in the setting of his defense of poetry as well as for what his approach has offered modern reading. It remains worth considering, as I shall be suggesting along the way, through the reflection on the condition of poetry with which it is involved.

It is within the main line of the development of modern English critical theory that the implications of Coleridge's meditation on language are realized, first by Richards and then by his followers, always in connection with the question of how we read now and of how to read Coleridge himself. Much of this can be shown to have been distorted, yet the distortions remain valuable considering the authority accruing to the main lights of Cambridge English. They are responsible for a view of Coleridge's poetics that is limited and calls for modification. In returning to Richards and Leavis, Empson and Williams we begin then a necessary task of revision. It is not the scholars but the leading critics who shape the view of tradition, literary and critical at once, by which we read and learn. Their voices remain authoritative only so long as they go unchallenged. By measuring them against a standard set by Coleridge himself, we put their claims in a long perspective, testing them in our own act of transmission. It is fitting that an initial idea of Coleridge on language should be introduced in the course of an exposition of this kind. For his meaning for readers now is inextricably bound up with the way that he has been presented to them.

Romantic Language and Modern Culture

Language is the general category of signification in Coleridge's thinking; it includes more than natural language, which is usually subordinated to a larger symbolic process in his reflection on the subject. The Berkleyan idea of a language of appearances made a lasting impression on him and is familiar from the poetry. It appealed to the easy naturalism of his early period and to his conviction that signification had a transcendental basis.[8] "Language is the sacred Fire in the Temple of Humanity" (*CL* III, 522)—a metaphor peculiarly apt to his conviction of its divine origins: "Words 'were from the beginning', nor would it have been possible, had the matter been left to our own invention, to have discovered or invented a medium possessed of advantages so many, so peculiar, and so appropriate, to all its various and numerous purposes" (*CC* 13:15). Appearances could be treated as a language of Godhead, but they were not the antecedent of human speech. Elsewhere he speculates that "besides the language of words, there is a language of spirits (sermo interior) and . . . the former is only the vehicle of the latter" (*BL* I, 191). Language was a zone of speculation, a resource for Coleridge's meditations, delirious as well as rational, on first philosophy. Linguistics in the modern sense does not apply, and "philosophy of language" scarcely encompasses what he was after.

The transcendental process of signification at work in his idea of language nearly from the beginning is expressed in various ways, often under cover of an assumed rationalism. The late *Logic* begins from a discussion of the role of words, and of grammar, in the development of the individual mind and the collective condition. Through words the mind grew into its educated lineaments; through an alphabet civilization grew "progressive and historical" (*CC* 13:15). For the childish mind fixed first on factors of likeness in the sounds of words, generating the system of language from degrees of phonemic likeness and difference. But the formal constitution of language in the individual mind was only the beginning of the story:

> In what way do we first draw or bring out the faculties of the nascent mind? We may reply without hesitation that *in substance* this is found in the question—"What is the *word* for such or such a thing?" Though *formally*, and as a direct *question*, it takes place more frequently in the teaching of a *foreign* language. And what is the form or law in the mind to which this first act of education corresponds? Evidently, that by which we remember things in consequence of their co-presence. The word "table" is sounded at the same time that the eye and the touch are directed to the thing, table. We begin δεικτικῶς, that is, *demonstrando*.   (CC 13:11)

Words were learned in a familiar world, in "co-presence" with what they signified. This was the base on which individual thinking was built, the first glimpse of a reason whose scope extended far beyond the things of the world. Reference was real but its vocation was limited by comparison.

At a moment of mounting controversy about the role of language in understanding, Coleridge's reliance on a transcendental Logos made him the enemy of materialist reductions of words to names of things— or more properly, of words to images. This emphasis is distinctive and important; as Part II will be concerned to show, it is the bridge which links his idea of language with his poetics in theory and in practice. Working from David Hartley and Horne Tooke back to Locke, and back again to Descartes and Leibnitz, Coleridge discovered where his allegiances lay and what the implications were. For present purposes it is sufficient to indicate that he came down with rationalist thinking against the empirical emphasis on language as nomenclature. The one saw language as the instrument of an active intelligence; the other as a reflection of nature mediated by a passive mind. Though his associationist phase drew him to a version of the latter position, he was won over to the rationalist orientation by his own first principles in the course of a tortuous investigation. In the end it was an expressive idea that dominated his thinking on the subject: "Language & all *symbols* give *outness* to Thoughts/& this the philosophical essence & purpose of Language" (*CN* I, 1387). In his developed understanding, language as an organ of mind does not compete with his feeling for its worldly employments, as the *Logic* shows. Living words, as he conceived them, represented an active mind at work in a common world known by a common terminology. It is this recognition which counts in considering the bearing of his way of reading, and the renovation of his conception of language under the auspices of Cambridge English.

"Semasiology" is the word Richards used to characterize Coleridge's achievement at the outset of the book which established him as the model for modern response:

> He was a semasiologist—aware, as few have been, that to ask about the meanings of words is to ask about everything. And I am assuming that his contributions towards this obscure, neglected, yet most central incipient science of the future are as important as he took them to be; that we still need to improve our understanding of language; that his unique combination of gifts enabled him to make some essential steps towards immense improvements; and that to attempt to take his work another step onwards is the best way of paying back a debt.   (*CI*, xi–xii)

What was this science of the future for which Richards found antecedence in Coleridge? It was distinguished from philology by its preoccupation with meaning. The semantic function of language, not lexical history and morphology, was to be the object. Richards was regressing here in search of linguistic footing, taking Coleridge as his guide in the absence of a more orthodox informant. The next year (1936) he would pay tribute to Hartley, recognizing that they had joined hands over the head of a century of distinguished investigation which saw the birth of linguistic science.[9] The deep historical awarenesses dominant in philological thinking, and in the institutional study of literature on this basis, were simply occluded in favor of "the meanings of words" encompassing "everything." Meaning in the new curriculum was to become an arena of association, psychologically constituted, largely uninformed by the learning of philology.

Semasiology as Richards imagined it would thus provide an alternative basis for understanding the language of literature. Coleridge was involved in the shift of ground, as a prototype and an example; he is still associated with its values. For he was the muse of this act of critical anamnesis, the apparent source of an idea of linguistic function on which Richards founded his school. But Coleridge on language, as Richards pursued the matter, had little to do with the understanding I have outlined. The stage on which he was made to perform had been set in an earlier book. In *Principles of Literary Criticism* (London, 1924) the matter was spelled out in a chapter on "The Two Uses of Language," beginning (under a Coleridgean epigraph) with an elementary distinction:

> There are two totally distinct uses of language. But because the theory of
> language is the most neglected of all studies they are in fact hardly even
> distinguished. Yet both for the theory of poetry and for the narrower aim
> of understanding much which is said about poetry a clear comprehension
> of the differences between these uses is indispensable. For this we must
> look somewhat closely at the mental processes which accompany
> them. (261)

Richards's "theory of language," the science of the future he called
semasiology, bore a casual resemblance to ideas current under other
names at the time. The cognitive turn suggests that something like
Saussure's inspection of signification was under way. In that event,
Richards might have been laying ground for a criticism based on a
modern sense of language as formally constitutive of meaning. Instead, he reinvented immanent reference, positing a scientific language
which makes meaning by referring to things, and distinguishing an
emotive language which "evokes attitudes without any reference being
required *en route*" (267). Poetry was the type of the latter, and the
prototype of all language; the scientific was derived from it. The modern confusion about poetic language stemmed from an inversion of
priorities which promoted the authority of science at the expense of
religion.

As hypothetical as these notions are, they point to something
worth considering in the modern condition. Literalism of the sort
Richards associated with science is a historical development related to
the rise of an empiricism bound to verification. Language had come to
be seen, in this spirit, as a catalogue of names. In the golden age of
lexicography, reference subordinated other linguistic functions. As
Richards saw it, readers who came to poetry were sure to be disappointed, since they would refer every phrase, every proposition to the
standard of the world. Poetry was threatened, its future jeopardized by
scientific assumptions. Like Eliot's "dissociation of sensibility" of the
same period, Richards's "scientific language" emerged from a tendentious historical tableau in response to a sense of crisis. He was concerned to preserve the possibility of reading at a moment when it
appeared to be under siege. His intuition was sound: the readers'
reports in his illustrative volume, *Practical Criticism* (1929), told a
story of disorientation and uncertainty. The formalism of the new
criticism of the thirties and beyond addressed this situation even when
it took issue with Richards. In the new criticism reference would be

banished from the precincts of the poetic text or confined to self-reference of one kind or another. Literature (poetry in particular) became the last refuge of language under the old dispensation. Here words carried on untroubled by mundane verification.

Reference is of course an issue familiar from more influential sources: especially from Saussure and Wittgenstein, whose moment Richards shares. Their very different understandings had the effect of isolating language — as a diacritical system, the object of a positive science, in the one case; as a Byzantine chess match full of ontological implication, in the other. Beginning from speech, both moved language out of the world, at least provisionally, and if their inheritors have sometimes taken reference as a starting point, the matter has seldom rested there. In such company, Richards's insistence on reference as the central fact looks like a case of intellectual regression. Even so, there is something worth saving here. What Richards isolated under the heading of "scientific language," Jakobson treated as the referential function. The defense of "emotive language" might be considered, then, a native version of the retreat from reference evident in authoritative accounts of poetry elsewhere — notably in the work of nearly contemporary Slavic formalists. Richards's dichotomy took a broader approach to the problem of defending the poetic function against encroachment. Behind it stood the Coleridge who, in a canonical formulation, defined poetry as "that species of composition, which is opposed to works of science, by proposing for its *immediate* object pleasure, not truth" (*BL* II, 10). When Richards turned Coleridge's definition into a schematic of signification, as he did with the specious splitting of scientific and emotive language, he invited dismissal. Yet he was motivated by a valuable idea, one which found corroboration elsewhere, as in Benedetto Croce's treatment of European literature of the nineteenth century under the generic title of "poetry."[10]

Richards was trying for a sense of poetry's special place, taking Coleridge as his guide — and taking his distinction too far. Against the background of Coleridge on language, the peremptory escalation to "two totally distinct uses of language" is simply inadmissible. Reference is as certainly a feature of poetic as of scientific language, even if the emphasis falls on evocation rather than factual description. This distinction was important to Coleridge, and he drew on it constantly. Reference is central to his thinking about poetic value, usually in connection with his war on "matter-of-factness" (*BL* II, 101), often with Wordsworth in mind. The hero of his argument was Shakespeare, who possesses "the power of so carrying on the eye of the reader as to make him almost lose the consciousness of words—to make him *see* everything—and this without exciting any painful or laborious attention, without any *anatomy* of description (a fault not uncommon in descriptive poetry) but with the sweetness and easy movement of nature" (*SC* I, 214). Great poetry conceals the machinery of signification, occluding the referential function. It addresses the world of objects without stooping to inventory. The language of poetry is indirect in this way, but it is hardly "totally distinct" from the language of reference. For poetry addresses the same world of experience that science does.

Formalist versions of poetic language mounted elsewhere do not indulge in Richards's diremptions. Jakobson's equilibration of linguistic functions, mechanical as it is, manages to include the poetic without sacrificing the integrity of the system. Reference has its place in Jakobson's scheme, but it is not a pivot on which everything else turns.[11] Richards's position remains interesting mainly for the way it situates the matter within a general cultural problematic: poetry under pressure of science.

Richards's rehabilitation of Coleridge on language was thin in part because of the limitations of his sources. The notebooks had of course been published only in excerpt, and sometimes in a misleadingly truncated form, as in the case of the entry on the metaphysical in poetry (*CN* I, 383). The philosophical lectures of 1819, which provide essential context, were not published until 1949. The marginalia, indispensable for the detail of Coleridge's reading, were scattered. These are the gilded veins of his long linguistic meditation. Where the materials were available, Richards did make use of them in an effort to discover the roots of the semasiology he was concerned to promote. This is the case, notably, in his account of the letters of 1800 and after, in which Coleridge works through some of the basic questions.

Even so, Richards's scholarship is deflected by his motives. It is colored by the behavioral psychology to which he habitually recurs, and by a mechanistic conception of linguistic process. Richards is a victim of scientific language in his own way. His apology for poetry presumes that we are committed by circumstances to immanent reference. He not only bears this burden, he embraces it. In the words of a typically querulous commentator of the period, "He attempts in effect to meet the friendly and intelligent Philistine on his own ground."[12] Where Richards is involved in special pleading, making the case for poetry to an audience of presumed agnostics, Coleridge had been concerned to defend the vitality of language in general, for common purpose. He was suspicious in advance of the sort of thing Richards would be about with his Basic English scheme, which reduced the tongue to a simplified set of 850 ciphers, because it debased language to a word game: "Ready Command of a limited number of words=playing Cat-cradle dexterously with Language" (*CN* II, 2722). This is astonishing in its prescience. It confirms the integrity of Coleridge on language, opening the horizon of his thinking on the subject.

Elsewhere he persevered in his quarrel with Wordsworth over the language of things because he suspected that nomenclature turned the primary instrument of thinking into a fief of nature. A question of principle which emerged in the wake of the "Preface" became the source of a leading idea, as developed in the *Philosophical Lectures*: "We are too apt to use words derived from external objects, that I verily believe: that many a man, before he asked himself the question, would imagine his mind made of thoughts as a wall is of bricks, till he asks whether he ever separated a thought from a thought, whether there was a meaning in the word 'thought,' except as the mind thinking in such a situation. . . . " (*PL*, 384). This approaches a critique of the language of science as Richards describes it. Nomenclature represented a limited conception of linguistic process, and of cognitive function in general. If we add that Coleridge was rehearsing Leibnitz's charge to Locke on the subject, the poverty of Richards's discussion becomes evident. He is vulnerable because he has so little sense of the "theory of language"—so little sense of its history, especially. The issues he raises are real ones; they have not gone away. His treatment of writing in an empirical climate throws us back on the thinking of his main informant.

The importance of Coleridge's example for the new criticism is an unexamined commonplace of revisionist versions of our institutional history. It is a part of my thesis that the real example did not take. In more favorable circumstances, his sense of language might have provided the basis for a principled modern criticism within the historical mainstream of English practice. His authority was in place, as Eliot's early observation shows. His critical intelligence was informed and responsive—neither prescriptive nor pedantic. The depth of his thinking about literature was beginning to emerge, and not only in Richards's eye. Coleridge's reflective understanding of how language means might have buttressed a critical institution under stress of science and literary modernism. Instead, it was compromised by problems of critical reception.

Coleridge on Imagination, Richards's effort to rehabilitate his position, was a crux. The summit, according to a sympathetic commentator, of a distinguished career, it became a dead letter.[13] The reviews tell the story of a missed connection, one that would have consequences for a later generation of readers. Nowhere was the failure of Richards's renovation more pointed than in F. R. Leavis's account of it in *Scrutiny*. *Coleridge on Imagination* turned Leavis against Coleridge himself. By 1940 he had concluded that "Coleridge's prestige is very understandable, but his currency as an academic classic is something of a scandal."[14] This was indicative, and self-defeating: Coleridge's grasp of poetry's past actually has something important to say to Leavis's view of tradition. His way of reading, productively reformed, might have saved Leavis from glaring problems of understanding which emerge in his consideration of romantic writing. More generally, Coleridge's understanding of language and poetry points to fundamental limitations in the criticism which followed in Richards's footsteps.

Richards's promotion of semasiology as a new science codified his own aspirations while presuming on Coleridge's. He followed his informant's meditation on language far enough to recognize its potential, but he was unable to realize its full significance. The "theory of language" which he floated as an answer to tradition in crisis was not in fact to be found in the Coleridge he knew. Recent effort to reconstruct the argument of *Coleridge on Imagination* on more effective ground evades the problem of its author's linguistic hypothesis.[15] His quandaries are worth considering now mainly in the context of an enduring critical orientation. For his book was the occasion of a chain reaction against the anomie of meaning conceived in psycholinguistic terms. The development of Cambridge English, the institutional locomotive of the new criticism, can be characterized through this reaction. Its values remain instinctive among professional readers despite the proliferation of methods derived from continental models. These are often, indeed, employed in defense of a new critical agenda, usually unwittingly. Semasiology provided the basis of this dominant idiom, and it remains an entrenched if largely unconscious model of institutional response.

Coleridge's allegiance to the language of the world in its integrity exposes the parochial simplicity of Richards's "emotive language." His sense of how poetry signifies—at a distance from things, yet intimate to them—undermines Richards's effort to identify reference with "scientific language": to do away with it for the purposes of modern reading. *Coleridge on Imagination*, a landmark of critical attitude, represents an understanding that is associated with its nominal source only casually then. In turning to consider the position which Richards details there, I want to lay stress on his modification of Coleridge's key commitments. The comparison of an original defense of poetry with its rehabilitation for academic purposes exemplifies the difference between romantic and modern reading. And it rehearses in an exemplary setting the real bearing of Coleridge on language.

Elements of Semasiology

Imagination as Verbal Coadunation

Coleridge's claims for poetry are based in part on his valorization of imagination, as realized in his distinction between imagination and fancy. Richards translates this cardinal but somewhat theoretic distinction into terms congenial to a modern mind haunted by language, verification, and validation.

Working from Coleridge's discussion of *Venus and Adonis*, he shows how fancy leads to the reader's disengagement from the poet's making of meaning (*CI*, 82). Readers respond to dense imagery by withdrawing the effort of understanding. Fancy is a sort of logorrhea which has little to do with "fact" in Richards's reductive sense of the word. Its effects are on the linguistic surface. Imagination, the higher activity of poetic making for Richards as for Coleridge, joins the separable meanings of words left dangling by fancy. It promotes active engagement by the reader, who makes connections as he reads among related meanings, realizing a significance which is more than the sum of the parts. Richards adapts Coleridge's terminology in this way to his own conception of reading as verbal processing.

Stylistic commentary in a linguistic vacuum is liable to sound ad hominem. Richards's formulations address this problem in Coleridge's critical discourse (a problem of verification, really) by substituting a linguistic base of meaning for Coleridge's ideal base. It is a rudimentary gesture, given the confusion which plagues his notion of meaning.

As John Crowe Ransom points out in his account of Richards's role in the formation of the new criticism, "Richards confines meaning in the strict sense to valid objective reference and denies it to the mere emotion that words may cause. Meaning is knowledge, not affective experience."[16] But Richards makes an exception in the case of literature, where the affective has a part in the production of meaning.

In *Coleridge on Imagination* the incongruity is bald. On the matter of "the parts of a meaning," Richards distinguishes among: (1) "awareness of the words as *words*: as sensory presentations"; (2) "sense," including related imagery; (3) "feeling"; and (4) "tone" (*CI*, 87–88). From this collocation of features with sparse attendant context it is possible to extract some premises. The language of the poem is primordial. Imagination cannot be considered apart from it. Literary meaning cannot be private to the writer, only a product of reading. For Richards will not distinguish between what is specifically linguistic in meaning and what is psychological.

Meaning is a social and conventional quality, then, dependent on the individual's inculcated ability to process language. The shift to the reader is important, even if Richards has only reorganized a familiar critical vocabulary under the heading of "meaning." He remains within the orbit of a settled terminology, but his understanding points in the direction of a criticism which will be resolutely affective in a behaviorist setting: a science of attitudes, to join two of his key terms. On Ransom's accounting, this affective emphasis exposes the romantic foundation of Richards's critical posture: "It is what the psychological bias would always tend to import into aesthetic theory" (*NC*, 15).

Richards's most promising development of the idea of imagination occurs where he compares fancy to language without syntax. The exercise demonstrates that fancy does entail propositional meaning of a kind. But it also suggests "that an absence of syntax is a favorable condition for Imagination"—to a point:

> It explains why languages whose syntax we do not understand sometimes seem inherently poetical: e.g. literal, word for word translation from "primitive" tongues or from Chinese; why ambiguous syntax is so frequent in Shakespeare; and why, in much of the modern verse which derives from Mr. Ezra Pound, it is easy to mistake a mere freedom to interpret as we will for controlling unity of sane purpose—that is, purpose integrated with and relevant to our lives as wholes.   (*CI*, 91)

Pound might be regarded as a test case for semasiology. Can a conception of meaning developed from romantic critical commitments respond effectively to the modernist challenge? Some of the problems are clearly indicated here. Shakespeare's syntactic congestion proves more congenial than Pound's refractive imagism, for reasons having to do with traditional standards of coherence. Imagination remains the measure of poetic value, coherence the measure of imagination. "Mere freedom to interpret" is not the point of imaginative reading. Valid affective response is Richards's concern.

Richards mounts, then, a modern version of the Coleridgean distinction between imagination and fancy, one displaced into elementary linguistic terms with the aim of monitoring reading and with implications for what is valuable in writing. The censorious tone directed at Pound muffles an act of some critical ingenuity. Its potential range would come clear years later, in Hugh Kenner's discussion of the development of symbolist and imagist poetics from the pursuit of linguistic effects in isolation. What Richards had seen as a defect in modernist writing Kenner writes off as a reflex of modernist reading: "The reading of the Pound Era, like its writing, discerns patterns of diction and gathers meaning from non-consecutive arrays . . . Pound's attention tended to fix on the constellated words in ancient texts, not on their syntactic connections . . . Especially in Greek lyrics he is sensitive to the boundaries of individual words, and apt to discern a talismanic virtue in relevant English words of his discovery. In the rare plural 'satieties' he found a Sapphic quality concentrated."[17] Pound's verse in its imagist moment aspires to the condition of the Sapphic fragment, every word a constellation of meaning free of syntactic constraint.

What Richards misses in applying his conception to Pound is not just a change of habit but the idea that reading is historically specific. His coherence is not the only coherence. And his linguistic approach to imagination, for all its air of the new, actually shores up an older sense of coherence at the expense of a more difficult modern one. Relating syntax to the activity of imagination provides Richards a promising point of departure. But in compressing primitive language, Chinese, Shakespeare, and Pound into a single discursive model he bypasses historical integrity. It is as though poetic function were a universal faculty in the empyrean of eighteenth-century psychology. At such moments he verges, indeed, on that Hartleyan automatism which so gripped Coleridge's thinking early on. And he exposes the period affinity of his enterprise with that of Roman Jakobson, for whom the poetic function would become an object of clinical investigation. Richards's version of poetic value is stripped in this way of Coleridge's deep historical awarenesses. Verbal imagination of a straitened kind practically defines his critical agenda. William Empson, Richards's student, is closer to the spirit of the original in his discussion of syntax in *Seven Types of Ambiguity* (1930). Where Richards regards ambiguous syntax as a generic feature of poetic language, Empson sees it as a stylistic device related to the development of a historically particular form. Thus of Shakespeare he observes that "these devices are particularly useful in managing the sonnet form because they help it to combine variety of argumentation and the close-knit rhythmical unity of a single thought."[18] Empson realizes a potential in Richards's thinking which was seldom realized elsewhere. *Seven Types of Ambiguity* remains a living testament of semasiology, early evidence that Richards's linguistic attention to meaning had a productive future in literary study.

Language as the Element of Literature

Coleridge's symbolic conception of language identifies the word as the basic unit of linguistic significance. This despite his later critique of the empirical vision of the mind as a wall of idea-bricks, each with a name (*PL*, 384; see discussion, p. 13). That he thinks in terms of unit-words is evident in his distinction of poetry and prose: "A poem contains the same elements as a prose composition; the difference therefore must consist in a different combination of them, in consequence of a different object being proposed" (*BL* II, 8). Richards objects to this distinction on the ground that "*words are not necessarily units of meaning,*" "that the literary conception of *words* as the elements either of poetic or prose compositions is inadequate for serious studies" (*CI*, 101–2). *Language* is the element of poetry as of prose—not words, which are abstractions: merely nominal, subpropositional particles subtracted from the field of force which Richards calls "meaning." Meaning transpires on many levels, including (but not confined to) the word in discursive context. Poetry cannot inhere in the individual word—this against Herbert Read's instance of Shakespeare's "incarnadine." "Only while we supply its context does it retain its poetic effect" (*CI*, 102). The familiar contextualism of modern criticism, with its stress on the relation of the parts to the whole, is the issue of the argument.

Richards's attention to the linguistic base in critical practice is his fundamental contribution to the field, the root of semasiology as he understands it. The "literary conception of words" as the elements of meaning practically defines a way of reading. At its most delirious, in Coleridge himself, reading becomes a meditation on the Word: "Words in original Languages are really sentences, each syllable certainly being a distinct symbol; but very often each letter being the relict of a syllable—perhaps of several . . . Suppose but a few words, these of course must come over and over again . . . Gradually, these sentences *wear out* into simple words—then they become like algebraic Symbols, & task the memory" (*CN* III, 3789). Here the word is everything *but* the sensory presentation. Not only a history but a proposition lies coded in its syllables. On the verge of the age of Grimm and Bopp, Coleridge's speculative etymology looks back to the old idea of reconstructing the original language of the Godhead. The goal of this exercise, as Barfield points out, is not "a feeling for words as distinct from the reality behind them," it is liberation from the idolatry of graven images: "In disciplining the mind one of the first rules should be, to lose no opportunity of tracing words to their origin; one good consequence of which will be, that he will be able to use the *language* of sight without being enslaved by its affections. He will at least save himself from that delusive notion, that what is not *imageable* is not *conceivable*."[19] The word against the image, the Logos against the world's light: such is the taproot of Coleridge's most expansive thinking on the subject of words and things. As I hope to show later in a discussion of "Frost at Midnight," the contest of word and image has poetic consequences of some importance. What a secular criticism must make of this, if it would take Coleridge as its guide, Richards's enterprise shows. He continues Coleridge's preoccupation with meaning on the basis of a modern conception of language as discourse.

Metric as the Motion of Meaning

Richards criticizes Georgian notions of meter as a musical supplement, attacking the idea of words as "sensory signs" divorced from meaning, "as with the bulk of eighteenth-century poetry for example" (*CI*, 111). He would include meaning within the purview of natural language, recovering meter as "the movement of meaning" (119). Meter would then appear a regular feature of language, not an artificial setting of it. And poetry would be defined by its relation to language in general. This part of his argument recalls again the period affinity to Slavic formalism. And it invites comparison with Saussure's conception of the sign as an integral association of sound-image and idea. What the Swiss linguist approaches in the spirit of positive science, with an eye to delimiting his object of investigation, Richards approaches with pragmatic ends in view. The case for poetry would have to be made on grounds more compelling than those derived in one way or another from Wordsworth.

Wordsworth's position—there is no "essential difference between the language of prose and metrical composition" (*LBP*, 163)—had liberated fresh poetic energies. But it had made meter the defining property of verse. Wordsworth treats meter as a secondary effect, something imposed on language, even if his own verse, in its better moments, tells a different story. His Victorian inheritors (so the argument goes) contrived a poetry of metrified ideas in Wordsworth's wake, an endlessly maundering *Prelude* on most modernist accounts, and buried poetry in the process. The divorce of meter from meaning, which Richards assigns not to Wordsworth but to the eighteenth century, was the beginning of the end.

Eliot's nearly contemporary claim for rhythm as the primordial feature of verse—a claim corroborated elsewhere by Paul Valéry—shows how current Richards's responses are.[20] They are typical of a modernist recovery of poetry as something which might have been spoken, on the basis of a conception of language as speech—something invested with meaning and rhythm by a human voice. It should be clear that such an attitude has much in common with the Wordsworth whose ear is fixed by the voices of others, who imagines his activity as a transposition of speech in extremis into the conventional precincts of poetry. Richards, with his romantic commitments, places the burden of blame on earlier poets, yet he cannot quite save Coleridge from responsibility by association. Coleridge's broader view of poetry as exciting equal and continuous attention by means including, but not limited to, meter does give scope to Wordsworth's argument. But it does not, on Richards's accounting, clearly break with the older sense of meter as a musical setting.

The crux of Coleridge's position, on this reading, lies in his claim for an intrinsic relation of poetry and meter not very different from Wordsworth's except in elaboration. "Equal and continuous attention" turns out to be a duplicitous formula. To make the intrinsic relation plausible Coleridge "would have to show that in no other way than by metre could we be forced to attend to all the parts in order to enjoy a whole" (*CI*, 116). Recourse to suppositious argumentation of this kind shows how Richards makes Coleridge perform on the scientific premises which he had set out to circumvent in the first place. The case for an essential relation between meter and poetry rests on the evidence of tradition. Coleridge's formula involves no logical claim of the kind for which Richards holds him accountable.

Richards proceeds to an egregious dismissal of prosody in toto, as if meter were a canker in the body poetic and the prosodist its apologist, or worse. The alternative he offers to Coleridge's careful and balanced remarks on the matter amounts to repression. Meter is an antique which shackles poetry to its primitive past—a view not unrepresentative of informed modernist opinion, to be fair to Richards. (Eliot's ambivalence stands out in this company: "Poetry begins, I dare say, with a savage beating a drum in a jungle, and it retains that essential of percussion and rhythm."[21]) He goes on to cite Coleridge against a mechanical view of meter as a way of preserving his authority for the future of semasiology.

At a point where Slavic formalism proved astute, semasiology would thus prove arid. Meter as the motion of meaning came down in practice to ignorance of metric convention: a feature of poetry's past so salient that Wordsworth had made it practically definitive. The preoccupation with linguistic meaning which is the legacy of semasiology was impoverished as a result by inadequate metric understanding. One measure of Richards's influence in the new criticism he inspired is the comparative (and mounting) failure of attention to metric features of poetry both old and new. The result has not proved a liberation from the shackles of poetry's past, rather a loss of poetry's claim to identity and a suppression of its history. In the readings of Leavis and Williams there is little apparent difference between poetry and prose. Without criteria of the sort maintained by Coleridge, imposing differences are readily (and naturally) dismissed.

The moment of semasiology was then a prosaic moment: a time when Eliot could maintain that "a great deal, in the way of meaning, belongs to prose rather than to poetry," and that "for us, anything that can be said as well in prose can be said better in prose" (*UP*, 152). He was speaking, as his prefatory remarks make clear, with Richards in mind.

Good Sense as a False Standard

Richards's scepticism about some of Coleridge's judgments of particular poems leads him to reflect that "Good Sense is a banner under which every kind of stupidity and every kind of prejudice willingly fight" (*CI*, 130). He regrets Coleridge's occasional lapse into "a trough of literalism" (*CI*, 136), notably in the critique of Wordsworth in the *Biographia Literaria*. Good sense comes down to adherence to fact, and to the standard of fact. It is a virtual instinct of English critical response. Richards is perhaps the most vocal, and influential, of English readers in his doubts about good sense, about fact, and about language as a record of fact.

On this point Richards must simply have lost his audience. As the case of Leavis shows, the standard of good sense survives even when critical reflexes change. The context of Richards's doubts is clear enough: his dichotomy of emotive and scientific language commits him in advance to judgments of attitude in poetry. Judgments of fact do not apply. Thus, "the judgment that a passage is good is an act of living" (*CI*, 140). Not quite ad hominem, yet informed by critical principles which can only be provisional, literary judgment will necessarily be subjective, without the consolation of universality which saves Kant's aesthetic judgment for philosophy. Taste in the old sense will be shorn of its aspiration to a standard. Literary criticism will serve as a propaedeutic to taste and be put to utilitarian ends. Reading will become a playground where the individual learns the rules of the game.

Occasional heresy apart, good sense remains perhaps the preeminent standard of English critical judgment. Yet it is a shifting standard. Intelligibility is a historical variable, informed first of all by the sense of what language delivers. What was good sense to Addison is already obfuscation to Coleridge, a matter of rhetoric. This is the key to his version of good sense: "True & easy Test of Poetry. If it relate to sight, might a well educated man born blind have written it—Examine Blacklock. And if to ear or sound, the deaf—if to feelings, a man utterly heartless?" (*CN I*, 1692) The language of sight, the language of sound, the language of feeling are so many "stereotype pieces," as he put it in the Biographia of current poetic diction: rhetoric as opposed to living perception—to reality. Good sense is not what adds up to an intelligible likeness, but what rings true. The blind poet employs formulas which do not rely on verification by sight; the living perception must be so far absent from his visual imagery.

Elsewhere, echoing Milton, Coleridge praises the language of Hesiod and Homer as "simple, sensuous, and empassioned . . . the desideratum or ideal of poetic diction of all languages . . . It is the language of poetry, not of speculation; an exponent of the senses and sensations, not of reflection, abstraction, generalization, or the mind's notices of its own acts" (*PL*, 71). Perception, in the expanded sense of the critical philosophy, is thus "the ineradicable *nisus* of poetry"[22] and a modern cognomen of good sense. Living perception is indeed precisely "good sense." Coleridge defends it without giving way to the documentary idea which Richards is concerned to suppress: "Poetry must be *more* than good sense, or it is not poetry; but it dare not be less, or descrepant. Good sense is not, indeed, the superstructure; but it is the rock, not only on which the edifice is raised, but likewise the rock-quarry *from* which all its stones have been, by patient toil, dug out" (*CL* III, 470). Committed to the world of collective representations, poetry is hardly an autonomous zone of discourse. His judgments of it proceed on broadly moral as well as technical grounds. Yet poetry remains distinctive through its primary allegiance to the pleasures of modulated meter, of imagery and figure. The ratio of truth to pleasure is a crux for his thinking about poetic value, as we shall see in considering Allen Tate's doubts about it in chapter 2. Richards's own doubts, about fact rather than a ratio of this kind, seem elementary by comparison.

It should be clear that the standard of fact involved in Coleridge's "good sense" is not an empirical standard of the kind Wordsworth sometimes seems to imply. Not the *Ding an sich* but the percept is the basis of good sense in poetry. How does a reader judge percepts? Such will be the difficult enterprise of modern critical practice, which cannot fall back on empirical mirages and will not be satisfied with "stereotype pieces." Richards turns it into something very nearly existential: a matter of intuition, of the heroic subjective. His account of the matter is plainly reductive, and unnecessarily so. Coleridge's version of good sense is less sceptical, more secure in the limited resources of human experience than Richards can afford to be. Science makes him wary of any claim to judgments of taste, and of reference as a standard of poetic judgment in particular. If poetry evokes attitudes by emotive language, it cannot be held accountable to a standard of fact. Richards is hoisted once more on his own petard, the scientific language which is his first premise. For it forces on him an untenable dichotomy and a defense of poetry as purely intuitional. Such a defense cuts poetry off from living experience, from society and history, consigning it to a limbo not unlike the aesthetic in the old sense. Even the consolation of subjective universality escapes him. Richards regresses to this barren plain while going forward with the question of language. His case does much to explain Eliot's claim that criticism *either* "seeks to find out what poetry is" *or* "assesses actual" poems (*UP*, 16). Like Pound's Mauberley, his early contemporary, Richards's relapse on the aesthetic is instinctive, and a symptom of sorts. The reaction against his semasiology would proceed as a recovery of the standard of good sense and of the possibility of judgment on the basis of a language which was, after all, of the world.

Poetic Meaning as Oblique

The propositions of poetry are pseudostatements which inculcated readers refer to attitudes, understanding them psychologically and dramatically rather than objectively. Poetry sounds propositional, yet it must be read as though the propositions were beside the point. Poetic meaning is oblique: "Poetry is not the thing said but a way of saying it," *pace* Housman (*CI*, 200). In fact there is no such "thing said" apart from the saying. Every speech act involves a distinctive act of ideation. Language is an indissoluble part of the process, as it is of imagination.

The citation of Housman is leading. It exposes as clearly as anything in his book Richards's real constituency, which is Georgian before it is modern, though he constantly elides the difference—by dwelling for instance on Eliot's antecedents (*CI*, 197). The ideology of modernism, "make it new," chafes at the suggestion; critical history has in fact scarcely caught up with Richards on this point.[23] His conception of poetic meaning descends from the romantic sense of poetic utterance as vatic, private, sui generis: something which cannot be reduced to a prose crib, nor even weeded much without snapping the flower. The organic idea which underwrites this Coleridgean metaphor is realized, in Richards, in linguistic terms, in a way Coleridge could not have imagined. Meaning for him was still a matter of statement, of an idea developed to a clear point in a language which was not too distracting. Alert to stylistic excesses, including his own, Coleridge subordinated rhetorical display to expression. Good style was for him the signature of good thinking; he exposed mannerism of every sort, not for impropriety but for problems of conception at the bottom of it. Meaning might indeed be oblique, but never simply "a way of saying it."

The divergence is fundamental. Meaning as a linguistic function leads naturally to a view of reading as verbal processing: nearly the opposite of reading as an exercise in reflection. Even on his own ground, Richards struggles with large forces he cannot contain. Thus, his concern with "structure of meaning" is related in passing to attitudes to language in general. The structure of signification as the foundation of meaning seems near, but Richards's sense of meaning includes so much which is only quasilinguistic that this avenue is closed to him. Poetic meaning remains specifically linguistic, he insists, yet he is unable to take the position to its limit. What he is left with is a poetic meaning which is oblique by definition: neither referential nor entirely self-referential. Poetic obliquity is traced to romantic ventriloquism and characterized in terms of persona, voice, and tone. This emphasis would yield, via the early Leavis, the most perspicuous response to *The Waste Land* in the period. *New Bearings in English Poetry*[24] led readers away from the red herring of meaning in the conventional sense of *vouloir dire*. Leavis noticed that Eliot's poem is not to be considered as spoken by the poet—that Tiresias modulates within his medium's voice the voices of an age. (Tiresias is, of course, Eliot's figure for such heteroglossia. Leavis follows his emphasis on consciousness rather than voice—the residuum of a cognitive conception of persona.) Leavis's semasiological reading encouraged Eliot's audience to read the poem dramatically, leading them away from dependence on his notes. Problems in the linguistic base notwithstanding, the new idea of meaning offered modern readers a way out of old habits.

In practice, Richards's semasiology actually extended Coleridge's commitment to poetic intelligibility, with the difference that language makes. For language was now an opaque medium at best; the medium had in effect become the message. Poetic obliquity might yield obscurity in modern verse, but this was to be preferred to structures of meaning which were plain because factual. The modernist prevails here over the Georgian in Richards. Comparison with Eliot shows him to have been sacrificing everything to save meaning—to save reading as he recognized it. He could not dismiss it, as Eliot did, as a pretext (*UP*, 151). The way out lay not in tossing meaning like a bone to the dog (Eliot's metaphor and solution), but in pursuing a more comprehensive conception of it. Only such a conception could save poetry from mis-understanding and disuse. Poetic obliquity was not an evasion of meaning but rather the pursuit of a more inclusive kind of meaning. With Coleridge in the background, Richards's enterprise would remain committed to imagination and the compact constructions of poetic art. Literary imagination was immediately involved in the condition of language; reading well meant beginning from that condition. Intelligibility depended on expanded linguistic awarenesses more than on direct experience, reflection, and historical sense. Poetic meaning was oblique ultimately because emotive language was oblique from the start. The evident circularity of Richards's argument is buried in the explanations of *Coleridge on Imagination*, a programmatic book which set out to extend the language revolution inaugurated by its subject, who was extolled as a Galileo of linguistics (*CI*, 232). In fact, it promoted an idea of language, and an idea of poetry on the basis of it, which misapprehends much of its informant's best thinking.

Semasiology thus amounted to an ambitious program for enlightened reading in the transitional cultural situation between the wars. As Mulhern shows, Richards imagined this program as a surrogate for the defunct values of religion and the bankrupt optimism of liberal social ideals. Poetry he saw as a life raft in the tempest: "It is capable of saving us, it is a perfectly possible means of overcoming chaos."[25] Coleridge was its muse, the original (with Arnold) of its moral seriousness about poetry and of the quality of its interest in meaning. Semasiology drew on the authority of Coleridge's name but made few concessions to his developed positions. True to its intellectual circumstances, it was committed to language as the basis of meaning. This was the source of its argument with evaluative criticism and of its influential modification of Coleridge on imagination. Richards's version of imagination dispensed with the cognitive machinery, substituting a linguistic machinery (itself cognitive at one remove) and an understanding of language as the irreducible ground of expression.

But semasiology involved nothing comparable to Heidegger's nearly contemporary pursuit of language as *Grund*, nor the exaltation of poetry as the expression of a narrowly national identity. A glimpse at German developments in the period shows how serious the claims for poetry might become and how sinister in the grip of the will to power. As Jochen Schmidt remarks of Heidegger's acquiescence in the ideology of National Socialism, it is one short step from *Grund* to *Boden*.[26] Richards's aspirations were cosmopolitan by comparison.

His future lay in China and America. Semasiology remained behind to become the basis of a new institutional criticism, one which would adapt its emphasis on language in the service of other ends. Coleridge's interest in the function of language had become in Richards an incipient linguistic theory of meaning. Their allegiance to symbolic ideas of language would be dismissed by Leavis and his associates in favor of a parochial identification with "English" as the basis of an exclusive national culture.

2

Semasiology Under Scrutiny

Among Richards's inheritors, Leavis stands out for the sustained development and influence of his position. He became the torchbearer of the new Cambridge English, its aspiring institutional builder. Through *Scrutiny*, his version of the new criticism attained to real and enduring authority among English educators, soon eclipsing the diffuse achievement of his mentor, who had gone off to pursue Basic English. Like Empson, Leavis was formed in the school of semasiology, and in *New Bearings* he realized its potential in his own way. The book made Richards out as a champion of the new poetry, of Eliot and Hopkins in particular. Leavis cited Richards's rationale of the poet's vocation ("He is the point at which the growth of the mind shows itself") as the basis of a somewhat different claim: the poet as "the most conscious point of the race in his time" (*NB*, 16). The shift of emphasis does not quite efface the Arnoldian idea. But Leavis's sense of time as particular, a fundamental condition, shows clearly against this background. It is characteristic.

Following Richards's lead, Leavis was concerned in *New Bearings* to defend poetry at a moment when its audience seemed to have lost the thread. The case he made for Eliot, Pound, and Hopkins posited a poetry of the modern condition. The Victorian inheritors of high romanticism were scapegoats of the argument, sacrificial victims of the new dispensation in English poetry. They were charged with poetic preciosity and retreat from history, or (in the case of Browning) with failure of intelligence, *pace* Arnold. So far Leavis appeared to be marching with Eliot, whose vision of tradition he virtually reproduced in the book. Semasiology showed itself as resolutely modern here, in its abuse of the antecedents of modernism as much as in its defense of the new. This too is characteristic of Leavis. He drew the line with Hopkins, whom he saw not as Victorian but as protomodern. His discussion of Hopkins in *New Bearings* shows how he adapted the semasiology already under way in Richards's earlier work to the needs of his version of literary history.

The situation he had faced, as he recalled in his "Retrospect 1950," was one in which academic readers regarded Hopkins as a freak. Bridges had hardly made the case in the original edition of 1918; rather the opposite. He sometimes emended Hopkins's text when he thought it would improve the sense. Of one such emendation Leavis observed, with righteous asperity: "[Bridges's] objection to 'combs' seems to be based on nothing better than a narrow conception of metaphor—the same misconception that prompts editors to emend the 'Tomorrow and tomorrow and tomorrow' passage in *Macbeth*: 'having regard to the turn of thought and the necessary continuity of metaphors, I am convinced that Shakespeare's epithet was *dusky*' (*Macbeth: The Arden Shakespeare*, p. 141). Good metaphor need not be a matter of consistently worked out analogy or point-for-point parallel" (*NB*, 142). Here is Richards's defense of obscurity in modern poetry mounted on first principles. It must have played its part in the general recognition accorded Hopkins within a few years of the publication of *New Bearings*. Yet Leavis would soon be promoting a literalist conception of metaphor not very different from the one he attacks in Bridges as a way of demoting Shelley. Of the second stanza of "Ode to the West Wind" he would object:

> The sweeping movement of the verse, with the accompanying plangency, is so potent that, as many can testify, it is possible to have been for years familiar with the Ode—to know it by heart—without asking the obvious questions. In what respects are the "loose clouds" like "decaying leaves?" The correspondence is certainly not in shape, colour or way of moving. It is only the vague general sense of windy tumult that associates the clouds and the leaves; and accordingly, the appropriateness of the metaphor "stream" in the first line is not that it suggests a surface on which, like leaves, the clouds might be "shed," but that it contributes to the general "streaming" effect in which the inappropriateness of "shed" passes unnoticed. What, again, are those "tangled boughs of Heaven and Ocean?" They stand for nothing that Shelley could have pointed to in the scene before him; the "boughs," it is plain, have grown out of the "leaves" in the previous line, and we are not to ask what the tree is.[1]

What can account for the apparent change of direction? Even allowing for critical development, and for differences of poetic setting, Leavis's partisan application of what appeared a first principle should be suspect. The claims he makes on the basis of these examples are large ones. If metaphor of this ambitious kind is heroically modern in Hopkins, how can it be a sign of poetic adolescence in Shelley?

The beginning of an answer is to be found in Leavis's ambivalence toward Richards, and to semasiology as a propaedeutic to good reading. Leavis turned sharply against Richards after the publication of *Coleridge on Imagination* in 1935. Outside *New Bearings*, which antedates the change, his work is weak in the linguistic base, where Richards had concentrated his attention. The sense of linguistic function is not very developed even there. Leavis's judgments usually proceed from a special sense of value in tradition. Though he invokes it polemically in his practical criticism, signification is a dead letter for him. His view of language is bound to a view of *the* language—of English of a special kind. Nothing alien impinges on his consciousness of it. Richards provided him with little more than shots in the dark; Wittgenstein, his Cambridge contemporary, with conundrums. He might have fallen back on others, but his limited sense of the literary precluded his considering anything overtly philosophical. So he reverted to literary habit, taking the word as his hard currency. The attack on Shelley exemplifies a growing attachment in Leavis's criticism to words as names—an attachment he had once resisted. It is evident in his disaffection with Yeats, whom he began to find "too elliptical" with *The Winding Stair*. Of "Byzantium" he complained that "the realm of time and sense is elsewhere in the book a more rich and positive presence."[2] The "masterful images" which he would praise in a review of 1940 as the mark of Yeats's achievement were transparent reflections of that realm, as his citations show: a way of naming an already familiar world.[3]

Reaction formation and an insistent parochialism conspired in this developing way of reading, which actually inverted the semasiology from which its author had begun. For Richards, it was the attitude, not the reference that counted for poetic expression. Ellipsis might be a problem for the empirical mind, but it was at home in verse. Emotive language, the element of literature, encompassed more than the naked word. A poetics of reflection was the point, as it had been for Coleridge and the early Arnold. Its horizon was expansive, like that of reflection itself, international in aspiration. Leavis's "English" was constricted by comparison: the English of literature, of one man's Great Tradition. Richards's defensive campaign to save poetry was promoted in his work to a cultural agenda: Fortress England. It was an agenda for which history would soon provide living justification. The authority of Leavis's critical judgment after the war must be accounted in part to his prescient sense of isolation, of England's green and pleasant land against the Babel across the Channel, and against the Philistines over the ocean. His conception of English as the stone wall of the island fortress virtually defines a critical style.

Terry Eagleton calculates Leavis's notion of language as "a naive mimeticism: the theory was that words are somehow healthiest when they approach the condition of things, and thus cease to be words at all."[4] On this hypothesis he was continuing Wordsworth's archaic emphasis on "the best objects from which the best part of language is originally derived" (*LBP*, 156). Leavis attacked a semblance of this understanding in *New Bearings*, denouncing the Georgian idea of the "intrinsically poetical" (*NB*, 70) while defending Eliot's use of modern imagery against its detractors. The intrinsically poetical is associated elsewhere in his work with the romantic, which he depreciated nearly by rote. And in a celebrated review essay of a sort he came to relish, he demolished F. W. Bateson's effort to see English poetry as a reflex of the development of the language, on grounds that Bateson's conception of words was simplistic. Words were not to be considered simply as reflections of historical experience, even if they were historical products.[5] With some qualification, Eagleton's contention stands inspection all the same. The best objects for Leavis are still familiar things, and the best part of language still displays them. His promotion of Lawrence might be measured by this documentary standard. Deeply empirical in his testing of poetic diction, he would dismiss the Georgians as vague in favor of the hard language of modernism.

The root of his difference with semasiology can be situated here, where Coleridge had parted ways with Wordsworth. For semasiology was committed to a language "derived from reflection on the acts of the mind itself" (*BL* II, 40), in Coleridge's formula. It was psychological in inspiration and temperamentally averse to a language of fact. The emphasis in Richards fell on meaning rather than naming. Empson's "ambiguity" had gone on to occlude direct signification in favor of all sorts of poetic obliquity. Leavis could subscribe to such commitments only so long as ordinary experience remained clearly in view.

After the break with semasiology, he would fight to recover fact as poetic ground. Hence, among other reasons, his attack on Shelley.

"English" of the sort he often invokes serves Leavis in ways that are reminiscent of Wordsworth. The idiom is his monument to a lost way of life: the lineaments of the ruined cottage of organic community, the last bastion of traditional English culture.[6] "Essential Englishness" (Eagleton's apt phrase) survives only in the language—or in his version of it. Another commentator puts a point to the case in a recent essay. An early defender of Joyce, Leavis deplored his pollution of this best part of language in *Finnegan's Wake*. Joyce's satire raised in a compelling way the question of the modern writer's relation to the tongue. In Colin MacCabe's rehearsal of Leavis's attack,

> What must be preserved at all costs is a space between the writer and the language, between the command and the expression, between the need and the medium. Joyce is rejected in so far as he tends to collapse these two areas into each other. His use of language tends to obscure the undefined "what they came from"—the individual consciousness autonomously producing works which "finish" within the social medium of language but which "start" somewhere else. But Joyce's work insists on the way in which the individual is always already constituted in language, always already given a place within stories he or she has not composed and Joyce insists that the effort of the writer is to remake that language and those stories.[7]

Saving English meant subordinating writing to an established discursive order instead of querying it from within. Faced with a radical poetics of language, Leavis was driven to declare himself. The defender of poetic obliquity in *The Waste Land* yielded to a stronger principle, abandoning modernism for the defense of this ideal order.

MacCabe's attention to the linguistic assumptions of Leavis's criticism extends a mode of argument familiar in Cambridge English from Richards forward. Literature as the elaboration of an attitude to language in general: such has been the working premise of the school. Eagleton and MacCabe rely on Leavis's example even as they deplore his literalism. For it is through the question of language that the sociality of writing has been formulated, affirmed, and criticized since semasiology. Leavis's late attack on *East Coker* bears witness to the persistence of the premise. In *The Living Principle* he would flay Eliot's "unintelligence about language—his inability to recognize its nature and significance," insisting that "the pre-existing English language, essential to Eliot's need, was a product and manifestation of creativity, and he hadn't, and couldn't have, created it."[8] Not very different from MacCabe's emphasis on the medium, in fact, though the latter makes something more cogent of it. What he sees as the necessary sociality of individual expression, Leavis puts in terms of the writer's particular consciousness.

Leavis's hostility to romanticism stands out in considering the fate of semasiology, since it broke a vital link between Coleridge and modern English criticism, and between romanticism and modernism generally. Coleridge had provided Richards with a sense of direction at a moment of crisis. The real strength of tradition becomes evident in such moments. Coleridge had sustained Richards even where his example had seemed inadequate to the demands of a new situation and a new literature. His formulations had served as a basis of argument; it remained possible to invoke standards, even if in a negative way. The modern poet who wrote vers libre could be seen to be reacting to the limitations of mechanical meter. Without a figure of Coleridge's kind, the standard becomes implicit, and ultimately a mirage. Eliot's strength as poet and critic made him a comparable exemplary reader, as Leavis noticed in his review of *Coleridge on Imagination*.[9] But the acolyte's ambivalence about the high priest of modernism would prevent his making of him what Richards had tried to make of Coleridge. The result was to be a critical idiom insistent on standards, but without the resources to defend them adequately. The voice of *Scrutiny* often seems to be wailing in the wilderness. The principles it is always articulating turn out (like the defense of Hopkins's metaphor) to be provisional, while laying claim on something larger.

Richards and Eliot both proved inadequate for Leavis's purposes, mainly on grounds of an untenable relation to language. They had once appeared the heroes of modern criticism. In the second number of *Scrutiny* (1932), under the title "What's Wrong With Criticism," he had made the case:

> [T]his age will be remarkable in literary history for its achievement in criticism. The histories of literary criticism contain a great many names, but how many critics are there who have made any difference to one — improved one's apparatus, one's equipment, one's efficiency as a reader? At least two of them are of our time: Mr. Eliot and Mr. Richards have immensely improved the instruments of analysis, and have consolidated

and made generally accessible the contribution of Coleridge. Mr. Eliot has not only refined the conception and the methods of criticism; he has put into currency decisive reorganizing and reorienting ideas and valuations. The stimulus of these two very dissimilar forces had already made itself felt, and there is no reason to suppose that Mr. Empson's book will prove to be the only important critical work produced by their juniors.[10]

Richards was already on the road to China when this was written; in the same number he reflects on developments in language and literature there. Eliot's lectures at Harvard, which drew the line with Richards, commenced in the course of the same year. Here Leavis would be confronted with a critical imperative: define poetry, or read and respond to it. A pragmatic distinction, to be sure, and one which will not bear much weight, yet sufficiently forceful to inspire Leavis's charge, just three years later, that Richards treated poetry as grist for his psycholinguistic mill. "Poetry has ceased to matter" (136), as he put it, echoing the mentor whom he would soon be dismissing. Only "authority" now drove readers to it.

This crisis of cultural faith is answered in his subsequent work by an effort to establish authority adequate to the end of saving poetry. Leavis's career might be characterized as a quest for authority within a literary tradition still sufficiently dynamic to have spawned modernism. Who could stand for its enduring values? Coleridge was regarded by Richards, demiurge of Cambridge English, as the name to conjure with. Eliot, the modern oracle, had recognized him as "the greatest of English critics, and in a sense the last." With Shakespeare, Milton, and Wordsworth at its cardinal points, Coleridge's version of high poetic tradition is the prototype of Leavis's own. The way back was plainly marked. Instead, this imposing model of response was abandoned in Leavis's abrupt dismissal of *Coleridge on Imagination*. Associated with the romantic at a moment when Eliot had defined himself as modern (and as classical, in sharp contrast to Richards's neoromantic commitments), Coleridge fell in with the wrong names. "Romantic" had become the evil which "modern" would redeem. Leavis's diatribe against Shelley is perhaps an extreme instance, but its extremity makes it paradigmatic. It is not untypical of his perverse readings of the romantics and their inheritors—readings which marched lockstep in the ideological advance guard of modernism. They were instrumental in turning a generation of readers away from early modern poetry in favor of the triumphant novelty of 1922. Leavis might profitably be regarded, with Pound, as the archpublicist of this schism.

Eliot's dyspathy for Shelley, to put the case in context, is altogether more honest.[11] His essays on Byron and Blake show him to be a sensitive reader of poetry which lay outside his own version of high poetic tradition. He could change his mind about Milton without fear of losing his way. It is difficult to imagine his employing a phrase like "Hopkins's anti-Tennysonian art" (*NB*, 174) to draw a line between poetic virtue and iniquity: a specious line, as Seamus Heaney's discussion of Hopkins between Keats and Yeats makes clear.[12] Eliot could appreciate the achievement of *In Memoriam* without incurring damage to the longer perspective imposed by his commitments.

In his insistence on the opposition of romantic and modern, Leavis was reacting under pressure of the modernist challenge, with his critical exemplars set plainly in the background. Instead of pursuing Language, as Richards had done, he chose to pursue Tradition, on the heels of Eliot. (He would end by pursuing language in another way, adapting the Ricardian emphasis on meaning to his crusade against alien intrusions on English).[13] He would make the case for Eliot's poetry on the grounds of Eliot's vision of poetic tradition, with some modifications. A natural conjunction with a distinguished precedent: Coleridge had of course turned his attention to criticism with the explicit aim of making the case for Wordsworth, the best poet of his generation. This entailed, in the labyrinth of the *Biographia Literaria*, a consideration of the past of English poetry — a scattered version of tradition, and the visible tip of a critical vision largely submerged in the notebooks and marginalia. Wordsworth figured in the *Biographia* as the poet who combined natural thought with natural diction, the culmination of a long development in English poetry. It was Coleridge who bracketed the rhetorical Augustan idiom, proposing as an alternative model Wordsworth's natural style. Coleridge made a place for Wordsworth which Wordsworth could not have made for himself. The new criticism of the 1930s and after would adopt the same posture toward the new poetry, ably defending its idiom on the basis of a valorization of ambiguity, irony, and paradox in literary tradition. But Coleridge, the antecedent of this mode of argument, would be shunted aside in the process. It was Leavis who was principally responsible for this occlusion of critical precedent and critical principle.

"Dr. Richards, Bentham, and Coleridge," Leavis's long review essay of *Coleridge on Imagination*, appeared in *Scrutiny* soon after the book's publication in 1935. Leavis distinguished Coleridge at the outset from Richards's treatment of him. Eliot was cited for his "purity of interest" in poetry, against Richards's "diagnostic attitude,"[14] which would make a science of Coleridge's critical practice. This is a crux: anything methodological, or speculative, put Leavis off. He demolished Richards from within an entrenched native empiricism (a Wordsworthian "matter-of-factness," to apply Coleridge's valuable term) without dealing with the book's real point: that Coleridge might provide modern readers a way of thinking about poetry. Leavis made it an occasion for dispatching Richards once and for all. He was not long in taking the same tone with Coleridge. His *Scrutiny* piece of 1940 finished the job begun in 1935.[15] Here the philosophical context of Coleridge's critical achievement was jettisoned immediately as extra-literary. The cardinal concept of imagination suffered accordingly, since Coleridge's definition of it relies on a critically developed sense of "perception." Such a sense might have gone far to correct Leavis's disabling myopia vis-à-vis figurative language. Instead, he indicted "imagination" by innuendo, citing Shelley's praise of Coleridge, "subtle-souled psychologist," as evidence of a bent which is colored, in context, by association with the fallen Richards. Shelley's honorific was thus inverted to insinuation. English culture's most compelling critical intelligence was stilled in this influential line of response through Leavis's distaste for expansive critical reflection and the sort of writing which it appeared to justify.

Leavis mistook Coleridge, evidently, because of his own commitments and what they entailed. Yet Coleridge represented, as I have proposed, a potential resource for Leavis's critical activity. A resource lost, in the event, with everything it might have conferred in the way of authority and continuity in tradition. Leavis could not recognize Coleridge's achievement because he had already made him over as proto-Ricardian, a theorist without a vital practice. Thus, when it came to considering Coleridge's extended treatment of Wordsworth in the second volume of the *Biographia*, Leavis could only shrug and pass on. For he had maintained that the theory was vain and the practice inconsequent. Yet Coleridge remains Wordsworth's most durable critic and that at a time when Wordsworth's prestige is considerable. He is the lasting source of the fundamental questions.[16]

As for practical consequence, there is no more penetrating account of the kind in the critical canon until modern criticism learned to perform on Coleridge's stage. The critique of Wordsworth amounts, indeed, to what Leavis had demanded of Richards in 1935: "Coleridge's theory can be developed only in an arduous and scrupulous exploration of the organic complexities of poetry by a developing analysis—by an analysis going deeper and deeper and taking wider and wider relations into account."[17] This is just what Coleridge *does* realize in moving beyond the question of poetic diction as it arises in Wordsworth's career to the horizon of the poetic as distinctive discourse, and on to the matter of the poet in the wider lens of human experience. Coleridge is there for Leavis, as a model and a resource, yet Leavis will not recognize him. The failure of critical transmission appears in this dismal moment a lapse of self-understanding.

What were the consequences? They might have proved worse, considering the authority accruing to *Scrutiny* and to its founder personally. "We need not, I think, take too seriously those who try to dissociate the poet and the philosopher [in Coleridge]": so wrote Herbert Read in 1949, before a symposium which counted among its speakers John Crowe Ransom, Allen Tate, and R. P. Blackmur, as well as Benedetto Croce.[18] It was not Leavis but the procrustean Quiller-Couch whom he adduced as the archdichotomist, a move which casts Leavis's dismissive exercise in very different light. That pragmatic temper, intolerant of any intrusion of the ideal in poetry—a pragmatism here assigned to America but also to an entrenched way of reading in England—precisely characterizes the Leavis who would debase Coleridge's critical activity to metaphysical brainstorming. Read's apology was not untypical, but the damage had been done.

Coleridge's mature critical practice began at a moment when he was concerned to discover the roots of his thinking. The developing critique of Wordsworth proceeded in tandem with his critique of empiricism and with his turn to the new German critical philosophy. The literary is constantly brought into relation in Coleridge's reading with larger ideas which confer range and scope on matters which might otherwise appear parochial. It is not necessary to make Coleridge's criticism rotate, like Hegel's wheels, within a metaphysical combine in order to appreciate what is gained by the propinquity of these very different investigations. Read maintains that "Coleridge made the criticism of *method* the basis of his aesthetics" (*LC*, 83): a difficult, unsubstantiated claim and certainly misleading as applied to the quality of Coleridge's habitual responses to writing. If he aspired on occasion to "a philosophical method of criticism" (*LC*, 88), even "a science of

Criticism," it remained one project among others, something expressed in the subjunctive or optative voice. His aspiration to method remained an invigorating force in his reading, all the same.

Coleridge as the exponent of philosophical method in criticism is less tenable, on the available evidence, than Coleridge as a reader of exemplary habit. Semasiology as conceived by Richards had attempted to promote the reading on the basis of a thin tissue of observations on language. Leavis dismissed the reading out of impatience with the immethodical method of Coleridge's thinking, and out of exasperation with Richards. Faced with the continued erosion of traditional reading habits, current practitioners could be forgiven for dismissing their contrary claims as survivals of a lost continent of sensibility. Yet they underwrite the kinds of claims that can now be made in Coleridge's name. Meanwhile, the arrival of the French new wave has inspired fresh attention to Coleridge on language — an attention compromised by an impoverished sense of the past. It is a sign, indeed, of the critical bind for which that past has come to stand that the inspiration has been largely imported.

Semasiology in America

Coleridge is the prototype of the analytic approach, and the prime literary source for the rationalist bent, of the American criticism which arose in response to the modernist enterprise. It was engaged criticism, concerned to make a place for what was new and interesting on the basis of a conservative view of tradition derived largely from Eliot's early essays. Variations in individual practice do not obscure the primary commitment of the new critics to poetry. With its own ground rules and long historical privilege, it was an epitome of good thinking in an illustrious form. Coleridgean features, in a familiar line of transmission: in Ransom's eponymous survey of 1941, the new criticism begins from Richards and Eliot. It occupies the place in American letters which Leavis and *Scrutiny* occupy in England. Differences of culture and temperament gave the American development a more speculative cast, opening it to influences from Kant to Veblen, keeping it abreast of modern thinking. But its notion of what was literary remained constricted, except perhaps in the work of Kenneth Burke, with consequences that came clear in a second generation of practitioners. The institutionalization of the new criticism proceeded through the consolidation of techniques of reading which codified its commitment to irony, paradox, and ambiguity.[19] The mainly conservative social ideals of its first generation — Ransom and Tate, Blackmur, Burke, and Winters — were sublated in the process. Understanding poetry in a historical vacuum would become the stock in trade of their inheritors.

The institutional form which the new criticism assumed in America changed everything while paying homage to the old gods, Coleridge foremost among them. The new emphasis on reading as technique simply inverted the basic values of his critical intelligence, which was expansive, synthetic, and inclusive. In the long perspective opened by recognizing the affiliations of his critical activity in modern thinking about literature, it is clear that analytic procedure was split off from historical motive in response to cultural forces which were widely recognized but seldom effectively confronted. Scientism stands foremost among these. Richards's move to America was emblematic: American thinking is of course hospitable to the diagnostic attitude which Leavis charged him with having adopted. Yet he met with resistance, and not only from Eliot. In an early survey of prevailing practices, Blackmur drew a parallel between the Cartesian reduction of philosophy to epistemology and the Ricardian reduction of criticism to linguistic science.[20] And he observed the abyss which it opens in critical practice: "Because it is possible to apply scientific methods to the language of poetry, and because scientific methods engross their subject matter, Mr. Richards places the whole burden of criticism in the application of a scientific approach, and asserts it to be an implement for the judgment of poetry. Actually, it can only handle the language and its words and cannot touch — except by assertion — the imaginative product of the words which is poetry: which is the object revealed or elucidated by criticism." That imaginative product, the object of criticism, was a historically constituted matter which yielded only to informed critical intelligence. The reification of poetry as "language" was a move which betrayed "the poem as it is read and as what it represents is felt" (*LG*, 390).

Despite resistance to the linguistic reduction performed by Richards, his approach to reading proved catching — in part perhaps because it seemed to address the large objections to Coleridge on imagination posed by Irving Babbitt. These are summarized in Babbitt's rather commonplace observation that "analogies to be of value should surely have validity apart from the mere shifting mood of the man who perceives them."[21] The subjective was under pressure, and imagination was vulnerable to the charge that it was the vehicle of merely private vision. In defense, Richards had tried to make it appear more responsible, even objective in its workings. Following Coleridge's lead, he presented it as a cognitive faculty; by implication it became a uniform process which could be repeated by readers nearly automatically. The linguistic function of imagination rescued the concept from abstraction, settling it in a medium which could be measured. As Babbitt observed in a summary judgment anticipating Leavis, Coleridge "does not succeed in disengaging his theory of the imagination sufficiently from the transcendental mist."[22] Semasiology brought it down to earth, opening it to verification, saving poetry by dispersing mists and sceptics at once.

Babbitt is germane here because of his influence on Eliot, who made his teacher's dyspathy for the romantic into a program for reading: at once a way of reading and a view of literary tradition, of what was worth reading. These are, in effect, interchangeable. Donne could be read as investing his ideas in objects: he was therefore good. At this basic level Eliot reproduced Babbitt's suspicion of imagination as something irretrievably subjective. Their concerns converge with Richards's effort to secure imagination in language in order to verify and control it. Liberty of imagination had become an intolerable hangover in the bright light of science. Poetry would have to be defended as a rigorous exercise if it were to survive at all.

On American ground the claims of tradition counted for less than they did in England. Though the political motive of the Southern Agrarians (Ransom and Tate among them) led them to recuperate poetry as a means of holding on to a lost past, their effort had nothing like the polemical force of Leavis's project. Southern agrarianism was obviously reactionary in a way that the cryptopastoralism of *Scrutiny* was not. As a substitute for the argument from tradition, recourse to high reason was an attractive, perhaps inevitable route to legitimacy. Against this background, the new criticism in America might be described as an effort to fill in the blanks of Coleridge's claim for a logic of poetry, "as severe as that of science" (*BL* I, 4). Ransom's book set out to pursue the analogy by disposing of the psychologism prevalent in current critical practice.[23] Richards served him as he had served Leavis, as a scapegoat for sins of the subjective. But he got a fair (and extensive) reading which exposed the behaviorist reflexes of his project without dismissing his aspiration to a coherent aesthetic theory. Richards was made to stand for the shortcomings of linguistic science as the basis of a theory of poetry, yet his position at the head of the new criticism was affirmed. The diagnostic attitude had found a home in America.

In the wake of *Coleridge on Imagination*, "semasiology" became a code word for the inadequacy of Richards as a model of critical response. For Blackmur, writing in 1951, it would be associated with semantics and semiotics, and buried with Basic English (*LG*, 428). But Richards's enterprise lived on under other names. The commitments of semasiology converged on the phenomenon of metaphor—with mimesis, the oldest matter of poetics. For Aristotle, it was a poet's most important resource. Coleridge had sketched, in the opening chapters of the *Biographia Literaria*, a summary history of the newer English poetry based in part on its changing metaphoric expression, with Wordsworth at the end of the argument. Semasiology had made a program of Coleridge's practice. The verbal conception of imagination, the suspicion of direct signification, the defense of poetic obliquity: Richards's positions pointed to metaphor as the touchstone of poetic value. One step farther and the meaning of the poem is the structure of its imagery. This is of the course the new critical step. Not a uniform step in the work of the American school, yet representative enough. It was Ransom who developed the cardinal distinction of structure and texture in poetry, and though Blackmur moved quickly to suppress it, the essentialist idea of structure became common coin in American critical practice. Poetry would be understood as a species of logical exercise expanded through the special resources of metaphor.[24] Ransom's discussion of Richards on metaphor, a crux of *The New Criticism*, acquires fresh value in this long context.

For it was at this point that semasiology was cleared through customs and domesticated. Ransom argues in effect that Richards was won over by Coleridge. By which he means that Richards had come to recognize the "cognitive office" of poetry and to defend "the logic of poetic discourse" (*NC*, 74):

> Coleridge's specific theory of poetry has to do with the act of the Secondary Imagination in composing the poetic metaphor, and with its consequence, the noblest poetic object which we can experience. If in the *Principles* Richards conceives metaphor as smuggling irrelevance into discourse, in the *Coleridge* he begins to accent Coleridge's special understanding of metaphor, and in the *Rhetoric* he has just about gone over. There will be a difference between the two conceptions. Coleridge in his doctrine is very close to Hegel's theory of poetry. He is continually talk-

ing about poetic imagination as an "esemplastic" faculty, reconciling opposites into a unity. Its work is a "coadunation"; and also furnishes a kind of "interinanimation" between the opposed parts of the metaphor, which are, as Richards would say, the tenor and the vehicle. He has a metaphysical prepossession on behalf of unity and synthesis, and naturally on behalf of relevance as better than irrelevance. But the point is that the new unit of discourse contained in the metaphor for Coleridge is still irrelevant to the rest of the discourse.   (NC, 76–77)

Ransom's reconstruction is fast and loose: it is not metaphor in particular, but poetic discourse in general that is a product of imagination for Coleridge. The shift is symptomatic. Semasiology fulfilled its vocation in converting Ransom to linguistic terms for understanding imagination. He had already dismissed tenor and vehicle—Richards's terms—yet they come back to inhabit his thinking about metaphor. For he distinguishes his own position on doubtful grounds. It is true that the local effect counts for much in Coleridge's (and Richards's) appreciation of poetry. Yet in principle at least, Coleridge subordinates the parts to the whole in considerations of poetic value.[25] Ransom's divorce of structure and texture only reorganizes these relations, defining terms, clarifying ordonnance. He embraces Richards at arm's length. In the end there is little real difference in their positions on the structure of metaphor, on its definitive relation to poetic discourse, or on the linguistic function of imagination.

"Wanted: An Ontological Critic," the concluding essay of Ransom's book, provides a conspectus of his revision of semasiology. It begins from a familiar sense of poetry as distinctive discourse. Distinctive in structure, but also in content: "It treats an order of existence, a grade of objectivity, which cannot be treated in scientific discourse" (NC, 281). The search for ontological ground leads him inexorably to language. He passes over Richards's aimless treatment of the matter in favor of Charles Morris, whose distinction of symbolic and iconic signs becomes the basis of Ransom's claim that "science deals exclusively in pure symbols, but art deals essentially, though not exclusively, in iconic signs" (NC, 287). This turns out to mean little more than that art is presentational, constitutive of what it signifies: "In the play, the icon is our image of Prince Hamlet, and it is never twice the same, so that the rule of consistent definitive reference is abrogated with each reappearance" (NC, 291). Hardly a radical revision of Richards. Rather a codification, or consolidation, of the point of view which he had promoted in the name of semasiology. The ontological critic would be concerned with poetry as semiosis. He would not be concerned—this is the real force of "ontology"—with semiosis as a social process, and product. The vestiges of social address lurking in semasiology (Empson at least had made something of them) were conspicuously eliminated in the revision.

Ransom's discussion of meter provides a more decisive modification of Richards's position. His adherence to meter as an indispensable determinant of meaning restores the Coleridgean emphasis. The poet-critic brought to the issue a sense of the mutuality of music and phrasing in poetic practice which disposes sotto voce of meter as "the movement of meaning." (Richards never actually appears as the occasion of the argument. His presence is indicated obliquely, in a chart with ciphers, a residuum of scientific aspiration which Ransom could not resist.) Instead of dismissing meter as a relic of the old dispensation, Ransom elevates it to iconic status. Its contribution to poetry is made indispensable in this way. The rejection of meter by modern writers is taken as a sign of their schismatic condition. Thus, Ransom follows Richards in linking the decline of metric practice to modern circumstances even if he deplores the result instead of approving it. Semasiology as a critical accompaniment of modernism gives way here to a poetic ontology in doubt of modernism's distinctive achievement.

While Leavis hectored Richards's diagnostic attitude, Ransom transformed it into the basis of his own. Both made of it what they needed for very different ends; both left Richards behind. A more disinterested response to semasiology, and one which remains essential reading for understanding what has become of the institution of criticism, appeared in Allen Tate's essay, "Literature as Knowledge." Writing in 1941, quite likely in connection with the publication of his mentor's book on the subject, Tate situated semasiology in an Arnoldian line beginning from Coleridge and culminating in the crisis of poetry in the positivist moment. Tate did not dismiss Richards out of hand. He considered him symptomatically, as the continuer of a long effort to accommodate poetry within a new cognitive order. "Literature as Knowledge" posits a canker at the root of the crisis of modern criticism. It represents indeed the most radical critique of Coleridge's position forthcoming in modern critical discussion. More thoughtful than Babbitt, dispassionate as Leavis could not be, Tate considered the project of semasiology without yielding to its programmatic aspiration.

Coleridge on Imagination, that great chimaera, he took as "the most ambitious attempt of a modern critic to force into unity the antithesis of language and subject, of pleasure and truth . . . an antithesis which has harassed critical theory since the time of Coleridge" (*LK*, 45). Not a successful attempt, yet instructive for what it said of the critical condition. Instead of dismissing the diagnostic attitude, Tate would commit it to the service of the "experience of the poem" which "we must never leave" (*LK*, 48). Poetry lost its raison d'être when debased to an object of investigation, as it was in Charles Morris's proposition that poetics be considered a branch of semiotic. Ransom had taken the bait. Tate did not, and he proposed, astutely, that Morris's "iconic sign" was merely an evasive formulation of the image (*LK*, 28–29). It was nothing new: Richards had been there fifteen years before. In "Literature as Knowledge," Tate showed himself better than a generation ahead of the critical resistance which emerged in the seventies to continental versions of Morris's claim.

Ransom and Tate on the future of Morris's semiotic: a proleptic enactment of structuralism and its aftermath. The susceptibility of American criticism to the structuralist enterprise, which seemed so new, shows that the lesson had been lost. Such is the price the American institution paid for ignoring its own history. Tate would salvage Richards's rational inquiry for a criticism that would not turn its back on the poem as aesthetic object. In this he differed fundamentally from Leavis, who lost the constructive force of semasiology when he condemned the diagnostic attitude out of hand. The strength of the new criticism in America would lie in its attention to textual detail. Its poverty of theory might be considered an advantage in this context, insofar as it kept the reader at the poem. The example of the criticism of two generations past suggests that this Coleridgean tenacity of response counts for more in the long run than critical empires built on foundations of tendentious reading. Literature has a way of surviving its allegorists, whether it is Tradition or Mind being constructed.

Coleridge was of course an allegorist of sorts himself, and so was Tate. "Natural thoughts with natural diction" presumes a great deal of nature. What makes Coleridge's criticism an example to which all of the new critics would recur, theoretical reservations notwithstanding, is its balancing of the claims of the reader and the text. Despite his air of abstraction, Coleridge approaches reading as an extensive activity which brings him into relation with the world: with history as it is condensed in language, with discourse as social formation. Reading is for him a form of relation, not of dissociation or escape. Yet he reads as a practitioner, with an eye for significant form, for the way meaning is invested in language, for the way it makes the case. Because he has always been read in bits—because even the *Biographia* is read in bits— it is inevitably the theoretic Coleridge who gets a hearing. Not mistakenly, but partially: for Coleridge the critical allegorist, fabricator of reason, understanding, and imagination, is possible only on the back of Coleridge the indefatigable reader, with everything he invests in the exercise of his living concerns. This Coleridge is buried in marginalia and notes. It is this Coleridge who confers the engagement and range which is missing in our sense of the other, the idealizing Coleridge of Chapter XIII of the *Biographia*. If Tate turned to Chapter XIII for the root of the crisis in modern criticism, he was only following the lead of informed critical intelligence.

What he found there was a sense of poetry's effect as a special ratio of pleasure to truth. Coleridge had distinguished poetry from science on this basis. Its immediate object was pleasure, where that of science was truth. Not that poetry was unconcerned with truth (nor science with pleasure); it was a question of priority. Coleridge's valorization of pleasure in poetry amounted for Tate to a valorization of atomistic reading, the whole as no more than a calculus of the parts. Concentrating on the single passage in Chapter XIII where Coleridge formulates these relations canonically, as it were, Tate lost sight of the vast project of reading from which it was abstracted. That Coleridge immediately contradicted Tate's construction of the passage in his remarks on Isaiah, Tate took as a sign of Coleridge's confusion—not of his own. He concluded, momentously: "There is, then, in Coleridge's poetic theory a persistent dilemma. He cannot make up his mind whether the specifically poetic element is an objective feature of the poem, or is distinguishable only as a subjective effect. He cannot, in short, choose between metaphysics and psychology. His general emphasis is psychological, with metaphysical ambiguities" (*LK*, 39). A radical critique indeed, if it were true to the spirit (or the letter) of Coleridge's criticism. Yet the dilemma Tate sketched never occurred to Coleridge in this form because reading was not riven for him by an inert opposition of subject and object. Tate made Coleridge a screen for Richards's quandaries in this way. And he concluded that "Coleridge's failure to get out of the dilemma of Intellect-or-Feeling has been passed on to us as a fatal legacy" (*LK*, 40).

Astute as he otherwise showed himself to be in "Literature as

Knowledge," Tate lapsed into a trick of projection in formulating a vanishing point of this sort in critical tradition. The canker was original, apparently ineluctable. But to put it this way was to indulge in an allegorical habit of longer pedigree than Coleridge's. The effect of Tate's summary judgment, taken with the suppression of Richards's erratic dialogue with Coleridge by Ransom, has meant divorce from a model of formidable critical intelligence just when criticism is most in need of one.

The Structure of Complex Words

While Leavis was defining his position against the example of semasiology, and Ransom was adapting Richards's approach to the setting of the American institution, Empson was involved in an early revision of his mentor's way of reading. *Seven Types of Ambiguity* (1930) appeared five years before semasiology was codified in *Coleridge on Imagination*; its precocious intelligence must have given Richards pause. The book was widely influential. George Fraser, in a fine essay in appreciation, takes it to be "at the roots of all that is most stimulating, as well as much that is most perverse in the American New Criticism."[26] Empson might indeed be regarded as the original of that contrary energy which so productively complicated the development of institutional criticism out of Cambridge English. As this past comes to be seen as the real topos of current critical argument — its prototype and enduring ideological resource — Empson's role in the formation of deconstructive reading will assume real importance. In *Seven Types of Ambiguity* he was deconstructing semasiology *avant la lettre* while turning meaning into a sphere of conflict. His "ambiguity" rived the simplicity of Ricardian "statement" beyond recognition. "Seven types" was an incantation, the hieratic number turned on textuality, which was about to become as transcendental as the White Goddess. The ingenuity of the book is still engaging, and not only for its premonitions about semasiology as a science of the future.

Empson began with the emphasis on rhythm characteristic of the best modernist thinking. He made it the basis of a novel discrimination of poetry and prose: the former was more elaborate in its ambiguity, encouraged by the devices of meter and rhyme, which "make it seem sensible to diverge from the colloquial order of statement, and so imply several colloquial orders from which the statement has diverged."[27] The discussion had taken off silently from Coleridge's insistence (against Wordsworth) on poetic procedure as conventional, a matter of the reader's knowing what to expect.[28] The equal and continuous attention which is in part a function of meter, and the crux of Coleridge's own sense of poetry's difference, was translated in this way into ambiguity, a textual property. The affective standard was in effect reified, and the polysemic quality of verse associated with rhythmic shifts from prose word order. The reader registered these as "a variety of statements in one order" (*ST*, 40). It was not only in a differential way that rhythm functioned but "as a means of insisting upon, and then limiting, the possible implications" (*ST*, 40). The stamp of the mathematical mind is clearly visible here, in the notion of meaning as a variable function in a field, subject to asymptotic control.

As a corrective in advance to meter as the motion of meaning, Empson's elegant exposition shows brilliantly. He was alert to the problem of subsuming sound to meaning as Richards had done. The book set out to break up the static opposition of poetry as Pure Sound and as Pure Meaning, the older and the newer dispensations. His effort to connect stylistic practices with signification at the theoretic base was leading, and recalls the direction of Coleridge's argument in the *Biographia* and elsewhere. It combined a reader's common sense with the ability to think broadly about how poetry signified, and what that implied of its uses. His discussion described a way of reading which was familiar, including for instance the subliminal comparison between prosaic statement and poetic elaboration. Yeats's compositional habits verified Empson's instincts: poetry might be built up from a prose statement just as readers work back, from their side, toward plain sense. Rhythm as a means of limitation responded, too, to Wordsworth's sense of meter as control. Rather than dispensing with it, as Richards seemed to urge, Empson celebrated sound under the rule of a motivation which could not be split off from the general process of poetic signification.

As rhythm led him to a preliminary formulation of ambiguity as the intrinsic property of verse, ambiguity led him in turn to a valorization of complexity and contradiction in the delivery of poetic meaning. Not for its own sake—"it must in each case arise from, and be justified by, the peculiar requirements of the situation"—but all the same, "it is a thing which the more interesting and valuable situations are more likely to justify" (*ST*, 298). Poetry became then the most developed form of verbal order, in a familiar sense. Empson conceived of it very much as Coleridge had done in his formulation of poetic pleasure as more than the sum of particular effects. He turned the Coleridgean insistence on whole response against Richards's quadrivium of Sense, Feeling, Tone, and Intention: "Thus to say a thing in two parts is different in incalculable ways from saying it as a unit; Coleridge says somewhere that the mind insists on having a single word for a single mental operation, and will use an inadequate word rather than two adequate ones" (*ST*, 302). Coleridge on language rose here against the Richards who would attempt to use his diffuse observations for a science of meaning. Empson's astute citation indicated in advance how specious semasiology would prove in rendering Coleridge's thinking serviceable. It showed also how he might be read instead: aphoristically, in the settled context of habits of reading recognized, if not always well understood, by experienced practitioners. This is how Friedrich Schlegel wrote, and was read, in a comparable setting.[29] Coleridge the romantic aphorist, as against the adept of philosophical method, offered something as yet unplumbed in a cultural situation which favored the large formulation. The contemporary concern for what the language of poetry said about the possibility of thinking underwrote the tendency of Empson's inquiry.

Eliot considered his work philosophical, under the aegis of Richards; to Fraser it appears methodological on account of its exceptional consistency.[30] *Seven Types of Ambiguity* provided a point of clear resolution in the general confusion of an emergent way of reading. Yet Empson's reading can no more be reduced to first principles than Coleridge's, despite the inchoate field theory of the one and the aspiration to philosophical method of the other. Both amount, rather, to a defense of reading *for something*: for understanding, initially, in a philosophically particular sense of the word. Coleridge was of course occupied in extracting Kant's "understanding" from reason. It is less generally appreciated that he came to identify human understanding with naming:

> Thus, in all instances, it is words, names, or if images, yet images used as words or names, that are alone the subjects of Understanding. In no instance do we understand a thing in itself; but only the name to which it is referred . . . the proper functions of the understanding [are those] of generalizing the notices received from the Senses in order to the construction of *Names*: of referring particular notices (*i.e.*, impressions or sensa-

tions) to their proper Name, and vice versa, names to their correspondent class or kind of Notices.[31]

Reading as a propaedeutic to understanding naturally led him to see poetry as more than an exercise in sensibility: as participating in a logic of imagination, working through sensation. Poetry might indeed be regarded as preparation for philosophy in this way, the language of the latter differing from common language only in precision and consistency.[32] If this approximates the course of Coleridge's own pursuit of understanding it explains how he came to see poetry and philosophy as essentially related. In the *Biographia* the relation was expressed, in the words of a recent commentator, as "the possibility of deriving from philosophy, the science of sciences, a guiding light to illuminate what would otherwise remain in the darkness."[33]

The philosophical critic begins from understanding, but always in connection with an existing problematic. For Coleridge it was Reason against Faith, the Kantian knot, and it was to this that he returned in *Aids to Reflection*. For Empson the understanding promoted by reading for ambiguity led to an alternative sense of English and its possibilities. This is clearly indicated where he writes of "the value of a detached and willing attitude to grammar" (*ST*, 301)—so different in tone from Leavis's catechism of the literal proprieties. When he goes on to observe that "the grammatical sentence is not the only form of statement in modern English" he evokes Wittgenstein, or even Walter Benjamin's "prompt language," of the same period.[34] It is against the enterprise of Leavis that he rings true at this distance, for there is a feeling here for the stifling insistences of institutional language, apparently in response to Cambridge English in its formative moment. Richards was his target, but what he concluded about critical dogma (*ST*, 324) and about the "position of the literary critic" as social more than scientific (*ST*, 310) applies to the founder of *Scrutiny* with different, but equal force. Richards had raised the question of language for Empson—this was the real subject of his book—but it was the abuse of language as an institution that he stood against in his conclusion.

Empson was then very much the product of Cambridge English, not just as Richards's student but in his preoccupation with language as the opening question. It should be clear that his approach actually had little in common with Richards's diagnostic attitude, despite Eliot's "philosophical" proposition. Empson's treatment of the question of English, and of poetry as its consummate expression, was quite different. *Seven Types of Ambiguity* set out to trace the "stages of advancing logical disorder" (*ST*, 62) in the phenomena of poetic ambiguity. The book took poetry seriously as a rational formation and attempted to understand both what it meant and what it said of ways of thinking. For the "stages of advancing logical disorder" replicated features of the historical development of English poetry. Not consistently, of course: Chaucer was conspicuous in the early stages of the process, but he also figured later on. And Shakespeare was conspicuous throughout, a deep mine of ambiguity of every description. With the romantics the story became dramatic, however. Shelley and Wordsworth, two key instances, showed signs of losing the thread in their verse. Their language carried them away: their thinking could not keep pace. This Empson turned, not into an inquisition, but into an advanced stage of logical disorder. It was of interest, both as poetry and as a reflection of a historical condition. It was not that poets had lost the ability to control and shape the language. Rather, it was being put to a different use, the formation of thought, with all the ambiguity entailed. The contrast with Leavis against romanticism could hardly have been more pointed — or more subversive, when this ambiguity was traced to the metaphysical idiom celebrated by Eliot and Leavis for logical integrity (*ST*, 208–9). Empson was concerned to get the sense of romantic language right so that readers could see what was involved in romantic poetry. His recovery of Swinburne, against the still familiar reduction of his verse to pure sound, was a virtuoso exercise of this kind (*ST*, 205–7). The point of course was a poetic "logic, severe as that of science," yet more variable than Coleridge's formula had perhaps envisioned.

The culmination of logical disorder occurred in the sixth type, sometimes in reaction to romantic shuffling, as Empson called it. Here, "a statement says nothing, by tautology, by contradiction, or by irrelevant statements, if any" (*ST*, 223). The dialogue of Wilde, the nonsense of Carroll and Lear, and Yeats's "Who will go drive with Fergus now" showed how good writers came by extraordinary effects with this terminal ambiguity, which promised meaning it refused to deliver. Prufrock's monologue sums up its ironic possibilities in modern verse, though Empson did not cite it. Nor did he situate this voice, as Kenner would, satirically, against its romantic antecedents.[35] The sixth type is of particular interest for showing what Empson made of the poetic potential of *various* employments of the language. It was in his adherence to what might be called verbal integrity — the way writers realized a vital way of thinking, not just a range of poetic effects—that his deep affiliation with Coleridge showed most distinctively. "Activity of thought in the play of words," as Coleridge noticed tersely of *Venus and Adonis* (*SC* I, 217): not a startling idea at this remove, but a crucial one for the formation of modern criticism and still worth considering against those who would turn the history of literature into a morality play.

In his survey of prevailing practices in 1948, Stanley Edgar Hyman characterized Empson's reading as "categorical," meaning something like generic, and referring principally to *Some Versions of Pastoral* (1935).[36] Empson does show interest in generic convention, but not in the prescriptive way which the term often involves. His chapters in that book on proletarian writing and *Alice in Wonderland* showed how far afield of prescriptive pastoral he was thinking. Hazlitt, adduced by Hyman as the prototype of such broadly generic reading, makes a more likely affiliate than the literary Darwinists with their teleological evolutionism. For it was not typically the process of transmission but the peculiar product which interested Empson—the transfiguration of the type (or types) in the inflections of the restlessly seeking imagination. Empson was possessed of such an imagination himself, and it defies the categories which Hyman tried out on him, one after another. Far from "the application of Richards's theories about the nature of meaning and poetic interpretation" (*AV*, 293), his early books represented a decisive turn away from Ricardian habits and terminology, as I have been arguing in the case of the first of them. Whatever his other sources (he was a syncretist of the best sort) it was Coleridge who supplied the integrative understanding which informed a long career. Empson followed Richards in attending to the notebooks, taking Coleridge at his speculative best. Coleridge the poet, of the "Ancient Mariner" especially, counted for more than meets the eye, as a long and responsive late essay shows.[37] And Coleridge the curious reader, of Shakespeare in particular, was never far from his instincts.

Empson's magnum opus is undoubtedly *The Structure of Complex Words*,[38] a study in linguistic context and an extraordinary theory of verbal dreamwork in English verse. It is a challenging book, one which gives the lie to the continental view of modern English criticism as plodding and parochial. Empson sets out to correct Richards at the base by showing that emotive language cannot be considered distinct from scientific, or cognitive language as he calls it. The language of verse is fundamentally similar to that of the drawing room or of diplomacy: it functions in a social context which is indicated in material ways in the forms and formulae of speech, and which modifies the sense of individual words. The discussion relies on current work in linguistics, but it qualifies its sources through the special commitment it brings to bear. The burden of the argument is that modern reading requires a better grasp of language; that the better grasp must be broadly social, not narrowly literary; and that poetry performs stunts of semantic speculation, or imaginative lexicography, which amount to consequent argument, or structure (in Ransom's acceptation). The first two positions no longer appear controversial, despite institutional resistance to thinking about language. The third binds poetry to the history of the language as reflecting (and creating) ways of thinking from within discrete semantic fields. The idea is appealing but hypothetical, a volatile combination Empson handles with tact.

The algebra of signification which he developed to simplify his discussion led readers to exaggerate its difficulty. Having resumed poetry's dependence on reference (and on the familiar world of human experience in the process), he now seemed to be sacrificing it to the scientific assumptions Richards had evaded by his declaration of independence. Yet Empson's algebra was devoted to the emotive factors associated with reference—to appreciative and depreciative pregnancies of sense "imposed by a play of feeling" (*SCW*, 16), to mood as it colored signification. The point was not that poetry could be reduced to symbolic logic. As his first book had suggested, readers were divided between poetry as sound and poetry as sense. In order to integrate their responses it was necessary to insist on the way that the feelings could be identified within the forms of the language as they appeared on the page. They were not superimposed from without, they were a part of the script. Directions for reading in this way were "given by the immediate context," so that the emotion associated with a word was "an extremely public object, practically as much so as the Sense; there is a presumption that anybody would feel it under the circumstances" (*SCW*, 36, 34). Empson's expanded arena of signification thus supplemented rather than supplanted Richards on sense. It retained the hierarchy of denotation and connotation, and continued his emphasis on the sufficiency of the text under a more inclusive idea of how poetry meant.

The next step was a different matter. Empson proposed an "equation theory" which formalized the relations between different senses of individual words as these appeared in poetic context. Words were affirmed in this way as propositional units of meaning, against the assumption of semasiology. They were themselves at issue in the development of poetic texts, as a sort of semantic unconscious telling the story in epitome. *King Lear* became a meditation on "fool," *Othello* on "honest." Considered as a modification of contemporary studies of Shakespeare's imagery, Empson's theory took the verbal basis of meaning to its limits. The meaning of the poem was not only to be isolated in the structure of its imagery, but in the semantic equations within its key words. A momentous step, as we shall see, for the future of Cambridge English, since it appears to have underwritten (if not actually to have inspired) Raymond Williams's recognition of the value of such words. The literary idea of words, celebrated by Coleridge, contested by Richards, rehabilitated by Leavis, rose again in Empson to define another way of reading, one which relied on old habits.

He was cautious about the implications of a position at once so rooted and so marginal. Richards, to be sure, but also Coleridge had to be placated. Rather than facing the doubtful master, he took on the grand inquisitor directly, defending the proposition that "a clear-cut equation theory is needed":

> Perhaps it would be more of a test to wonder whether Coleridge would agree with me, not whether Professor Richards would in a Coleridgean frame of mind. Coleridge would be likely to despise any equation theory as trying to reduce the absorption of the living water of thought to a manipulation of "fixities and definities." I don't myself think that there is a fundamental difference here . . . I do not see that Coleridge need have objected to such an account; indeed I think it gives a reasonable basis for some very bold suggestions by Coleridge, to the effect that too much definiteness of terms is a bad thing, wasting "the vital and idea-creating force" and preventing "originality." (*SCW*, 57)

The tactic of recurrence to Coleridge in this context is as remarkable as the claim of solidarity with his thinking about language. For it exposes with rare clarity the authority of his example for the practice of Cambridge English. This was the voice by which reading was tested, even for those who, like Empson, made no large claims on his name. If Richards were to be challenged effectively, it could only be through his own informant. It is a measure of Empson's fealty that he proceeded in this way. For the effect was affirmative; the Coleridgean foundations were in place, even if the institutional superstructure appeared shaky.

Empson's recourse to Coleridge on language was astute conceptually as well as tactically. For Coleridge read with an attention to words as units of meaning even as he insisted on the symbolic function of language in conveying the process of thinking. No contradiction surfaces between the practice and the premise, perhaps because he could consider words as potentially propositional in the way I have suggested. They were not distracting from sense because they were already constitutive of it. Words were signs, participating actively in what they represented. Unlike names, which really were "fixities and definities," the element of signs was the living water of thought, and they could hardly be abstracted from it. Names might be defined—"Horse: Quadruped. Graminivorous"—but living words, as signs, exceeded naming. Empson's key words, despite their lexicographic coordinates, are signs in just this sense. His point about them might indeed be put in these terms: that the lexicon glosses names while thinking constitutes signs. Empson may be said then to have extended Coleridge's commitment to symbolic language to a critique of lexicography, on his way to a specifically linguistic conception of poetic value.

Specifically linguistic, yet social still, inasmuch as language was irrevocably social. Equation theory was not just a reformulation of metaphor, for "a metaphor is the opposite of an equation. A metaphor goes outside the ordinary range of a word, and an equation 'argues from' the ordinary range, treating it as a source of traditional wisdom" (*SCW*, 332). What Empson was about could not be considered a modification of the Ricardian thematics of metaphor, nor a cognate of Ransom's pursuit of it. For metaphor as they conceived it was very much a matter of names rather than signs—of tenor and vehicle (even if these terms had their uses) rather than a process of thought. Equation theory dealt with the intrapropositional nature of the sign: the senses of the word became significant through the equation, not as they referred to one idea or another in particular. The apparent difficulty of the conception came down in practice to a tenacious defense of the symbolic because the most interesting thinking was that to which the symbolic resources of language were fully committed. The full word against the empty name vindicated Sissy Jupe's humiliation at the hands of Gradgrind, the dismission of living experience under the rule of Richards, and the reduction of poetry to metaphor in the new criticism in general.

Although it precipitated no crisis in Cambridge English, *The Structure of Complex Words* mounted a substantial challenge to its central assumptions on Coleridgean principles. The book was not neglected, yet its force was scarcely realized in spite of its importance. Equation theory looked like symbolic logic; the reaction against scientism exacted a fresh toll here in shunting Empson's argument aside. Poetry would continue to be read, for a generation to come, as structure embellished by texture — as ornamented logic. The split between poetry as sound and poetry as sense was confirmed as essential to the institution. Subsequent efforts to breach the gap proved no more successful than Empson's. The institutional standard proved a force in its own right, greater indeed than the force of its authorizing voice, and of its own best voices. The next inside challenge to its hegemony would be mounted from a very different point of view, but with a like sense of Coleridge's bearing on the case.

3

The Etymologic of Raymond Williams

Coleridge's distinction between cultivation and civilization is counted among the important desynonymies which he introduced, or at least circulated in English parlance in a form that became influential. At first, in the 1818 recension of *The Friend*, it expressed the difference between two ways of knowing, and the consequences flowing from them. "Cultivation of the reason and of the will" was opposed to "observation of outward and sensible things as the only realities." The one led via means as purely "intellectual" as possible to a spiritual idea. The other led to refinement of "the means of sensual gratification, and the conveniencies of courtly intercourse" (CC 4:1, 501). Paradigmatic, an opposition without a middle term, the two ways were made to signify a falling-off of "the truly *human* in human nature." This Coleridge treated as typological: "Thus, both before and after the flood, the vicious of mankind receded from true cultivation, as they hurried towards civilization" (CC 4:1, 502). The obvious bearing on modern minds and modern mores went unelaborated, but it was not lost on ears that could hear. In "Signs of the Times" (1829) Carlyle treated "the two great departments of knowledge" in association with Coleridge's terms: "the outward, cultivated exclusively on mechanical principles; the inward, finally abandoned, because, cultivated on such principles, it is found to yield no result. . . ."[1] If cultivation now applied indifferently to the pursuit of both ways, "all civilized nations" referred ironically to those who would order society mechanically, according to *mere political arrangements*." This debased sense of "civilization," as against the positive values represented by cultivation or culture, became sufficiently influential to make a strong appeal to Leavis some one hundred years later.[2] Coleridge's diremption had taken root in the cultural politics of the period.

"Civilization" as a term of opprobrium and "cultivation" of the only culture worthy of the name recur late in his career in an overtly political connection. Writing in 1830, perhaps in response to Carlyle's piece of the preceding year, he expanded on his original paradigm, bringing the two ways to bear on the living situation of church and state: "[c]ivilization is itself but a mixed good, if not far more a corrupting influence, the hectic of disease, not the bloom of health, and a nation so distinguished more fitly to be called a varnished than a polished people; where this civilization is not grounded in *cultivation*, in the harmonious development of those qualities and faculties that characterise our *humanity*. We must be men in order to be citizens" (CC 10:42–43). The shift from the vatic voice of 1818 to the politic voice of 1830 shows how he applied his critical investigation to ends of more than metaphysical interest. He had been making the effort since the prospectus of *The Friend* in 1808, addressing himself to the condition of late Georgian England from a broadly critical base. Carlyle's reliance on his example is noticed in passing by Raymond Williams in a celebrated argument which situates Coleridge's achievement in a long cultural perspective very different from the constricted aesthetic appreciation of Richards and his inheritors.[3] Here he is cast as a key source of the critical reflection on the state of society continued by Carlyle and Arnold. Leavis had recognized his contribution through Mill's important early essay, making Mill's understanding the fulcrum of his own.[4] Following this lead, Williams would grasp Coleridge's position in counterpoint to Bentham's, but he would go beyond Leavis's satisfaction with Mill's division of things to recover something vital to his own practice in Coleridge's way of thinking. The recovery amounts to a new sense of Coleridge on language, and the difference of approach epitomizes Williams's role as the marginal man of Cambridge English.

Williams is of the school, yet he has always been at odds with its institutional insistences and political diffidence. He was instrumental in challenging the dismissive account of the romantic movement which was a corollary of the triumph of modernism. His emphasis in *Culture and Society* on the revolutionary ideals of the romantic poets, on their principled opposition to church and state in the worst moment of the modern English monarchy, effectively answered the Leavisite inquisition of their otherworldliness and abstraction.[5] But what of Coleridge the literary respondent, the one who wrote from a settled sense of poetic possibility and value? It was this Coleridge who had spoken to Richards, and whose name underwrote the new critical agenda. Formed by Cambridge English, Williams might almost have missed out on him in the turn away from semasiology. Yet he found the missing link indispensable, even for a resolutely reformist treatment of literary value. Coleridge the critical reader has remained a constant resource for Williams, while the poetry and philosophical enterprise have counted for very little. This scission of concerns has proved productive in ways not fathomed by Richards and his followers.

The change of direction is important for seeing how Coleridge might be brought to bear on modern reading. For it is not as an exemplar of critical method, rather as a model of response to writing in society that Coleridge has come to stand for Williams. In his "Notes on English Prose" he situates Coleridge at the head of a modern stylistics concerned with verbal integrity: "One of the marks of a conservative society is that it regards style as an absolute. A style of writing or speaking is judged as a question of manners, and appreciation of this style as a question of breeding and taste. In important literary criticism, since Coleridge, this conventional assumption has been set aside. Style is known, not as an abstract quality, but as inseparable from the substance of the ideas and feelings expressed."[6] Style as a sign of social grace yields to style as an index of intellectual force everywhere in Williams's thinking about writing, and to larger effect than in most of the important literary criticism which he derives from Coleridge. Of a strongly worded passage from Leslie Stephen's *Agnostic's Apology* (1893), Williams remarks in the same piece: "But as Stephen approaches a climax of his argument, in the last sentence, he begins to use 'utter' as a repetitive adjective: 'utter want', 'utter ignorance', 'utter incapacity'; and we catch in this a kind of domineering scepticism, which has since been widely prevalent: in some serious argument, but more generally in a persistent type of conservative journalism" (*WS*, 110). It is the Leavisite tone which he identifies in Stephen's style. The illiberal scepticism of its modern affiliates is exposed in this way, in a voice recognizably Coleridgean.

The resonance of so fine an observation reaches from Victorian periodical literature through *Scrutiny* into current polemic. Williams's idiom shows its descent from the Coleridge of *The Friend* by its attention to style and attitude: to revealing inflections and tone of voice. When Coleridge deplores the modern taste for "skipping, unconnected, short-winded asthmatic sentences, as easy to be understood as impossible to be remembered, in which the merest commonplace acquires a momentary poignancy, a petty titillating sting, from affected point and wilful antithesis; or else in strutting and rounded periods, in which the emptiest truisms are blown up into illustrious bubbles by the help of film and inflation" (*CC* 4:26), he is attacking a way of writing (and reading) for its poverty of intelligence. Not the style itself, but the inadequacy of the style as a vehicle of meaning is the point. It reveals, like Stephen's too emphatic "utter," a posture toward its object—a mincing posture, in this case, a triumph of manner over substance. Coleridge was preoccupied with this very characteristic problem in his survey of current practices in the opening installments of *The Friend*.

Williams's debt to the argument from style as Coleridge pursued it is mediated several times over, even if he recognizes its original source. Not so his idea of prose, which relies directly on a familiar formulation of the matter: "It is still remarkable, in a persistently narrow critical tradition, that the contrast between verse and prose can be made as if it were self-evidently a contrast between the 'imaginative' and the 'prosaic'. This is related to the still-common habit of using 'poetry' as a normal and adequate synonym for 'literature', and to such symptoms, even in some of the best critical writing on the novel, as describing its organization as that of a 'dramatic poem'" (*WS*, 73). It was Coleridge who defined poetry broadly for the English, and who read prose not as "prosaic" but as fully imaginative in possibility. The Arnoldian disappointment in romantic and Victorian literature is exposed on such a premise for its failure of range and sympathy. Where is the novel in his consideration of the fate of poetry? Where is the essay for Richards's semasiology? In his appreciation of the novel Williams bears passing resemblance to Leavis, who exerted an indirect influence on his critical training.[7] But it should be clear that his place in English criticism is not ancillary to Cambridge English. He is perhaps Coleridge's most original modern inheritor—an exemplary reader in his own right, in the mainstream of English critical practice despite his institutional marginality.

Marginality might almost be regarded as essential to the role. The Leavis of *New Bearings* was marginal in this way. *Scrutiny* began life, precariously enough, as an organ of reform. Its series of revaluations lay at the heart of the enterprise. Williams has recognized the achievement despite the temperamental gulf which separates him from its collaborators. Yet his second-generation revaluations have not fared well among the old revaluers. His recourse to social principle is easily dismissed as "ideological"—a charge he does not discourage. The immethodical method of his criticism is vulnerable as well, for reasons worth taking up at length. His marginality, associated in recent commentary with the problem of his method, is only the other side of his commitment to something larger than English. If Coleridge's name stands for anything now, it should stand for the possibilities of this sort of marginality.

In his retrospective account of Cambridge English, Williams lays stress on the shadowy language component of "English Literature, Life and Thought"—out of sight, yet very much on the minds of Richards and Leavis, in different ways. For Williams too language was the necessary anchor of such a curriculum, for the evident reason that "it is in language that the decisive practices and relations which are projected as 'literature', 'life', and 'thought' are real and discoverable" (WS, 188). To start elsewhere meant settling for a restrictively literary notion of the language or evading the question entirely. Institutional English has proved, indeed, congenitally susceptible to restrictive versions of the tongue. The continued vitality of the discipline has depended on a sense of the language as hard evidence in the absence of anything else that might serve. This in turn has made the idea of language high ground, contested over and over again as the discipline has developed. This is where the decisive battles are fought. Here Williams chose to take his stand with "language in history: that full field." Against the background of the sort of reading promoted by Richards—"naked reader before naked text"—he proposed "a newly active social sense of writing and reading, through the social and material historical realities of language, in a world in which it is closely and precisely known, in every act of writing and reading, that these practices connect with, are inseparable from, the whole set of social practices and relationships which define writers and readers as active human beings, as distinct from the idealized and projected 'authors' and 'trained readers'" (WS, 189). An older conception of literature as immediately social in this way—and of language as speech in a living world—underwrites such an idea. Writing has of course always been of and in society. This much is so plain that it should hardly have needed emphasis. Yet Cambridge English had obscured the social vocation of writing and reading by turning it into laboratory work. Literary modernism, to which it had tried to respond with this program, had led the way out of vital social relation. Professional readers were aware of these things, but regarded them as beside the point. They had little enough to do with institutional work.

"Language in history" readily became language *as* history in Williams's criticism, and it authorized a reading of literature as social documentary. Blake became the poet who had seen the industrial city in its integral social and economic relations for the first time; while John Clare's "green language" constituted a pastoral Albion of the mind when the land had been enclosed away. Clare's case shows how the forms of language could be related to ways of seeing on a foundation of social history.[8] Only against such a background, recognized as it was associated with later events, did Clare's haunting voice acquire force and resonance for modern readers. The search for historical value in literature led Williams to see language in this way: as the expression of historical conditions deeply continuous with our own but occluded by institutional interference. Learning to read in this belated moment meant recuperating the language so that the common reality could be seen for what it was and finally changed. It was bound to appear a subversive enterprise in a culture so instinctively conservative and temperamentally committed to established practices.

Yet the social idea of criticism is a dominant orientation of the English school, not the dangerous alternative its institutional antagonists would see in it. Its roots lie in a familiar past. Writing in *Blackwood's* in 1859, E. S. Dallas made the case for literature as a public resource in these terms:

> It is, indeed, too much the custom to regard literature as mere literature. We speak of a republic of letters, and the phrase seems to imply that every other form of republic may be in allowance more or less close with it, but is essentially to be treated as a foreign state . . . Literature in this light loses half its importance. It is only when we come to see it in the fine blossom of history that its full meaning can be caught. It is nothing if it is not a reflection of the period in which it flourishes,—its active as well as its meditative life, its politics as well as its romance; and we may rest assured that there is not a movement in it, not a force, not an atom of life which has not its counterpart in contemporary history.[9]

Dallas was no crusader. The son of a Scots planter in Jamaica, his formation under Sir William Hamilton, at Edinburgh, inclined him to a psychological understanding of poetry—one which he spun out at length in *Poetics: An Essay on Poetry* (1852) and *The Gay Science*

(1866). He might indeed be thought a Victorian antecedent of Richards. Yet his account of the *primarily* social and historical value of literature, and the defense of popular forms of writing on this basis, look forward to Williams's reaction against psychologistic reading — a reminder of how novel Cambridge English had been in its initial historical oblivion, and how deeply traditional Williams's recovery of writing in society would be in reaction. The last Victorian sage, as he has been called,[10] would see literature as valuable for its historical intelligence, in the setting of the dramatically altered circumstances of postwar English society.

Against this longer background it is Williams who appears representative of the traditional vocation of English criticism. It has been a journalistic vocation since Addison's time, despite academic incursions[11] — a fact worth recalling in considering Williams's institutional difficulties. For the problem of his method is largely academic; it arises where his discussion of the forms of language can be challenged on philological grounds. If his appeals to the history of the language rely at points on intuition, it is hardly surprising. Etymological judgments are usually intuitional, as a cursory look at the OED shows. The depth of Williams's philology matters less for the future of criticism than the approach he has recovered. With Coleridge, he affirms the function of criticism in shaping the forms of expression on the basis of a developed historical understanding. Large features of Coleridge's practice come into focus when considered through the lens of Williams's undertaking.

Social Language

In its late Victorian origins semasiology was a science of the sense-development of words, an outgrowth of the rampant philology which consumed the nineteenth-century imagination. As practiced by Carl Abel, it shifted emphasis from the study of grammatical forms to the ideal content of words. Scientific in aspiration, it had a moral aim — "to contribute towards rendering philology a comparative conceptology of nations."[12] Coleridge's occasional effort to characterize styles of national thinking through the words of the native tongue[13] might be regarded as a primitive version of Abel's semasiology, which depended on a notion, now familiar, of ways of thinking specific to linguistic groups. The idea has been extended in various directions, most pro-

ductively perhaps by the prodigious Emile Benveniste, whose treatise
Le Vocabulaire des institutions indo-européennes (2 vols., Paris, 1969)
attempted to reconstruct the social fabric and collective practice of the
proto-Indoeuropean group by the comparative method. Despite its
psychological tendency, Abel's semasiology retained the rudiments of
historical method, and the enterprise reflected an emergent European
consciousness for which mutual understanding would be of para-
mount importance. Language appeared in this optimistic moment a
sort of universal solvent, the decisive means of breaking the grip of
human misunderstanding.

The historical constitution of language, brilliantly confirmed in
the Indoeuropean hypotheses of Franz Bopp and Jakob Grimm early in
the century, had grounded words and their grammar in an evolving
world. When Richards appropriated "semasiology" for his new science
of meaning, he dispensed summarily with the philological quest for
historical value in language. Its futility was practically a first premise.
Meaning was to become a psycholinguistic quantity, with the example
of Coleridge conspicuous in the background. His prephilological sense
of language suited Richards's purposes, presuming as little as it did on
a historical grasp of the matter. Coleridge's reading at Göttingen made
sufficient impression to interest him in the idea of language considered
historically, and he was constantly responsive to the period resonance
of the forms and meanings of words. But this aspect of his understanding was suppressed, symptomatically, by Richards. In the work of
Empson and Leavis there is some effort to recuperate historical value
within the new conception of meaning. Leavis might even be said to
have recovered something of the original force of semasiology by making the language the infrastructure of an English conceptology. The
culmination of these revisions of Richards occurs in a quite different
form in Williams's pursuit of the history of English words for other
purposes. His recourse to etymologic argumentation is distinctive, and
definitive of his critical style. It represents, on this reading, an effort to
reintegrate elements of the lost philology in order to restore the historical basis, and thus the social vitality, of modern criticism.

"Etymologic" I take in a sense recently devised to associate Coleridge's paronomastics with his style of verbal thinking: "In Coleridge's
reformed usage, etymology could link words, and so thoughts, without involving the fetters of material objects and images. Etymologic
is a process that depends upon etymology for the linking of ideas
. . . a special way of getting from one point to another in a

sentence, paragraph, or argument. In Coleridge himself, it was more than a principle of style; it was an habitual way of thinking."[14] Etymologic is the legacy of Hartley's association psychology and of Horne Tooke's queer word games — a delirious residuum in Coleridge's thinking. Hartley and Tooke inhabited the form of his thought long after he had exorcised them from its substance.[15] Their enduring presence marks as clearly as anything in his work Coleridge's situation at the threshold of the critical philosophy which he professed. He could see through it to the new world which lay beyond, yet he remained instinctively attached to old dispensations. Etymology was for him not a science but a discursive art. Its value lay less in its testament of a developing way of thinking than in the confirmation of his own understanding. Etymologic promoted the association of ideas to the status of ideological supplement.

It is characteristic of his situation that Coleridge should have insisted nevertheless on the science of word-formation. One of the philosophical lectures of 1819 begins from this premise:

> There are few pursuits more instructive and not many more entertaining, I own, than that of retracing the progress of a living language for a few centuries, and its improvements as an organ and vehicle of thought, by desynonymizing words. Thus as late as the Restoration, for instance, "ingenuous" and "ingenious," "ingenuity" and "ingenuousness" were used indifferently the one for the other. "Propriety" was the common term for propriety of behaviour, for instance, and for property in the sense of estate or ownership.   (PL, 368–69)

The attention to the development of sense in words is real enough in such a passage. Yet Coleridge moves on to consider, not the social or intellectual history which might be inferred, but desynonymy as an essential office of philosophy.[16] Material history is not the point. What counts is the way the mind arrives, through "the progress of language" (PL, 369), at a larger understanding of reality. Material history provides illustration of a process in which it is involved as, precisely, matter, in the most reductive sense.

Etymology has heuristic value for Coleridge only insofar as it gives latitude to his ideas. Yet he writes in what sounds, occasionally, like a philological spirit. In the "Preface" to Aids to Reflection (1825) he proposes "to direct the reader's attention to the value of the Science of Words, their use and abuse, and the incalculable advantages attached to the habit of using them appropriately, and with a distinct knowledge of their primary, derivative, and metaphorical senses. And in furtherance of this Object I have neglected no occasion of enforcing the maxim, that to expose a sophism and to detect the equivocal or double meaning of a word is, in the great majority of cases, one and the same thing."[17] Coleridge's linguistic understanding might then be described as protophilological, with an equivocal sense of historical value. An epitome of his liminal position: in an early letter he projects a work on the "History of Phrases," but it would not be long before this assumed the form of a "philosophical Romance to explain the whole growth of Language" (*CN* I, 1646). From the very beginning it was language as evidence of mind which compelled his attention. The historical motive is real enough in his consideration of language, but its scope is limited by this emphasis.

As a qualification from the late manuscript on logic shows, Coleridge understood this: "I am not speaking of language *historically*, or pretending to narrate etymological *facts*."[18] His preoccupation with word-formation through desynonymy, the real subject of his long-running romance with language, includes historical process all the same. But it is characteristic that the form is what matters:

> It is a delicate question concerning the comparative richness of Languages, and their consequent aidance or hindrance to Thought & progressive Intuitions—which must depend on the state of the Language, in which some one or more great minds had fixed and rendered it classical—. . . the mind catching at a new intuition will be impeded by its want of a verbal symbol, paralysed by its not daring (in the formed state of Language) to invent or rather to *generate* a symbol representative of the intuition . . . and assuredly, tempted to corrupt & alloy the *purity* of the new Intuition by the attempt to express it by some false analogy thro' some former symbol . . . And tho' this be but a *name* for the new thing, yet in which instance do not names react upon our conception of things & if false more or less falsify or at last perplex them.   (*CN* III, 3954)

Postmodern readers will be tempted to assimilate such a reflection to the deconstructive conviction of the impossibility of signification. What it yields in the context developed here is something nearly opposite: an adherence to the congruence of understanding, as it grows through the expansion of language, with "our conception of things." Understanding was not an arid abstraction but a living engagement, forming the infrastructure of perception. It is at this point that the historical becomes important to Coleridge: as an achieved system ("the state of the Language") and an incentive to reform the language as "great minds" had done before him.

The reform of language was of course one of the great enterprises of the enlightenment—a desideratum from both the rationalist and empiricist ports of entry. Language, as we shall see, could be made to bear responsibility for those defects in human understanding which so exasperated Locke and his inheritors. In Williams's work, to put the matter in a modern setting, the reform of language remains the first step to that larger understanding which he calls consciousness. His etymologic functions, like Coleridge's, as an ideological supplement, contesting the suppression of historical value in Richards and the distortions of Leavis. This long context is revealing not only for what it says of the affiliations of Williams's idiom, but of the critical institution as we know it. For it suggests that the critique of language is its deep legacy and permanent means. Critique, as a method of indirect affirmation,[19] has been occupied since Kant in preserving a traditional bond against the encroachment of ratiocination. Conservative by design, it would save the organism by isolating the parasite: the sleep of reason, breeding monsters. Richards's defense of emotive language was critical in this original sense, saving poetry by splitting it from the conditions of reference and the expectations of science. Williams would back off the implications while adopting the method, displacing the abortive critique of language in general with a more limited critique of the terms of critical discourse. Literature grasped what science could not imagine, but its peculiar power became available only through a reading which knew enough to see who it spoke for—and why.

Williams's investigation of what he would call key words reverted, on his own account, to a reading of Eliot's *Notes towards the Definition of Culture*. Eliot's expansive, apparently anthropological sense of the word concealed a bias. In his memorable list, culture "includes all the characteristic activities and interests of a people: Derby Day, Henley Regatta, Cowes, the twelfth of August, a cup final, the dog races, the pin table, the dart board, Wensleydale cheese, boiled cabbage cut into sections, beetroot in vinegar, nineteenth-century Gothic churches and the music of Elgar."[20] Far from a cross section of common practices, this sketch of English life honored an exclusive ideal. Eliot's notion of culture was different from that of Clive Bell, whose elitism remains exemplary for Williams, mainly for its identification of culture with religion. Culture as class is conspicuous in both Eliot and Bell. It was against this assumption that Williams wrote *Culture and Society* (1958), where "the selective version of culture could be historically controverted by the writings of the thinkers who contributed to the formation and discussion of the idea."[21]

The reformation of the idea of culture under pressure of the industrial revolution Williams assigned to Coleridge, *On The Constitution of Church and State*:

> Here, clearly, Coleridge is trying to set up a standard of 'health', to which a more certain appeal may be made than to the 'mixed good' of 'civilization'. He defines this standard in the word *cultivation* — the first time, in fact, that this word had been used to denote a general condition, a 'state or habit' of the mind. The word depends, of course, on the force of the important eighteenth-century adjective *cultivated*. What Coleridge here calls *cultivation* was elsewhere, as in Mill, to be called *culture*. (CS, 61)

Tracing the idea thus became a semasiological enterprise. The change of sense was materially available through the history of "culture," "cultivation," and related words: "industry," "democracy," "class," and "art" to cite only the instances elaborated in his introduction. Proceeding from the history of words to the history of ideas was unproblematic in Williams's treatment. He moved back and forth with conviction, anchoring the argument for a larger sense of "culture" in the certitude of a material history in a verbal nutshell. The book's case was provocative and influential, and it depended on the authority of semasiological thinking. Semasiology as a practical science was perhaps most familiar to professional readers through the OED, which both expressed and reinforced a deep-seated conviction of the truth of the language. It is a conviction available throughout the critical network I have been describing. At its most pronounced, in Leavis and Williams, "English" became a reified form of community or, alternately, a material trace of the dissolution of community. Williams challenged Leavis on linguistic grounds, contesting the lay of the language. An embattled fortress or the cipher of a long revolution: two versions of the collective condition, of modern England itself.

The semasiology which Williams developed to make his case was historically interested from the beginning. His aim was a new anatomy of British experience:

> In the last decades of the eighteenth century, and in the first half of the nineteenth century, a number of words, which are now of capital importance, came for the first time into common English use, or, where they had already been generally used in the language, acquired new and important meanings. There is in fact a general pattern of change in these words, and this can be used as a special kind of map by which it is possible to look again at those wider changes in life and thought to which the changes in language evidently refer.   (CS, xiii)

Taking its bearings from a politically charged vocabulary, this map would chart a social sea change. The unrecognized history of a familiar lexicon proved a useful heuristic for his vision of Britain in transition. The choice of terms indicated in advance the direction of his inquiry. He was not elusive about this: rather the opposite. His purposes have made his method more liable to objection than it might otherwise have been. It is possible to dispute some of his emphases, certainly. The growing idea of culture in the period he treats was inflected by popular biographies of Goethe, as David DeLaura has insisted.[22] Coleridge cannot be accounted the sole, nor even the most influential source of the word's rising currency. His place in Williams's treatment is largely allegorical in any case. He stands for a transformative vision of modern experience. His distinction between civilization and cultivation underwrites a process of understanding which Williams plots genetically, through the development of the idea of culture as it is reflected in the semantic development of the word.

DeLaura's objection points up the liabilities of this approach all the same. Organic in its grasp of historical process, it is accordingly "romantic," with all that implies of the dominance of the idea over the fact. This is of course disturbing to Williams's materialist critics and comforting to his institutional detractors. He is disarming in talking about the defects of his work—in professing, for instance, no attachment to *Culture and Society* after twenty years. But he makes the characteristic point that "it is the very success of the book that has created the conditions for its critique" (POL, 100). In other words, it succeeded in what he set out to accomplish: to raise the question of culture against prevailing notions of culture as class. The strategy was effective even if the tactic was problematic. In his understanding of the essentially rhetorical nature of critical argument, Williams confirms his sense of the polemical vocation of criticism. Semasiology remains for him what it was, in an incipient form, for Coleridge: a rhetorical art whose claim on historical validity is not scientific but discursive. If his account is congruent with "our conception of things," it is as true as history can hope to be.

This is more explicit, certainly, than Williams can afford to allow. Semasiological argument depends for its effect on a tacit claim to historical verisimilitude, if not scientific validity. Thus, in contesting Leavis's nostalgia for "organic community," Williams turned on his employment of "organic," which had been made to bear an ideological burden against the mechanical institutions of the modern state. Leavis had hypostasized Coleridge's famous opposition, originally applied to poetic form, as a historical tableau: organic community supplanted by mechanical industry. Williams dismissed the simplification as conjectural, weighing the value of "organic" on a scale which would recur later, at the outset of *The Country and the City* (1973): "organic community" was simply the past, seen from whatever later vantage point, and as such had little real historical value. Yet rural life, on his own account, *was* organic in the most important sense of the word: "[T]he one thing that such a community teaches is that life is whole and continuous—it is the whole complex that matters" (*CS*, 260). The problem with Leavis's version of "organic" was not so much the word as the pastoralism it was made to serve. The "Note on 'Organic'" at the end of this chapter added nothing essential to the case, though it did show how the word came to be employed (usually as "organize") to describe very different social ideals. Williams's conclusion was anodyne: the word was loaded, we should attend to its history—and "perhaps all societies are organic (i.e. formed wholes), but some are more organic than others" (*CS*, 264). The force of this was mainly negative: it would not do to use the word as Leavis used it, as a shibboleth. Its actual history told a different story.

Williams's semasiology began then as a *critical* semasiology, concerned to dismantle a familiar vocabulary as a way of exposing the social, intellectual, and especially the political history of a dominant way of thinking. The negative function of his analytic eased the evidential burden. For what he had typically to demonstrate was not the precise semantic development of key words, but how their institutional abuse dissimulated a material history. *Culture and Society* has been criticized for its failures of attention to the political sphere—Williams has regretted it himself—yet the case of "organic" shows how the political was included in his critical procedure through the treatment of individual words as their meanings had arisen, expanded, and changed in response to broadly political circumstances. The advantage of such a procedure was considerable: what might otherwise have been regarded as purely political discourse acquired critical range through its seeming scientific aspiration. In practice the relation between means and ends was circular. The democratic view of culture was supported by the etymologic treatment, while the latter was motivated by the wish to discredit a dominant account of culture. A familiar paradigm of scientific discovery, in fact. As applied to historical inquiry, however, it was bound to be regarded as a partisan operation.

Leavis was both a model and a rival for Williams's critical activity, probably the immediate source of his sense of the social possibilities of critical discourse as well as of his focus on the large linguistic question. Later he would make an example of Leavis on language from the perspective opened over the course of his own career:

> This also involves the rejection of idealist accounts of language as a common possession—at its best, Leavis's notion of language as a continuous legacy through the ages that carries the finest insights of the community. For while Leavis was right to stress the cultural importance of language, his notion of continuity was quite false, since it rested on an abstraction from what were always extraordinary historical transformations and reversals, and then on proposing a single heritage of meanings which were held to sanction particular contemporary values. (*POL*, 176-77)

The idealist position, anthropological in inspiration, would abstract language from the living community, treating it as a metonymic equivalent of the tribe. Speaking with structuralism in mind, Williams thus associates Leavis's idealism with a much larger development: a social scientism which posed an immediate threat to English studies, insofar as it would abstract the language (and its literature) from the concerns of a community in crisis.[23] So comprehensive an idea of English had proved limiting. "A single heritage of meanings" was the legacy of Leavis's version of semasiology. Against such single vision Williams proposes a semasiology which would include the semantic contradictions deleted by Leavis, incorporating alternative worlds in a single word: "[It is] generally assumed that language is merely the instrument or record of the changes which have happened elsewhere; whereas it seems to me that certain shifts of meaning indicate very interesting periods of confusion and contradiction of outcome, latencies in decision, and other processes of a real social history, which can be located rather precisely in this other way, and put alongside more familiar kinds of evidence" (*POL*, 177). English becomes, on this account, not simply a documentary of social history but rather one stage among others on which historical conflicts are acted out. Such a view would confer extraordinary potential on semasiology. For it might then aspire to something more than collecting the facts: an active interrogation of the process of history.

In discussing *Keywords* (1976), the "Vocabulary of Culture and Society" which grew out of the earlier book, Williams observes the novelty of the enterprise while allowing that careful readers had always considered meaning in this way (*POL*, 175–76). He speaks of "historical semantics" and of the "social history" of words (*POL*, 179) in reference to his work. Novel it certainly was, in the form he devised for it, yet it should be clear that a long semasiological tradition underwrote his predisposition to regard words as a thesaurus of meaning. Williams may be said to have raised semasiology, not so much to consciousness (for it had become conscious in other forms), as to an effective method of historical investigation and critical argument. It becomes increasingly philological as it assumes a life of its own in his work, more exact and also more liable to specific objection. Without philological training, and uninterested in pressing scientific claims in any case, Williams invites the charge that he is (like Richards) a dilettante out of his depth in the science of language. It is possible moreover to speak of idealism, of a kind quite different from Leavis's, in his pursuit of a social history of ideas. For Williams attends to concepts as concrete integers, and to the history of concepts as distinct from (though available only through) the history of words.[24] His linguistic understanding thus represents a prephilological survival, or postphilological anamnesis, something akin to Coleridge's desynonymy. I want to suggest that Williams's semasiology remains valuable despite its problems of method; that it answers legitimate cultural needs in a way that the old philology, by its nature, did not and could not; and that it represents a viable way forward for a criticism which would be socially alert and not merely appreciative or normative.

Culture and Civilization

Williams wrote the entry for the *Encyclopedia of Philosophy* (1967) under this rubric, and though he treats both words at greater length in *Keywords*, their conjunction here is leading.[25] The subject is, conventionally, one for an anthropologist. Williams performs a summary survey of anthropological discussion of the matter after a bit of etymological groundwork, an account of the modern semantic development, and division of the semantic field of "culture" into three competing concepts. True to the vocation of the encyclopedia, there is no consideration of the emergence of civilization as a historical event. Civilization referred to an "actual social condition," without elaboration, in contrast to barbarism, another social condition. Relational definition of this kind underscores the nominalizing force of Williams's semasiology. It links his enterprise with the long tradition of language reform. His apparent motive is to avoid a prescriptive sense of "civilization" of the sort associated with Clive Bell and Bloomsbury. The discussion exemplifies the way his semasiology responds to ethical conditions.

"Culture" is the fulcrum of his ideological lever, the central term for his reconstruction of the language of critical discourse. Its etymon is Latin *cultura*, cultivation of the fields, and from this its metaphorical senses derive. Cicero's *cultura animi philosophia est* shows how readily it was adapted to the idea of mental (or spiritual) cultivation. Williams makes the point that Latin uses in this sense refer to a process rather than "an achieved state." The reification of the process is what interests him: how "cultivation" became "cultivated," with the implication of class superiority. "Cultivated" and "civilized" (in the Bloomsbury sense) are virtual synonyms at the end of this semantic development. Culture and civilization are thus collapsed into a single concept as they had been before Coleridge. Williams's effort of desynomymy follows in his footsteps. It would restore distinct senses to distinct concepts, depriving the new Barbarians of their proprietary claim on civilization by evacuating it of any but relational content, while exalting "culture" as the morally significant term.

The crucial development of the idea of culture occurred in the course of the industrial revolution. The word underwent a complex transformation. Williams distinguishes four senses at the end of the process:

1. Culture as "'a general state or habit of mind,' with close relations to the idea of human perfection." This is the sense of the word for Arnold in *Culture and Anarchy*—a conspicuous instance of idealization in reaction to democratic insurgency (*POL*, 109). The elite sense.

2. Culture as "a general state of intellectual and moral development in a society as a whole."
3. Culture as "the general body of the arts and intellectual work."
4. Culture as "the whole way of life, material, intellectual, and spiritual, of a given society." This is the anthropological sense.

Williams traces pressure on the term to romantic sources. Coleridge's organicism, and his distinction between a mechanistic conception of civilization as material progress and an organic "cultivation," were primordial. They introduced a broadly social, as against a normative, idea of culture, as he had emphasized earlier (*CS*, 62f.), underwriting the claim of (2) against (1). Though DeLaura is surely correct in finding German sources for the idea of culture in the period, the force of Williams's argument remains: Coleridge's distinction between cultivation and material well-being undermined the association of "culture" with merely external conditions of development.

Other sources cited for the semantic development of the word include the romantic attention to "folk life and national tradition"; the new orientalism of the period, with a growing awareness of the integrity of non-European civilizations and a corresponding limitation of the normative idea; and "a new emphasis . . . on the strong connection between the ways of ordinary social and material life and the styles and assumptions of imaginative and intellectual work." The last of these is so general as to invite qualification and perhaps dispute. The emergent dialectic of the individual and the social is more often seen from the point of view of the individualism of the period than from its acute awareness of the social sphere. Williams had disputed the individualist emphasis in his discussion, in *Culture and Society*, of the romantic artist (*CS*, 30f.). It would perhaps be more apt to suggest that the tension between a normative "civilization" and an organic "cultivation" was informed by the dialectic as a whole, and that (1) and (2) were inextricably involved with it. Williams observes the tension but fails to resolve it into the romantic matrix at the source.

In *Keywords* the semasiology becomes paradigmatic of the largest movements of history. Williams tells the story of the new industrial order through a chronicle of its words, from aesthetic and bourgeois to wealth and work. Here, the verbal sign as a materially available epitome is extended to its limits, with a constant oscillation between word and concept as constituent features of a single formation. The analogy to the Saussurean sign is unavoidable. But apart from the pronounced difference in elements (Williams's word is much more than a sound-image), there is nothing of the dualism of signifier and signified in sight. The sign for Williams is simply the written word, and it has an integrity beyond semiotic splitting and historical dispute. His semasiology might be described as a semiotic before the fall: before positive science, before the abstract materiality of phonemics. Its interest in meaning restores the sign to its functional vitality and to the world of ideas. That is, for his purposes, its great value. Language ceases to be the property of linguistics with its endless formalization and reverts to the common resource it has always been.

What is lost in the reversion to an older idea? Not only the illusions of positive science (precision, for instance) but the conviction of secure historical knowledge. This too might be regarded as a liberation, from the tyranny of "fact" conceived in positive terms. What are the facts of the history of "culture?" As soon as they are plotted, they become conjectural narrative. Williams's plot does not escape this condition. As the history of a word, it is both more and less than intellectual history. Alert to various strains of informed opinion, Williams still refers everything to a semasiological core, as though the struggle of ideas were a gloss on "culture":

> What mainly happened in the early nineteenth century, under the influence of Herder and many other writers of the Romantic movement, in Germany, England and France, was a social and historical application of an alternative idea of human development: alternative, that is, to the ideas now centered on 'civilization' and 'progress.' This application was exceptionally complicated. It was used to emphasize national and traditional cultures, including the new concept of folk-culture. It was used to attack what was seen as the 'mechanical' character of the new civilization then emerging: both for its abstract rationalism and for the 'inhumanity' of current industrial development. Politically, as so often in this period, it veered between radicalism and reaction and very often, in the confusion of major social change, fused elements of both.[26]

"What mainly happened" converts a confusion of data into a capsule history in conformity with (and in confirmation of) a teleological idea. It is not enough to maintain that the idea derived originally from the semasiology. *Culture and Society* shows it fully formed, before the semantic tracing had been accomplished in such detail. And the difference between the two accounts of the word "culture" shows how Williams's sense of its development responded to the growth of his dissenting valorization of cultivation against a dominant "civilization." For he realizes in *Keywords* a more integrated understanding of the emergent senses of "culture" than he had before. Here the word appears as more than the trace of a change of mind. It is contested ground in a continuing struggle for power.

It is this struggle which Williams has continued in his long consideration of "culture" and what it will bear. On the basis of this example his semasiology can be said to have begun as a heuristic procedure—a way of working from the dictionary back toward lost distinctions. Yet it was always more than desynonymical in intention, as the argument of *Culture and Society* indicates. It became a historical method of sorts, a way of plotting an elusive change of thinking. In the end it appears as both while assuming an openly political function: the word is not a passive object of investigation, but a basis of argument. As Williams grew conscious of the implications of his procedure, he modified his practice to reflect his sense of its possibility. Without retracting the modest claims he had made for semasiology as a historical method, he came to see what the limits were, as the introduction to *Keywords* testifies. In fact he proves his own best critic.

What sort of knowledge are we left with, then? Not, I think—contrary to what his institutional critics will maintain—something ideologically suspect. For his semasiology had from the beginning, as I have been arguing, a negative force: it showed how problematic the prevailing terminology of criticism was, beginning from its fundamental category. Williams's approach to literature through its key words harrowed the ground of Cambridge English as Richards had once harrowed philology. But it should be clear that semasiology as an agent of reform is a very different matter from semasiology as a science of the future. Its aim has not been the institution of a method but the adoption of a historically responsive critical discourse—one which would be polemical in vocation. To criticize Williams's philology on particular grounds is to engage his project, not to reject its basis.

This is true, I will argue, even when the semasiology functions openly as an ideological supplement, as it did in his discussion of culture in *Marxism and Literature* (1977).[27] This, for many readers, was the sticking point of the analytic, since it bound Williams to an unpalatable view of history and, more generally, of cultural politics. In this definitive context, the semasiological detail came to matter in a more than negative way. It became, indeed, the necessary starting point for a new conceptualization of writing in society—the root of a "cultural theory" on reformed Marxist principles. Cultural material-ism as he describes it would take existing concepts as "problems, not analytic problems either but historical movements that are still unre-solved" (*ML*, 11). Culture, language, literature, and ideology were the cardinal points of his new geography of modern feeling. His treatment of them relied on the semasiology, but no longer remained confined by it. The Coleridgean idea of cultivation was adduced against the nor-mative "civilization," but now it was abetted by an emergent socialism. The religious understanding of spirit was shown to have been displaced by a secular grasp of the subject and his inner life:

> 'Culture,' or more specifically 'art' and 'literature' (themselves newly gen-eralized and abstracted), were seen as the deepest record, the deepest impulse, and the deepest resource of the 'human spirit.' 'Culture' was then at once the secularization and the liberalization of earlier metaphysical forms. Its agencies and processes were distinctively human, and were generalized as subjective, but certain quasi-metaphysical forms—'the imagination,' 'creativity,' 'inspiration,' 'the aesthetic,' and the new positive sense of 'myth'—were in effect composed into a new pantheon. (*ML*, 15)

Culture sublating religion: a contentious way of putting it, certainly, yet true to a recognizable history, beginning from Coleridge himself, and available explicitly in Arnold and Eliot on the elusive incarnation of religion in culture.[28] For believers, Williams formulated in an acces-sible way assumptions which were widespread but seldom spoke their names. He provided in such a passage a clear point of divergence for a different formulation of the matter. For materialists, he created a bridge to the genuine religious feeling which they have been inclined to regard as cant. History (and first of all the history of literature) then became available as something more than a record of superstition. Semasiology served in such a setting not only the reform of Cambridge English but of belief in the widest sense, as Richards meant it. Of relation, that is, to a living world and all it includes.

As grounds for engagement and exchange, this account of culture differed from what Cambridge English had offered. In closing his discussion of culture, Williams characterized the school obliquely through its own conception, observing that "the significance of the alternative concept of culture, defining 'intellectual life' and 'the arts,' was compromised by its apparent reduction to 'superstructural' status, and was left to be developed by those who, in the very process of idealizing it, broke its necessary connections with society and history and, in the areas of psychology, art, and belief, developed a powerful alternative sense of the constitutive human process itself" (*ML*, 19–20). The Cambridge concept of culture—in reality the dominant concept for half a century—presumed a transcendental subject, stripped of the intrinsic value conferred by religion, in search of sustaining relation in a world of alien and often threatening others. Culture as an existential quest for value was contested by Williams's insistence on the social as the primary source of human identity and belief, whatever these might be. Identity was relational, extensive rather than intrinsic, irreducibly collective. His cultural materialism is plural in its vision of historical process, deeply rooted in modern circumstances, tempered by the quality of his engagement. If it is ideological, it remains open to inspection and modification in ways that subvert what the word connotes of doctrinal rigidity. In fact, Williams's notion of what "ideology" might bear is at odds with the practice of the Marxist tradition, which he criticizes for confusing Destutt de Tracy's valuable neologism with the odiously dogmatic "false consciousness" (*ML*, 56f.). In its place he proposes "a general term to describe not only the products but the processes of all signification, including the signification of values" (*ML*, 70)—an acceptation which relies on Voloshinov, the enigmatic linguist who may or may not have been Mikhail Bakhtin writing under cover.[29] Ideology as a general semiotic situates Williams in a familiar world: searching, like Richards and Leavis, for an idea of language which can save literature for modern thinking without sacrificing its broadly social vocation.

What I am concerned to emphasize in this context is the plurality of his affiliations. Formed by Cambridge English, but inspired by a Coleridge it had not recognized, Williams represents a singular convergence of the most important thinking about literature in the language. His exposure to Marxist dialectic refined an orientation which was already pronounced in his early work, one which may be called, simply, democratic. A trying of this kind by the fire of a larger and more comprehensive idea was just what Cambridge English had resisted—as though the problems of reading in English were sui generis. The vitality of Marxist thinking permitted Williams to proceed with his inquiry where others found limited scope for development. A review of his expansion of "culture" over the years shows how much it brought to his sense of the relation of disparate semantic fields. Other semasiologies—those of Owen Barfield and C. S. Lewis, for instance—simply did not go far enough to make an enduring impression.[30] It was only in taking semasiology into ideology, as a historical science of signification, that its potential as a method of investigation and argument was realized.

The Coleridgean roots of his semasiology count for less, in the end, than Coleridge's example for his comprehensive vision of modern experience. Writing of John Stuart Mill's failure to understand poetry as a mode of *thinking* (not just of feeling) Williams had observed in *Culture and Society* that

> Coleridge, if Mill had attended to him, could have made this issue clear; made it clear, at least, as an issue, even if his own method of organization could not have been transferred . . . A whole position like that of Coleridge cannot be offered for conviction; it is not, and could not be, a suasive element. The most that a man like Coleridge can offer is an instance, but, to the degree that one realizes Coleridge's position, one realizes also that an instance is indeed the most valuable thing that can be offered. The kind of thinking which we observe in Coleridge centres our attention, not on Mill's rationale of a society, but, almost wholly, on the *relations* between personal instance and social institution.   (*CS*, 68)

The enduring force of this instance showed here far afield of its conventional affiliations. It raised indeed the question of who Coleridge was against the background of a critical institution which had used his legacy for its own purposes, then disposed of him, as far as it could, on grounds of *his* inconsequence. What Williams noticed of Mill holds true, I think, of Cambridge English reading Coleridge: he might have made the claims of poetry clear if he had been accorded a real hearing. Coleridge must bear some responsibility through his insistence on a system he could not conjure, yet continued to bruit as though he soon would. The failure of self-understanding was reproduced in his later readers as a failure to grasp what he was about. For it was not as a methodical reader that Coleridge proved exemplary for his contemporaries and followers, but as a reader of responsive view. What was self-evidently true of Eliot as a reader has not always been clear in the case of Coleridge.

Williams has then recovered a sense of his informant's achievement which is fundamentally different from what has prevailed elsewhere. On this basis he has surveyed the critical institution in its largest relations while reading and revising the canon. The conspectus of critical tradition realized in his work is brought to bear against the limitations of the Cambridge English by which he was formed. It was by returning to the Coleridgean roots that Williams was able to exert this decisive influence. I should like to conclude by recalling the terms in which he mounted a challenge to the Leavisite position at a moment when it appeared triumphant. Against Leavis's postulation of a modern clerisy Williams weighed Coleridge's original example of "a class whose business was general cultivation, and whose allegiance was to the whole body of sciences." By contrast,

> For Leavis, the minority is, essentially, a literary minority, which keeps alive the literary tradition and the finest capacities of the language. This development is instructive, for the tenuity of the claim to be a 'centre' is, unfortunately, increasingly obvious. '"Civilization" and "culture" are coming to be antithetical terms.' Leavis writes a little later. This is the famous distinction made by Coleridge, and the whole development of this idea of culture rests on it. Culture was made into an entity, a positive body of achievement and habits, precisely to express a mode of living superior to that being brought about by the 'progress of civilization.' For Coleridge the defence of this standard was to be in the hands of a National Church, including 'the learned of all denominations'. Since this could not in fact be instituted, the nature of the defending minority had continually, by the successors of Coleridge, to be redefined. The process which Arnold began, when he virtually equated 'culture' with 'criticism,' is completed by Leavis, and had been similarly completed a little earlier, by I. A. Richards. Of course Leavis is right when he says that many of the 'subtlest and most perishable parts of tradition' are contained in our literature and language. But the decline from Coleridge's allegiance to all the sciences is unfortunately real. (*CS*, 254)

Cambridge English had begun from a splitting of emotive and scientific language, shadowing the Mill who recovered his capacity to feel by reading Wordsworth. Once the special claim obtained, poetry simply lost sight of the social horizon, or was read as doing so. It was no longer responsible to any condition but its own. Poetry then became, indeed, as Williams charges, a substitute for feeling (*CS*, 67). When its private status was an accomplished fact, Leavis's literary clerisy became an inevitable institution. Judged by prevailing circumstances, it would appear perfectly legitimate despite its insularity.

In order to circumvent so unsatisfactory an outcome, it was necessary to retrace the steps by which it had become inevitable. Coleridge appeared at the vanishing point, measuring the situation's historical density while offering an alternative idea. The man of letters as a man of the world, judging writing in its social integrity, by the light of a shared experience and a common language: such was Coleridge's example as it would appear to Williams. As an answer to Leavis's "minority culture," Coleridge's original conception was more inclusive on principle and in practice. It was this Coleridge to whom English criticism would have to turn in its search for a socially responsible orientation and identity.

II

COLERIDGE, LANGUAGE, POETICS

4

Expressive Language and the Commitment of Poetry

In the beginning romantic language was expressive language, "a selection of the real language of men in a state of vivid sensation" (*LBP*, 153), charged with the spontaneity, power, and feeling of its origin in private emotion. Familiarity has dulled the formula, and vicissitude the force of the premise, but the emphasis on impassioned speech is important enough to have come to stand in the modern imagination for the condition of poetry. An expressive ideal joins the initial feeling to its realization in an existing tongue at every turn of the "Preface." In this primordial context, the medium is more than a medium, it is the element of poetry, the source of its pleasures, even of its values. The "plainer and more emphatic language" of "low and rustic life" (*LBP*, 156) made what amounted to a moral claim on the art. It was a novel, not to say radical proposition, and its defense of ordinary life and speech inspired a controversy that has been continued under other auspices by modern readers. Wordsworth's ideal, and Coleridge's modification of it, participate in the long critique of language undertaken in the Enlightenment, promoting colloquial against contrived diction, and familiar against extravagant expression on grounds reverting to first principles. Their collaboration and its consequences represent an invaluable resource for later thinking about the language of poetry, and about language as it is conceived in modern criticism.

Large questions of language consumed the English eighteenth century, as recent studies have showed, providing a platform for argument about knowledge as well as expression.[1] Against this background, the litany of romantic ideas about poetry describes a contentious version of the tongue. Abrams cites, among the cardinal points, poetry as instinctive utterance, drawing vatic strength from figures of speech and from rhythm, from ordinary rather than ornamented diction, and speaking to men in a language they would recognize and respond to.[2] The change of air had everything to do with a changing sense of the possibilities of public discourse. It was apparent from the opening hypothesis of the "Preface"; *Lyrical Ballads* depended on the force of the vernacular and tried out a range of voices illustrating the idiom its authors postulated at the outset. As an experiment in writing against expectation it was hardly less daring than "The Wreck of the *Deutschland*" or *The Waste Land*.[3] It took as many chances, and failed as often as Eliot did in his manuscript draft. In the process, Wordsworth and Coleridge realized something more than a new poetic aspiration; they realized their situation in the language. The one presumed the other.

The sources of the expressive language they sought were to be popular rather than traditionally poetic—"the language of conversation in the middle and lower classes of society," as the Advertisement to the first edition proposed. As for the *idea* of such an idiom, there were antecedents of various kinds. Abrams, again, lists "eighteenth-century speculations on the emotional origin of language, prevalent ideas about the nature and value of primitive poetry, together with the results of a century of developments in Longinian doctrines" (*Mirror*, 104). These he associates with Wordsworth alone. Gerald Bruns supplements them with Coleridgean organicism as it applied to language, and as it drew on the classical *energeia*—"the power by which a speaker's utterance moves an audience not to delight only but to understanding."[4] His emphasis on the persistence of Locke's discussion of words is perhaps more compelling for a consideration of how romantic language is situated within local cultural processes. For it was not through *energeia* but through his approach to Locke's position, and to that of his inheritors, that Coleridge arrived at a linguistic understanding of his own poetic assumptions. Expressive language was not so isolated a pursuit for him as it was for his collaborator. What he brought to bear on the new poetry was quite different, and it leads to a significantly different way of seeing romantic language.

The central context for this development is Coleridge's protracted struggle with the claims of the "Preface", arising out of differences which were already forming at the time of its publication in 1801. It has been usual to consider the "Preface" Wordsworth's work, yet Coleridge's voice sounds unmistakably through parts of it. This has led to problems of attribution. "'Much confusion,' Wordsworth complained, 'has been introduced into criticism by this contradistinction of Poetry and Prose, instead of the more philosophical one of Poetry and Matter of Fact, or Science'" (*Mirror*, 101). Not only the idea, but the expression bears Coleridge's stamp. Wordsworth did of course adopt this line of argument, laying the foundation for his new poetics of prose; but the principle can hardly be described as his own, considering what Coleridge would make of it. Still less can the remarkable claim that a full treatment of the subject would demand that the authors consider "in what manner language and the human mind act and react on each other" (*LBP*, 154).

As I hope to show, an inquiry of this kind is nearly what Coleridge was about at the moment the "Preface" was first published. His participation in its composition is an open question, and the evidence brought to bear by Norman Fruman is indicative if not quite conclusive: the emphases and diction are consistent, on the whole, with Wordsworth's prior writing.[5] There was no reason for Coleridge to have claimed it as his own, and he did not do so. That does not preclude, even on Fruman's telling, the persistence of his ideas, assimilated or subversive, in the finished piece. This much Coleridge *did* claim: "[T]he first passages were indeed partly taken from notes of mine" (*CL* II, 811) — a minimal and credible assertion, on the evidence of the opening. McFarland's tracing of the symbiotic relation of their voices shows how prevalent such mingled measures were in their work of this period.[6] With the linguistic proposition in mind, I hope to show how Coleridge went about developing a conception of language, and an idea of poetry, in response to the dominant values of "Preface." His still tentative understanding was complicated and extended by his differences with Wordsworth, and it acquires its enduring value for modern criticism in this context.

Wordsworth's sense of language has recently attracted attention both inside and outside the field. Hans Aarsleff, the linguistic historian, set out to correct Abrams's misapprehensions about its antecedents in a brief essay which argues that Condillac was "the central figure who brought about the change that lies behind the romantic aesthetic and the role it assigned to language."[7] It was not the German but the French connection which supplied the model for the turn away from imitation toward expression. Condillac stood indeed behind Herder, the source of most German thinking on the subject. And the observation from the "Preface" on language and the human mind, just cited, showed the principle of linguistic relativism at work in Wordsworth's thinking. Important as the argument is for grasping the transmission of the idea, its bearing on Wordsworth's poetic theory remains problematic. Aarsleff makes no specific plea of influence, though he observes that Condillac's ideas were in circulation in France during the period of Wordsworth's residence. What he offers is a seeming analogue in intellectual history for *some* of Wordsworth's pronouncements.

Aarsleff does not cite what Coleridge took to be an essential component of Wordsworth's idea of poetic language: that the idiom of "low and rustic life" was adopted "because such men hourly communicate with the best objects from which the best part of language is originally derived" (*LBP*, 156). Such a notion is not easy to square with the linguistic relativism of Condillac, which makes words refer to ideas, not things, and very private ideas at that. Where there are signs of linguistic relativism in the "Preface," they are more likely connected with Coleridge, who showed himself responsive to the idea as early as 1799: "In Nature all things are individual: but a Word is but an arbitrary Character for a whole Class of Things; so that the same description may in almost all cases be applied to twenty different appearances" (*CL* I, 503). This is the first significant reference to current linguistic philosophy in the *Collected Letters*, and it was written from Germany. Whatever the source, it shows that before the "Preface" was underway, Coleridge was actively engaged in thinking through linguistic relativism — and drawing conclusions from it. Aarsleff's assumption that the "Preface" sketches a self-consistent position identifiable with Wordsworth alone leads him away from a real foothold in intellectual history established by Coleridge.

A quite different adaptation of intellectual history to the problematic relations of the authors of the "Preface" is pursued in a recent book on Wordsworth's narrative experiments. The antecedents adduced by Don Bialostosky are Plato and Aristotle, who stand in by analogy for their English representatives.[8] Influence is not in question — a welcome circumvention, such influences having proved very little in the past. Nor does Bialostosky work out in detail the congruence of Aristotle's *Poetics* with Coleridge's criticism, or of the *Republic* with Wordsworth's. His contentions are limited by the scope of the analogy, but they are valuable within a narrow range. "Wordsworth's affinities with Plato's poetics of speech" (*MT*, 11) vindicate the expressive language of his lyrical ballads against Coleridge's objections to their representativeness. The poetics of speech honors the collaboration of the poet's voice in the presentation of characters, against the Coleridge who would complain of their peculiarity, relying on Aristotle's formulation of poetry as ideal. The argument defends Wordsworth's poetic mimicry, and it rings true of the ventriloquism apparent in much of his poetry, not just the early ballads. What Bialostosky misses in the "Preface" is less important than what he gains by avoiding diversion into the question of language as it arises there.

Yet the question *is* related: the poetics of speech, taking no interest in the mimetic function, is unconcerned with what the words stand for. They are constituted intersubjectively, as it were, and have their ground in the relation of the poet and his speaker. This emphasis seems altogether more responsive to Wordsworth's feeling for language than the linguistic relativism of Condillac,[9] even if it discounts "the best part of language" as proposed in the "Preface." And its corollary holds generally true for the Coleridge who found it necessary to go to the ground with language:

> Coleridge makes the category of medium, which distinguishes Aristotelian poetics from the poetics of speech but remains a subordinate category in Aristotle's analysis, the primary category of his poetics. The poet's modifications of ordinary language become the signs of the faculty that makes the poet, and the deliberate attempt to avoid those modifications appears as a perversion of the deliberate cultivation of them that is the poet's art.   (*MT*, 18)

The art for Coleridge lay in the relation to the medium (if not quite the medium as a category), and it was indeed from this position, broadly realized, that he would draw the line with Wordsworth in the *Biographia*. Expressive language remained bound, for him, to a world more resonant than the orphic whirl-blast of his own voice—or the voices of others. "No necessary connection to the representation of an action" (*MT*, 14) burdens the poetics of speech, but it is worth noticing, as a qualification, that Wordsworth shouldered that burden voluntarily by constant documentary allusion, inviting the sort of reading performed by his associate.

Coleridge's attention to the requirements of representation hardly makes him Aristotelian, though it does indicate a source of difference from Wordsworth's approach. The symbolic function of language as he would develop it linked words both to thinking and to a familiar world in which thinking took place. He was especially concerned to preserve the autonomy of thinking, to secure it against reduction to impressions. Language was the resource which freed thinking from the bondage of images. But living words as he would conceive them did not exclude reference to images and all they brought with them of worldly assumptions. The deep affiliations of this version of expressive language lay closer to home than either Condillac or Aristotle, as Paul Hamilton's recent book proposes in discussing native traditions which raised these issues.[10] Expressive language against the idolatry of sensation: such was the English context of Coleridge's philosophical poetics. Extensive antiempiricist and common-sense argument preceded his turn against reductive accounts of language. Yet they do not anticipate the form his conception took as it developed.

Hamilton's hypothesis is important but tortuous in its treatment of Coleridge on language and poetics, with consequences I shall be considering in concluding this discussion. For the moment, it will be sufficient to indicate what I take to be the bearing of his argument. The British antecedents which he cites for Coleridge's position are precursive rather than informative—they identify current lines of thinking without committing Coleridge to anything. His German sources, on the other hand, are informative, but not of much direct use for thinking about language. Hamilton's eventual disappointment with the critique of Wordsworth is based on his endorsement of "a radicalism whose methodological implications were repressed in the *Biographia*" (CP, 97)—an endorsement which disfigures Coleridge's real commitments. Instead of supporting Wordsworth's poetics of speech, Coleridge is seen to have relapsed on the "unfair" charge of literalism, regressing from radical argument to a conventional insistence on representativeness. Hamilton thus concludes rather as Bialostosky does, while attempting to rescue Coleridge's readings of Shakespeare and Milton on the ground that they fulfill the promise evaded by the *Biographia*.

What is lacking here is balanced commentary on Coleridge's thinking about language as it developed and came into relation with his larger occupations. For it was in the setting of his initial approaches to reason and understanding, as well as of his search for critical principle, that the investigation of language was conducted. On the evidence in context, Coleridge cannot be counted simply a continuer of the radical position, even if he shared its suspicion of empirical habits of mind. To press this affiliation to its limit is to insist that he prove a Galileo of linguistics in another mode. The role does not do justice to the achievement. His commitments were expansive ones from the start, and it is in this setting that his approach to language should be considered: "What is it, that I employ my Metaphysics on? . . . To expose the Folly & the Legerdemain of those, who have thus abused the blessed Organ of Language, to support all old & venerable Truths, to support, to kindle, to project, to make the Reason spread Light over our Feelings" (*CN* I, 1623). Language was more than the medium of his aspirant critique, it was an essential element of the truth he was determined to discover: "But above all do not let me forget, that Language is the medium of all Thoughts to *ourselves* of all feelings to others, & partly to ourselves—now a thing cannot be a medium in the living continuity of nature but by essentially partaking of the nature of the two things mediated. Hence our native language, by this incessant process of unification without loss of distinction becomes indeed επεα Ζωοντα—*living words*" (*CN* III, 4237). "Living words" represented the redemption of natural language through the expansion of a progressive reason. They were the stuff of thought, the material realization of the Logos.[11]

So boundless an idea has obvious liabilities. Its transcendental assumptions are alien to a materialist critical imagination. This, surely, is the real force of Leavis's objection. Richards's effort of renovation shows what somersaults were required to make it signify at all in the modern setting. It should be clear that for poetry to amount to more than a case of special pleading, the justification must extend beyond Richards's defense of distinctive discourse—beyond a faculty psychology and an idea of language based on it. For these only displace one sort of transcendence with another, confirming the religion of art on archaic grounds. Coleridge's sense of poetry's vocation was less grandiose despite his German phase. It partakes of the nature of its medium, a conventional bond, the instrument of a progressive reason. Balanced between the privileges of the past and the realities of the present, this idea represents a profound act of mediation. For a critical institution committed at the theoretical base to the idea of language, it remains a valuable resource and the model of a settled understanding.

Idols of the Marketplace

Coleridge's first productive engagement with the philosophy of language dates to the period following his return from Germany in 1799, when a crisis of vocation led him to renounce poetry in favor of a career as a practicing critic. Earlier research made a great deal of the

German background, and it does appear to have attracted Coleridge's attention to words as a source of historical value.[12] He seems to have been bent on a study of older vernacular languages when diverted into a very different line of inquiry. The diversion took him back into questions of linguistic reference raised and treated in the course of the century. Sorting the relations of words and things opened a fresh line of approach, bridging the gap separating poetry from the general philosophical questions to which he was increasingly drawn. J. A. Appleyard has related this formative investigation to Coleridge's incipient metaphysical views,[13] but the evidence points in the more urgent direction of his critical aspirations. The investigation of language served as a basis for argument with the "Preface," and for settling some preliminary issues of poetic value. At this remove, it has considerable precursive appeal, since it can be seen as an early effort to mount a defense of poetry on linguistic principles. Richards made much of an elusive body of evidence to this effect, and so have his inheritors.[14] A crossroads of romantic and modern understanding, Coleridge's obscure effort to get to grips with language participates in an ongoing revaluation of enlightenment thinking.

Accounts of language in Coleridge's England lay under the long shadow of Locke's *Essay*. Despite a straightforward approach the argument of Book III ("Of Words") is more complicated than it was supposed to be. Murray Cohen summarizes its author's achievement in these terms: "Locke, whose first responsibility was to retrieve words from their association with things, not only redefined them in terms of ideas but added to what might have been a mechanico-corpuscular theory of ideas the notion of relations between ideas (that is, between words). Locke did not simply reidentify words as ideas; he proposed a grammar of thought expressed in the logic of linguistic functions."[15] Locke's argument reacted to received notions of language as nomenclature. Words, he postulated, were not the signatures of things, but "sensible marks of ideas."[16] They were arbitrary in relation to ideas (sounds signified by convention, not by nature); and these ideas were themselves arbitrary in relation to objects (ideas were for the most part abstractions). Ideas anchored his conception, as their priority in the *Essay* predicts. Words were only their outward and sensible tags.

Locke distinguished three classes of ideas. Simple ideas, like that of motion, derived immediately from phenomena, and the words attached to them were clear to anyone who had experience of the phenomena in question. Complex ideas (Locke cited adultery and incest) were made up of the association of a number of simple ideas; they did not derive from phenomena directly and were correspondingly abstract. The words that designated them could not be verified like those attaching to simple ideas, and they were divorced in this way from substantial reality.

Of this distinction between simple and complex ideas Locke made a qualitative distinction between simple and complex names:

> From what has been said, it is easy to observe what has been before remarked, viz. that the *names of simple ideas* are, of all others, the least liable to mistakes, and that for these reasons. First, Because the ideas they stand for, being each but one single perception, are much easier got, and more clearly retained, than the more complex ones, and therefore are not liable to the uncertainty which usually attends those . . . in which the precise number of simple ideas that make them up are not easily agreed, so readily kept in mind. And, Secondly, Because they are never referred to any other essence, but barely that perception they immediately signify. (*Essay* III, 9:18)

The clarity of simple ideas, reposing on their natural derivation, accounts for the epistemological superiority of simple names. Conversely, it was because complex ideas *"want standards in nature"* (*Essay* III, 9:7) that they were arbitrary: their names lapsed into *"insignificant terms,"* "empty sounds, with little or no signification" (*Essay* III, 10: 2). In this way, simple names were seen to "immediately signify," while complex names did not. Thus, although it was ideas that all words designated, it was the world of things that conferred value on them. Nature remained the basic measure of language. This unarticulated premise was the residue in Locke's argument of the nomenclature he was doing away with. Its implications were extended to a third and intermediate class of ideas, that of substances. An example is the idea of man, which refers to an archetype of nature. The word "man" will evoke only an approximation of any individual to whom it may refer, and it is accordingly abstract and corruptible.

Locke isolated words from things, scrupulously partitioning mental and material; but he left a back door open. Through it words still resembled the things they were popularly thought to name. Such associations remained an embarrassment to be suppressed: a "great abuse of words, is, *the taking them for things*" (*Essay* III, 10:14). Modern philosophy was enjoined to conventionalize the use of language, "which was given us for the improvement of knowledge and bond of society" (*Essay* III, 10:13), and so to convert it from rhetoric, "that powerful instrument of error and deceit" (*Essay* III, 10:34).

The rising empirical understanding thus joined an attack on empty terminology conducted under the other auspices by Bacon, Descartes, and Hobbes among others. The object was neoscholastic bombast, but it amounted to a general inquisition of language.[17] It was this complex tradition that Coleridge would be engaging in his pursuit of language. Through it, in the *Philosophical Lectures* of 1819, he would expose the inadequacy of Locke's position. There the argument would be conducted against words as images: "Locke told us, in defining words, we ought to have distinct images or conceptions, and therefore we ought to have an image or a conception of an idea, which Cicero never heard of and which was a strange thing to Plato" (*PL*, 379). Such was the conclusion to which his consideration of the matter would lead him in time. But Coleridge had found his way to Locke's back door long before, as I shall be proposing, recognizing what it meant for words to be confused with things. He identified the surreptitious naturalism of Locke's analytic, and he would flay it not only from the point of view of Leibnitz[18] but from a growing animus against the tyranny of images in human understanding.

Coleridge's focus on the rather subsidiary treatment of words and things in Locke's *Essay* is an indication of his special interest in the language question, as well as of the tendency of his thinking on the subject. His orientation had considerable precedents. It descended in English transmission from Bacon's *Novum Organum*:

> But the idols of the marketplace [*idola fori*] are most troublesome [*molestissima*], insinuating themselves in the understanding [*in intellectum*] from the association of words and names with things [*quae ex foedere verborum et nominum*] . . . Words for the most part are imposed by the will of the vulgar, and divide things by lines most conspicuous to vulgar understanding. When however a sharper understanding or more diligent observation wishes to shift those lines, to make them more in accordance with Nature, then words cry out against it.[19]

The words of the common tongue corrupted understanding with delusive images of the things of the world. Coleridge saw that simple and substantial names, as Locke defines them, enshrined such images. Locke's glorification of these names as the best part of language involved a fundamental distortion of the role of language in human understanding. For it was not to hold a mirror up to nature that men and women spoke, nor poets wrote. Language was the "sacred Fire in the Temple of Humanity" (*CL* III, 522), a providential resource against naturalism.

Bacon's attack on Aristotle in the *Novum Organum* extended his suspicion of common parlance to a suspicion of terminology in general in the process of understanding. This passage exposes the native root of Coleridge's disaffection with the empirical school:

> An example of the sophisticated kind is most plainly seen in Aristotle, who corrupted Natural Philosophy with his logic; for he made the universe out of his Categories . . . [The Greeks — Anaxagoras, Parmenides, Empedocles, Heraclitus &c.] have all something of the Natural Philosopher in them; and have a savour of the nature of things, of experience, and of bodies: whereas Aristotle's Physics for the most part are nothing but a sound of Dialectical Terms.   (*NO* I, 63; pp. 34–35)

It is clear from Coleridge's discussion of Aristotle in the fifth lecture of 1819 that he followed Bacon's argument in his own way, making Aristotle the Genius of Generalization, with all this implied of a merely categorical understanding (*PL*, 180f.). That he was familiar with the *Novum Organum*, and attentive to Bacon's idols in particular, is a matter of record. They appear in passing in the *The Friend* (*Essay* VIII, *CC* 4:1, 482–87) and again in the *Philosophical Lectures*, where Coleridge took on their author by name (Lecture XI, *PL*, 331–37). Yet he did not conduct his attack on empirical understanding directly from Bacon's position, as he might have done, because he had already come to terms with the issues in his own way. The *Novum Organum* provided ballast for an orientation which was long established in Coleridge's thinking.

His divergence from Bacon on the idols of the marketplace confirms the originality of his position. Where Bacon differentiated vulgar from philosophical language, the Coleridge of the lectures would find only a distinction: "For active philosophical language differs from common language in this only, or mainly at least, that philosophical language does more accurately, and by an express compact, which is unconsciously, and as it were by a tacit compact, aimed at and in part accomplished by the common language, though with less precision and consistency" (*PL*, 369). Here is the justification in his conception of language for a philosophical appreciation of poetry reverting to his own early practice of the art. For the words of common speech, and of the writing associated with it, were the real basis of the understanding cultivated by philosophy. The long continuity of concern for the integrity of the language, evident through Coleridge's developing career, found initial expression in his tentative treatment of words and things at the turn of the century.

Coleridge's change of vocation proved more complicated than his resolution to make it. At first he planned to give up poetry for a critical defense of the works of Wordsworth and Southey. This evolved into an "Essay on the Elements of Poetry" which "would in reality be a *disguised* System of Morals and Politics (*CL* I, 623, 632 — September 17 and October 9, 1800). Yet he felt the need to settle his commitment to poetry in other principles. A letter of December 17, 1800, to John Thelwall, written while his resolve was fresh, suggested as a first step a "metaphysical Investigation" of language and mind:

> My literary pursuits are, 1 the Northern languages, the Sclavonic, Gothic, & Celtic, in their most ancient forms, as an amusing study, & 2. as a serious object, a metaphysical Investigation of the Laws, by which our Feelings form affinities with each other, with Ideas, & with words. As to Poetry, I have altogether abandoned it, being convinced that I never had the essentials of poetic Genius, & that I mistook a strong desire for original power. (*CL* I, 656)

What was involved here was a shift from poetry to the beginnings of reflective understanding on the common ground of language. He had a model at hand whose interest in language provided him with a starting point. The letter to Thelwall, with its proposed investigation of the laws of affinity governing words, ideas, and feelings, establishes Coleridge's reliance in this area on David Hartley, whose Law of Association he had been trying out for some time.

Coleridge's debt to Hartley was fundamental, yet equivocal. Hartley was familiar, and he had asked some of the questions even if he had not answered them in a convincing way. Writing to Godwin in another letter of this period Coleridge took on some of Hartley's mechanistic assumptions. It is of interest both as the most detailed record of his early approach to language and as an epitome of his struggle with Hartley. In it he urged Godwin to write a book on the power of words, and the processes by which human feelings form affinities with them—in short, I wish you to *philosophize* Horn Tooke's System, and to solve the great Questions—whether there be reason to hold, that an action bearing all the *semblance* of predesigning Consciousness may yet be simply organic, & whether a *series* of such actions are possible—and close on the heels of this question would follow the old 'Is Logic the Essence of Thinking?' in other words— Is *thinking* impossible without arbitrary signs? &—how far is the word 'arbitrary' a misnomer? Are not words &c parts and germinations of the Plant? And what is the Law of their Growth?—In something of this order I would endeavor to destroy the old antithesis of *Words & Things*, elevating, as it were, words into Things, & living Things too. All the nonsense of vibrations etc you would of course dismiss. (*CL* I, 625–26)

As the lapse into the first person suggests, this was a line of argument Coleridge was thinking about pursuing himself in the autumn of 1800. Here for the first time he was concerned with something more than words in particular: language as an organ, in its deep relations with thought. While dense, his proposal is neither "an immense heap of *little* things" (*CL* I, 349) nor inarticulate brainstorming. The letter is a celebrated one, but it has usually been considered topically.[20] Its sources confirm the English context of Coleridge's meditation on language, situating it in the aftermath of Locke's *Essay* and Hartley's *Observations on Man* (1754).

The letter to Godwin establishes Horne Tooke as the second muse of the investigation. Coleridge knew Tooke principally as the radical pamphleteer who had weathered a trial for treason in 1794. He must have felt a political kinship, for a letter of 1796 includes enthusiastic "Verses Addressed to J. Horne Tooke and the Company Who Met on June 28th, 1796, to Celebrate His Poll at the Westminster Election" (*CPW* I, 150). There Tooke figured as

> Patriot and Sage! whose breeze-like Spirit first
> The lazy mists of Pedantry dispers'd . . .

Coleridge explicated the former line in a note consisting of the two Greek words (᾽έπεα πτερόεντα) by which Tooke had named his long, quixotic dialog on language, known as *The Diversions of Purley*.[21] The "breeze-like Spirit" of Tooke's wingéd words wore as badly as his politics, though. Just two years later Coleridge was exclaiming from

Göttingen, "My God! a miserable Poet must he be, & a despicable Metaphysician [whose] acquirements have not cost more trouble & reflection than all the learning of Tooke, Porson, & Parr united" (*CL* I, 494). Two notebook entries of the German period suggest that Tooke had made his mark nonetheless, and they are worth considering for what they reveal of the foundations of Coleridge's understanding. The first entry, derived from material in Adelung's *Dictionary* (2nd. ed., 1793), tries out Tooke's speculative etymology for the first time in the notebooks:

> Mind — min — meinen — mahnen — mahen
> vibratory yet progressive motion.   (*CN* I, 378)

The reduction of complex names (like "mind") to simple etymons ("motion") by phonetic association was Tooke's basic weapon in his assault on Locke's complex ideas. For him there were only simple ideas, derived from the data of sensation. Complex ideas, or abstractions, were not constituted by the association of a number of simple ideas, as the words which expressed them could be made to show (*DP* 19, 600). Whatever Coleridge thought of this simplification of Locke's theory, Tooke's voice appealed to his verbal imagination. Years later he was still exercising it: "[W]ords as distinguished from mere pulses of Air in the auditory nerve must correspond to Thoughts, and Thoughts is but the verb-substantive Participle Preterite of *Thing* . . . " (*CN* III, 3587 f43ᵛ). In view of his reservations about Locke, this is a remarkable survival — the more so as it carries with it a suspect nest of assumptions about language, including the direct dependence of words on phenomena.

At about the same time, Coleridge proposed "Grammatical Essays in respect to Gender, & the Harmony of various Languages — a good subject for a study for 3 months at Cambridge" (*CN* I, 382). Now Tooke discusses gender in an important context in the first volume of his book. James Harris, author of *Hermes* (1751), an influential organ of rationalist language theory, had assumed the assignment of gender to object to be universal, and had given as his first examples the masculine sun and the feminine moon. This was grist for Tooke's mill. He was quick to point out that in the northern languages the sun was feminine and the moon masculine, but he made little of the fact, contenting himself with denouncing the habit of drawing evidence from the classical languages alone (*DP*, 26–27). Coleridge's proposed study of linguistic gender probably found its inspiration here. Though he seems not to have followed it up systematically, some results were forthcoming in his conversation years later in a discussion of Tooke's book. There Coleridge followed the matter beyond his source, tracing the articulation of gender in modern German to Luther and arguing that the sun remained masculine in conception despite the feminine article. In the meantime, he had versified the controversy, adapting an existing German epigram on the subject.[22]

This skirmish epitomizes Coleridge's ambivalence about Tooke's work. In the long run the amateur philologist seems to have served him the way Harris had served *The Diversions of Purley*: as an antithetical figure, attractive for the issues he had raised but threadbare in the main lines of his argument. His "system," as Coleridge followed him in calling it, was founded on an unwarranted induction: "Tooke affects to explain the origin and whole philosophy of language by what is, in fact, only a mere accident of the history of one or two languages" (*TT*, 70). That accident, the fulcrum of Tooke's argument, was the supposed loss of the original meanings of the particles of the English language. The term included for him all the parts of speech except nouns and verbs. Locke had been baffled by the particles in his discussion of language, Tooke argued, because he had failed to see what had become of them. He had been obliged to fall back on the suspicious contention that they reflected "operations of the *mind*" (*DP*, 21–22). Tooke corrected this apparent problem by collapsing the main English particles into nouns and verbal participles in a flurry of wildly speculative etymologizing. "If" became a form of "give," "awry" the past participle of an Anglo-Saxon verb meaning "to writhe," "more" the abbreviated past participle of another verb meaning "to mow" and suggesting "*any* heap" (*DP* 78f., 259, 278–79). On the basis of this exercise and analogues from "savage" languages, Tooke held that "every word in all languages had a separate meaning of its own" (*DP*, 297), reducing the speaker's role to verbal bricklaying. An uncompromising mechanism was the philosophic trophy of the argument: "The business of the mind, as far as it concerns Language, appears to me to be very simple. It extends no further than to receive impressions, that is, to have Sensations or Feelings. What are called its operations, are merely the operations of Language" (*DP*, 25). So it was that Tooke's account of the English particles was made to bear the burden of proof for a general theory of language.

And so it was that Coleridge proposed, in the letter to Godwin, that he "*philosophize* Horne Tooke's System." By this he meant not to supply Tooke's inductive leap the solid grounding it lacked, but to "solve the great Questions" about language and its relation to thought. Tooke had raised but not dispatched them with his cranky machinery, and it was against his answers that Coleridge was reacting. When he asks, "Is *thinking* impossible without arbitrary signs?" he seems to be responding to Tooke's identification of the operations of mind with those of language. And when he goes on to question the arbitrariness of the sign, he sets himself against Tooke's view of the "artful contrivances of Language" (*DP*, 32). This leads in turn to his antithetical characterization of words as "parts and germinations of the Plant," as "living Things" for which there was a law of growth in an explicitly organic sense. It was within this reactive process that Coleridge felt his way toward a preliminary understanding.

Through Tooke, Coleridge came back to Hartley and his influential Law of Association. Jerome Christensen traces Hartley's impact on Coleridge's thinking to 1794, showing how pervasive it was despite an ambivalence already fully developed in the letter to Godwin. Coleridge paid particular attention at some point to the chapter in Hartley's *Observations* in which he applied his association theory to language. It is a remarkable fact that this chapter was the only one in the three volumes of the 1791 edition which he marked up.[23] "Words and Phrases must excite Ideas in us by Association," Hartley proposed, "and they excite Ideas in us by no other means."[24] And, as a corollary, "the Arts of Logic, and rational Grammar, depend intirely on the Doctrine of Association. For Logic, considered as the art of Thinking or Reasoning, treats only of such Ideas as are annexed to Words" (*OM*, 270). He went on to detail the processes by which children learned language, building on primary associations between sense impressions and the sounds of the words that named them. From these it was possible for the child to guess the meanings of both adjectives and verbs from their repeated association with established names. Particles, on the other hand, were learned in association with whole sentences. Abstract names were learned in all three ways, the choice depending on the nature of the concept. Language, thus constituted, was "one Species of Algebra," its words "arbitrary Signs" comparable to algebraic variables (*OM*, 280). Hartley's conception of the role of language in thought represented a significant complication of Locke's, though he did not develop it at length. It was not just in words that thought proceeded, it was through them: "Diversity of Languages does also both help the

Invention, and correct false Judgments. For we think in Words, as appears by the foregoing Theory, and invent chiefly by means of their Analogies; at the same time that a servile Adherence to those of any one Language, or the putting Words for Things, would lead us into many Errors" (*OM*, 305; cf. *Essay* III, 10:14). Language was not identical with ideation, as it was for Horne Tooke; it was only the principal tool of ideation. As such, its place in the *Observations* was a modest one, as it had been in Locke's *Essay*.

Whenever Coleridge writes of affinities (as he often does in connection with language), of arbitrary signs, of words and things, and especially of vibrations, he evokes Hartley's argument. The project he describes to Godwin would begin nearly where Hartley's discussion of language had done: with a consideration of "the processes by which human feelings form affinities with" words. Coleridge retreated from ideation with "feelings" and subverted the mechanistic "association" with "affinities." The result was to make Hartley's associational process more subjective. But revising Hartley is hardly the same thing as philosophizing Horne Tooke's system, as Coleridge's next phrase would lead us to believe. What he was about here amounted nevertheless to a sublation of Tooke. To consider language in Hartley's terms was to consider it psychologically, from the point of view of someone learning and practicing it. To consider it as Tooke did was to consider it pseudohistorically as an institution with a life of its own. The proposal outlined in the letter to Godwin would respond to Tooke from Hartley's psychological viewpoint, though not from his stated positions. It would refute a relentless mechanism by an insistence on the activity of the mind in language. This was how Coleridge would philosophize Tooke. What was left of *The Diversions of Purley* was little more than a paronomastic game — a sort of superior punning.

Some of Hartley's positions came under attack in the process. The first of the "great Questions," "whether . . . an action bearing all the *semblance* of pre-designing Consciousness may yet be simply organic," answered Hartley's notion that association was automatic, not intentional. The plain implication was that language *was* more than simply organic: that it involved thinking. In addition, Coleridge took Hartley's warning against the confusion of words and things to task, proposing antithetically to "destroy the old antithesis" itself. By this he meant *not*, as it has sometimes seemed to his readers,[25] to treat words as reflections of things — the identification suppressed formulaically but preserved in practice by Locke and his followers. Rather, he meant to accord language an independent status *like* that of things. Living words remain altogether different, for him, from images. In effect, Coleridge went the long way round to affirming Hartley's antithesis in his own terms. Finally, he closed by characterizing Hartley's vibrations, the physiological mechanism of association, as nonsense. Despite the reservations, Hartley can be said to have provided Coleridge with a model of psychological argument, one he adapted in his attack on Tooke.

The letters to Thelwall and Godwin, taken with associated passages in the notebooks,[26] are slight evidence of what amounted to Coleridge's initiation in the philosophy of language. The project he envisioned was indicated only schematically, but the effect was lasting, for in coming to terms with Hartley and Tooke he found a principle to conjure with. Their related versions of language as a second nature which stocked the unformed mind with ideas, operating mechanically by association within it, presumed a passive intelligence which Coleridge could not admit. Ideas were not impressions made by words, and words were not the signatures of natural form. As "living Things" they count for more too than an early instance of his organicism. Coleridge's incipient conception situated the medium of language between image and idea, in an independent organ involved with both but bound to neither except by convention and the individual will. The larger vocation of language, and its value for an expanding human understanding, would depend on its essential autonomy.

"Some New Combinations of Language"

Coleridge's engagement with the philosophy of language was inspired, I have suggested, by his need to make a move in the direction of critical principle without leaving poetry behind. His notebooks and letters of the autumn of 1800, and occasionally of the two years following, exhibit renewed awareness of language as ground for argument. This is sometimes allied to poetic concerns:

> A Poet's *Heart* & *Intellect* should be *combined, intimately* combined & *unified*, with the great appearances in Nature — & not merely held in Solution & loose mixture with them, in the shape of formal Similies. I do not mean to *exclude* these formal Similies — there are moods of mind, in which they are natural — pleasing moods of mind, & such as a Poet will

often have, & sometimes express; but they are not his highest, & most appropriate moods. (*CL* II, 864)

Here, the simile is more than a rhetorical figure; it corresponds to a way of thinking, and by so conceiving it Coleridge measures the limitations of Bowles's poetry—and perhaps of his own. An indicative context, for he was moving in this period toward a more general investigation initiated by a reading of Locke. What had begun as an attempt to consolidate his concerns in a philosophical essay on poetry was turning into a study of the origins of modern epistemology. Later, in the *Biographia Literaria*, he would try to reconcile poetry and metaphysics by "an application of the rules, deduced from philosophical principles, to poetry and criticism" (*BL* I, 1). The double vision of the *Biographia* is the legacy of his early commitment to integrated understanding.

In the wake of the republication in January 1801 of *Lyrical Ballads*, with its polemical "Preface" in place for the first time, Coleridge made some effort to relate his version of the new poetics to the idea of language he had been developing. He was in effect exploring "in what manner language and the human mind act and react on each other" (*LBP*, 154) as this bore on poetic value. A letter of February 3 shows him determined to pursue it: "I fear . . . I shall not be able to do what my heart within me *burns* to do—that is, *concenter* my free mind to the affinities of the Feelings with Words & Ideas under the title of 'Concerning Poetry & the nature of the Pleasures derived from it'" (*CL* II, 671). No public treatment of the subject appeared, but the burning impulse found an outlet in a letter of advertisement composed over Wordsworth's signature and posted to William Wilberforce on the appearance of *Lyrical Ballads* in its new form. This letter shows how the meditation on language erupted in the margins of the "Preface":

I composed the accompanying poems under the persuasion, that all which is usually included under the name of action bears the same proportion (in respect of worth) to the affections, as a language to the thing signified. When the material forms or intellectual ideas which should be employed to represent the internal state of feeling, are made to claim attention for their own sake, then commences Lip-worship, or superstition, or disputatiousness, in religion; a passion for gaudy ornament & violent stimulants in morals; & in our literature bombast and vicious refinements, an aversion to the common conversational language of our Countrymen, with an extravagant preference given to *Wit* by some, and to outrageous *incident* by others; while the most sacred affections of the human race seem to lay no hold on our sympathies unless we can contemplate them in the train of some circumstances that excite *curiosity*, or unriddle them from some gaudy phrases that are to attract our wonder for themselves.   (*CL* II, 666)[27]

Coleridge's rendition of Wordsworth's voice in this contentious context epitomizes the paradox of their collaboration. The "Preface" was their joint production, yet Wordsworth took full credit for it. Coleridge did his best to make the case, yet he had never concurred with some of it, as he would later claim (*BL* II, 7–8). By 1802, in a letter to Sotheby, he would acknowledge "a *radical* Difference" (*CL* II, 812). This curious letter to Wilberforce shows how Coleridge tried to express that difference on linguistic grounds nearly from the beginning.

There is a great deal of Wordsworth in it. But the tone is peculiarly brittle — stiff-necked and emphatic in a way that exceeds the "Preface," even the occasion. Wilberforce makes a likely recipient for so didactic an exercise: Coleridge was undoubtedly playing to his audience. Even so, what the letter offers is Wordsworth as Coleridge must have seen him. The opening ratio suggests as much: "language to the thing signified" glosses the Wordsworthian formula which favored "the best objects from which the best part of language is originally derived." It represents a Coleridgean interpretation, in terms taken from his investigation of language. "Thing signified" is a revealing choice of words — the things to which Coleridge refers are not "the best objects" but "the internal state of feeling." His interpretation thus performs the elementary shift from direct signification, familiar in an unsatisfactory form in Hartley. Words relied on feeling — not things, nor even ideas in the usual sense. On this modified basis Coleridge set out to explicate Wordsworth's commitments.

The new ratio of "language to the thing signified" is an interesting one not only as it documents the advent of the idea of language in Coleridge's thinking, but as it reflects his poetic commitments at this important pass. A related statement of his position would appear in the same letter to Sotheby, of 1802, which suspected out loud the difference with Wordsworth. There the reliance of language on feeling would approach the status of critical principle: "In my opinion every phrase, every metaphor, every personification, should have it's justifying cause in some *passion* either of the Poet's mind, or of the Characters described by the poet" (*CL* II, 812). This was not itself the source of the difference with Wordsworth, though it included the point from which (on Coleridge's understanding) they diverged. The Wordsworthian emphasis fell, in Coleridge's rehearsal of it, on the corruption of speech — on "Lip-worship," "bombast and vicious refinements," "an aversion to the common conversational language of our Countrymen."

It was at the point where rustic speech became an exclusive ideal for Wordsworth's poetic idiom that Coleridge would take exception. As he continued in the letter to Southeby: "In my opinion, Poetry justifies as *Poetry* independent of any other Passion, some new combinations of Language, & *commands* the omission of many others allowable in other compositions/Now Wordsworth . . . has in his system not sufficiently admitted the former, & in his practice has too frequently sinned against the latter" (*CL* II, 812). The context is a familiar one, but it acquires new resonance against the background of Coleridge's argument from language. For the difference with Wordsworth appeared to him, at the moment he went public with it, a difference of "system" — of comprehensive understanding, as he employed the term. And the ground of the difference he isolated in an attitude to language in general.

Wordsworth's suspicion of everything artificial in speech and expression was measured, in the letter to Wilberforce, against the norm of common conversation, which was associated with "the most sacred affections of the human race." This contrast is clearly available in the "Preface," though more tentatively. By exaggerating its temper, Coleridge drove Wordsworth to an extreme adherence to the model of speech, uncontaminated by the contrivances which he deplored in literary language. Like the opening ratio, this characterization represents Wordsworth as Coleridge made him out: the dogmatic antagonist of every sort of poetic device. Wordsworth's real commitment was to an *expanded* idea of poetic expression, not to an exclusive one, of course. The exaggeration served to make an emphatic point.

The letter to Wilberforce thus reveals what seemed salient and potentially dangerous to Coleridge in the attitude of the "Preface." Signification was a thin patch in the armor; so were the comprehensive dismission of rhetoric and the rustic language Wordsworth would adopt in its place. His poetics of speech seemed to encourage a mindless documentary function, abdicating the imaginative latitude which poetry cultivated — first of all through "some new combinations of Language," as he would soon put it to Sotheby. Wordsworth reneged on poetry's ancestral charter when he subscribed to common conversation as the fundamental resource of poetic expression. His literalism (as Coleridge would later develop this idea) violated generic expectations; but more than that, it committed poetry to the limitations of common language.

It was, for Coleridge, a matter of balance. Common language was protophilosophical, as he would argue later in the lectures, a valuable resource for poetry. He was aware of its possibilities from his own practice. But he was also sensitive to the consequences, as his changing attitude to Bowles shows. Poetry on the conversational model typically degenerated into chatter. To be successful, it demanded the participation of poetic judgment informed by traditional values. Such an emphasis is available in the "Preface," and poetic refinement is obviously at work in the poems of *Lyrical Ballads* in varying degrees. But in relying as he did on the truth of "the common conversational language of our Countrymen" Wordsworth risked losing his balance. Even *his* poetry was not, after all, sui generis: he inherited and vitalized the great past of English verse. In Shakespeare and Milton it had been a poetry of vigorous thinking, of "activity of thought in the play of words." Wordsworth could not rise to such heights on the language of leech-gatherers.

Such was the crux of Coleridge's difference as it seems to have struck him in the beginning, against the background of his defense of the free mind in language. This connection was elusive, but important for the way he imagined his role as apologist and critic of the new school. He would play inquisitor to Wordsworth's common sense, defending the language of mind (conditioned by feeling) against the language of circumstance—"some new combinations of *Language*" against the idols of the marketplace. Broad accord with Wordsworth, as well as a certain diffidence about his grasp of the large issues, perhaps prevented his taking the argument to its limit. Instead, he turned to Locke for a longer view of the situation. Before considering the bearing of his excursion into the empirical mind, I want to look briefly into the "Preface" to see what it yields to this reconstruction of Coleridge's critical understanding in its formative moment.

As I have been urging, Wordsworth proposed to adopt the language of rustics because it derived from the best objects, in a distinctly primitive theorem which Coleridge was at pains to revise. The name appeared to Wordsworth the exemplary part of speech, as it had to Hartley and Tooke. Language was nomination; at its most authentic, it respected this function. The best language was to be found on location, as it were, in communities whose long practice had worn it down to essential expression: "[These rustics] convey their feelings and notions in simple and unelaborated expressions. Accordingly such a language arising out of repeated experience and regular feelings is a more permanent and a far more philosophical language than that which is frequently substituted for it by Poets, who . . . indulge in arbitrary and capricious habits of expression" (*LBP*, 156–57). If objects lay at the origin of language, human experience conferred value on it. Rustic language was the product of a long *askesis*. The force of this last idea is considerable, and potentially radical. Charles Altieri assimilates it to Wittgenstein through the attention to repeated experience;[28] Walter Benjamin's *Erfahrung* perhaps approaches it as well, in a more expansive setting.[29] But it shares something important, as the context suggests, with Coleridge's later defense of common language as protophilosophical. The familiar expression of the idea in the "Preface," at once assertive and sparse, taken with the outright attack on poetic diction, makes it Wordsworth's thinking despite the community of interest.

The primitive linguistic theorem was not the point, as the long influence of the "Preface" attests. What Wordsworth was getting at counted for more than the shortcomings of his understanding of how language worked. Still, these affected his conception of what he was about and complicated his claims again and again. For it was on this basis, in part, that he mounted his radical argument: "[T]he more industriously [the poet] applies this principle [of selection] the deeper will be his faith that no words, which his fancy or imagination can suggest, will be to be compared with those which are the emanations of reality and truth" (*LBP*, 166). A documentary poetry would be the ideal product of such a conviction. For the poet could add nothing meaningful to words emanating from sources so pure. Elsewhere, of course, Wordsworth wrote of expressing his ideas "in language fitted to their respective importance" (*LBP*, 161). The change of idea is abrupt, but ultimately irrelevant — the conviction of the value of common speech survives its imperfect formulation, and we make allowance for the demotion of the poet to recording folklorist. The poems themselves tell the story best, and they reflect both the triumph and the shortcomings of common language as applied to verse. Penultimately, however, it is fair to notice — as Coleridge did, in detail — that it was the practice which mattered for understanding Wordsworth. The letter to Wilberforce intimates, at the beginning of the process, how stentorious, how problematic, he found Wordsworth's pronouncements on language. They consumed everything else in the "Preface," as he echoed it there.

It is more than coincidence that Coleridge was thinking about language at this time. His investigation appears to have taken root in the conflicts surrounding the reissue of *Lyrical Ballads*. Within a month, he was composing "the result of my meditations on the relations of Thought to Things" in three long letters to Josiah Wedgwood. These took the form of a critique of Locke, whose *Essay* he was reading carefully for the first time. Here he lit on the prototype of the empirical idea he had been resisting all along. He singled out the discussion of language for exemplary abuse, citing a passage which recalls the argument he had contrived as Wordsworth's in the letter to Wilberforce: "[A]ll the figurative application of Words, Eloquence hath invented, are for nothing else but to insinuate wrong ideas, move the Passions, and thereby mislead the Judgement; and so indeed are perfect cheat" (*CL* II, 695; from *Essay* III, 10). Here is sustaining evidence that the tirade in that letter against "vicious refinements" in the language of contemporary literature was meant to represent Wordsworth's voice alone. Dismantling Locke's position on language was straightforward because the implications were clear from the earlier skirmishes with Hartley and Tooke, as well as with Wordsworth. Locke's position became the prototype of the conception which accorded language a merely mimetic function, condemning its figurative (or eloquent) use as interference. And Wordsworth's became, by implication, the conception of poetry founded on this puritanical debasement of words to labels. New combinations of language were a threat to Locke's nomenclature because they insinuated "wrong ideas." In Wordsworth, this attitude was reproduced as a principled adherence to norms of speech and a concomitant suspicion of poetic innovation.

Coleridge's sense of the connection to Locke's empiricism was fleeting though not I think merely subliminal, for it had a future in his thinking even if it was not developed in this form. There are good reasons for him to have resisted the logic of the comparison. The poetics of speech as Wordsworth developed it plainly violates Locke's strictures on the idols of the marketplace. Its faith is a breath of fresh air. There was little enough to be gained from linking Wordsworth to Locke's censorious Book III in any case. The philosophical defense of poetry was not yet current, so that linkage would have had no real meaning for contemporary readers. For Coleridge himself, it meant only that he was confronted with an alien idea of language. The next step would involve identifying its premises and affiliations.

The presumptive analogy to Locke contained a considerable insight all the same, worth expanding on briefly as a way of imagining what Coleridge was getting at. It is useless to observe that Wordsworth was empirical in his thinking, and certainly misleading. On the matter of language, he was not even close. Locke's analytic grasped the mental function of language, going far beyond the simplicity of best words and best objects. Yet its reliance on verification made it subject to the same sort of judgments, as I have suggested: words were valuable insofar as they could be validated in sense experience. A perfected language would thus consist of simple names only. This was Tooke's desideratum. Existing, or natural, language bore the brunt of Locke's resentment of the imperfection of ideas. The calibration of human understanding could only come to pass through a vast reform of language — a new nomenclature to sweep out the idols of the marketplace. It was in his attack on distortion in expression that Locke resembled Wordsworth in Coleridge's eyes. Here was where he found the type of his collaborator's energetic dismissal of rhetoric, as the letters to Wedgwood must lead us to suppose. So extreme and contrary an attitude was only the underside of an ambitious idealization in both Locke and Wordsworth. What language might be for human understanding, what it was in the event in a fallen world: such a view sacrificed a living language for an imaginary order. The idealization became a problem the moment it was submitted to modern circumstances. Understanding could never be as clear nor language as pure as they imagined.

Coleridge was hardly alone in wondering about the basis of Wordsworth's attack on poetic language. It bore passing resemblance to informed contemporary response, as Mrs. Barbauld's anonymous review of Lamb's *John Woodvil* shows:

> A School of Poetry has within a few years been set up by Sir Lamb and some others whom it would be indecorous as their Works are not before us [*sic*], where all Harmony of Numbers is despised, all the regularities of Rhythm & Variety of Cadence are disregarded, and from which all the Graces of Language are contemptuously banished. This Harmony of Numbers, these regularities of Rhythm, and Varieties of Cadence, have, it is true, in many Instances been more attended to than chastity of Sentiment and Vigour of Expression. Disgusted probably that these Ornaments should have been distributed with an ill-judged Profusion, this

School, in order to reform the Taste, and enamour it *with* the charms of Simplicity, not content with stripping Poetry of her superfluous Embellishments and arranging tastefully those which would really adorn her Person, and set off her Beauties, has absolutely deprived her of the common decencies of Dress . . . An affectation of plainness and simplicity, which is the flimsiest covering for Incapacity that was ever assumed/ which is nowadays offered to us as the very essence of Simplicity & Pathos.   (*CN* II, 1848)

Coleridge cited it thus in his notebook, resolving in a letter to Southey of about the same time to "cut her to the heart" (*CL* II, 1039). His own allegiance was firm, even as he doubted Wordsworth's harrowing of the resources of poetry. His convergence with some of Mrs. Barbauld's doubts about simple language did not constitute capitulation to the forces of the past in English poetry, as Hamilton and Bialostosky, among others, would imply.[30] His separate allegiance to a language which "carries within it a human history that can enter into new, subtle and precise expression"[31] only qualified his support of Wordsworth's rhetoric against rhetoric. Language continued as the fundamental source of their difference of understanding. Coleridge's version of expressive language would lay stress on its function as an instrument of thinking—and that in the theoretical base, not only in the poetic superstructure.

For support of such an idea he had only to turn to the rationalists, and this he did as soon as he had done with Locke. Drawing sustenance from Tooke's suggestion that Locke's discussion of words should have subsumed his account of ideas, Coleridge skipped back to consider the Cartesian alternative. There he found what he conceived to be an improved version of Locke: "Words (according to Des Cartes) are to be considered in three ways—they are themselves images and sounds; 2. they are connected with our Thoughts by associations with Images & Feelings; 3. with Feelings alone, and this too is the natural Tendency of Language" (*CL* II, 697–98). It was in fact a very different idea of language that he sketched out. Here were words as things in a sense anticipated in the letter to Godwin. They were not identical with images as Locke's primary names were, but instruments in their own right: an intermediate order, connected with thinking on the one hand, "Images and Feelings" on the other. The emphasis on feeling recovered ground squandered by Locke, dispersing the categorical assignment of names to ideas. And it set the stage for a defense of poetry on the basis of the "natural Tendency of Language."

Against the solidarity of names and images promoted by Locke, Coleridge would stand for living words. He developed the idea in the course of this reading of Descartes, with Hartley's association psychology driving him to his own conclusions:

> For as words are learnt by us in clusters, even those that most expressly refer to Images & other Impressions are not all learnt by us determinately; and tho' this should be wholly corrected by after experience, yet the Images & Impressions associated with the words become more & more dim, till at last as far as our consciousness extends they cease altogether; & Words act upon us immediately, exciting a mild current of Passion & Feeling without the regular intermediation of Images . . . Words therefore become a sort of Nature to us, & Nature is a sort of Words. (*CL* II, 698)

The word against the image: a crux of his approach to language, at work nearly from the beginning of his thinking on the subject. Their opposition is a deep premise of his long quest for critical understanding. As he treats it here, the contest of word and image constitutes the real ground of poetic creation. Language is the horizon of this second Nature, "a sort of Words" inscribed in the world.

Words and Things

The importance of language for Coleridge's reformation of reason and understanding is attested by plans at the end of his life for an *Opus Maximum*, "beginning with the Propyleum, On the Power and Use of Words, comprising Logic, as the canons of Conclusion, as the criterion of Premises, and lastly as the discipline and evolution of Ideas. . . . "[32] This prolegomenon stands unfinished in manuscript, the stunted growth of a seed sown over thirty years earlier: "Not only words as far as relates to speaking, but the knowledge of words, as distinct component parts, which we learn by learning to read—what an immense effect it must have on our reasoning faculties?—Logical in opposition to real" (*CN* I, 866). Coleridge's attention to language in the autumn and winter of 1800–1801 proved germinal for the growth of his "whole system," which the *Opus Maximum* was to have incorporated. It represented a second crescendo in the movement of his reflection on language. The first had come halfway between initiation and system, with the *Biographia* and the philosophical lectures. In the former Coleridge addressed himself not just to poetic diction, but to the larger relations of language and thought in poetry. In the latter he sketched a history of philosophy, ancient, scholastic, and modern, drawing on resources derived from his investigation of language. In both, a presiding conception of language is so intimate to the conduct of his argument that it is difficult to isolate as a distinct feature of his thinking.

Coleridge's symbolic view of language, as Richards called it, emerges in the process I have been tracing, but it is not yet explicit in his reactions to Tooke and Hartley, Locke and Descartes. The notebooks of this period are helpful in filling in the blanks, and taken with notes and letters of the three years following provide a preliminary idea. A note of early 1801, important for its introduction of the symbol, shows how deeply the investigation of language cut: "It seems to elucidate the Theory of Language, Hartley, just able to speak a few words, making a fire-place of stones, with stones for fire. — four stones — fire-place — two stones — fire — /arbitrary symbols in Imagination" (CN I, 918). David Hartley arrived at his sense of language through reflection on childhood acquisition. Coleridge interprets the play of the son named after him in the same spirit. Two principles appear to be involved. The first is the primary association of words with ideas: it is the idea of fire, not the material thing, which the symbol designates. Lacking fire, infant Hartley substitutes stones. They bear no resemblance, but he still calls them "fire" because that is what he has in mind. It follows that the relation between words and things is indirect, hinging on ideas. Words are arbitrary because they do not correspond directly to phenomena: "fire" designates two stones standing for the missing thing. This is the second principle — a corollary, really, of the first. Words are symbols insofar as they "stand for" phenomena at one mental remove. Coleridge thus confirmed the force of Condillac's linguistic relativism empirically, at the beginning of his career, in his symbolic view of language. Words do of course participate indirectly, through the mediation of ideas, in the world of things, even if they are not reducible to things. But the emphasis falls on the autonomous order of the symbol, its instrumental role in thinking. To observe that words are symbols "in Imagination" is to insist that the connection between words and things is a volitional one arising in the process of thought. Before the child had mastered the conventions of language he had already grasped the symbolic function underlying them.

The arbitrary sign reverts to Locke of course, but the function of the symbolic—the Imagination and all it includes—is just what Locke and his inheritors were concerned to suppress. For the proliferation of symbolizing interfered with the conventional operation of language—of human understanding as they would promote it. Words could hardly be trusted if they were "arbitrary symbols in Imagination." As such, they were not names at all, nor could they deliver the clear images of things as required. Threadbare idols of the marketplace, these words had their basis in the sorry history of human confusion. Coleridge would embrace the process that Locke despaired of: "Language & all *symbols* give *outness* to Thoughts/& this the philosophical essence & purpose of Language" (*CN* I, 1387). The primary association of words with ideas became for him the foundation of a personal symbolic. Language in its outness was a social medium, the way the subject went public. Its "philosophical essence" lay in its symbolic function, and this in turn found its purpose in performance. Language was not after all a scientific algebra. Its vocation was symbolic in a human world, with all that included of uncertainty, negotiation, and the difficulty of understanding.

Coleridge soon went public with his new-found fire, trying out the idea in his letters and notebooks. To Humphrey Davy he recorded his progress in chemistry, noticing ironically the mirage of scientific terminology: "As far as *words* go, I have become a formidable chemist—having got by heart a prodigious quantity of terms &c to which I attach *some* ideas—very scanty in number" (*CL* II, 727). Empirical knowledge was as easy as mastering the names. Getting the ideas was another matter. But what, in that case, did names really come to? Later he would put a point to it: "Ready Command of a limited number of words=playing Cat-cradle dexterously with Language" (*CN* II, 2722). Empirical (or Aristotelian) understanding dealt in terms of specific but doubtful significance. It played games with language on the way to a narrowly circumscribed version of knowledge. At this point he was still entertaining the empirical idea, at least for Davy's consumption, but with a clear notion of what was involved.

Not long after he would complain from his sickbed that "all but dear & lovely Things seemed to be known to my Imagination only as Words" (*CL* II, 737)—a delirium of sorts, the sign of a growing abstraction. Words were occluding images as thinking consumed his living experience. The displacement of his natural faculties, as he would call them in the *Biographia*, was here related to the dominion of language. What that could be made to bear would soon become an issue of magnitude: "Examine minutely the nature, cause, birth & growth of the *verbal* Imagination of which Barrow is almost the Ideal" (*CN* I, 1275). The investigation of language thus led him back to his critical aspiration, its original setting. Verbal imagination was to prove significant for his developing idea of poetry and of style in particular, as I shall be proposing in chapter 5. Before considering what became of it, I want to draw some preliminary conclusions about this first stage of Coleridge on language, and about expressive language as it emerges from his difference with Wordsworth.

It was against Wordsworth that he had conjured the idea of living words—against the primitive linguistic theorem, and, as it would appear in the *Biographia*, against the idiom it authorized in some of the lyrical ballads. Coleridge appreciated the possibilities of common language, and he was broadly sympathetic to Wordsworth's experiments with it. His qualification was of a different order from Mrs. Barbauld's, as the investigation of language should make clear. It had less to do with Wordsworth's simplification of poetic means than with his retreat from philosophical vocation in the dramatic line of his verse. Wordsworth's voice was Coleridge's ideal. What troubled him was the sort of mimicry which debased it to simple language and simple thinking.[33] For language found its vocation in the expression of the speaking subject, and preeminently in that of the poet. There was a considerable difference between the poet's language and "the real language of men," as Wordsworth called it, not because the one was an elite dialect but because it gave voice to a reflective consciousness. At their best, poetic thinking and poetic diction were inextricably associated, the one finding essential means in the other. It is this association that characterizes Coleridge's evaluation of poetry in the *Biographia*, and looking back from his discussion of Wordsworth there it can be seen to have been at work in his consideration of the matter from the beginning of his career.[34]

What is excluded by such an understanding is evident in Bialostosky's defense of Wordsworth's narrative experiments. Coleridge's idea of expressive language was heroically monologic. The voice of the inspired subject was his model; his poetry explores its possibilities, taking it to limits which Wordsworth sometimes dismissed but often exploited in his own way. Where Wordsworth practiced this resonant voice, Coleridge recognized him as the great modern poet. Where he tried out the voices of others, Coleridge usually missed the point. So, to put it in perspective, did Lewis Carroll, among Wordsworth's distinguished parodists—a sign of how novel his dialogic vein really was in cultural context. Its most striking employment among his inheritors is to be found in the heteroglossia of *Alice*, where a ludic potential barely suppressed in some of Wordsworth's experimental narratives is brilliantly realized. The dialogic was indeed a potent source of poetic fire, but it needed severe keeping.

Coleridge would express his dyspathy for Wordsworth's dialogism by recourse to Aristotle, a move that has troubled his modern inheritors since Richards. There is an evident conflict of interest between expressive poetics and the canons of representation, a conflict felt and even confronted, if not decisively resolved, in the *Biographia*.[35] Its sources are clearly indicated in the early language investigation, its consequences in the conundrums of Cambridge English. Expressive language is one answer to linguistic relativism: the conviction of the truth of poetry compensates the failure of language as a reliable bond. Living words, "arbitrary symbols in Imagination," could hardly sustain Locke's aspiration to an order based on a stable linguistic currency. In this setting, the symbolic appears to be a form of withdrawal—even, as in the case of later symbolist poetics, of escape. It has usually been transmitted in modern criticism as an adherence to imagination where society proves inadequate to human needs. The evacuation of historical content in modern versions of language might be said, on such a premise, to respond to disappointment in the collective condition. Once the value of language became (for institutional purposes) mainly symbolic, Coleridge could be seen as a progenitor. A tenuous connection, to be sure, but one that sustains his place in the modern critical mind. In his reformulation of language, he seemed to Richards to have found a way past disappointment—past the horror of history and loss. Expressive language, in the form of poetry, was "capable of saving us; it is a perfectly possible means of overcoming chaos."[36]

Yet Coleridge had never seen it in quite this way, and his long engagement in the largest issues, social, political and religious, confirms the conviction of Raymond Williams that the romantic source was not after all the root of the modern retreat from engagement. Expressive language, the organ of thinking, was forcefully committed in Coleridge's practice to the social process from which it would later appear to be withdrawing. Is the contradiction original, or a product of transmission? Was Coleridge's symbolic idea a private one, as modern readers have long believed, or more inclusive?[37] The investigation of language points to the latter, and to a more integrated understanding of his poetics than is usually admitted. His recurrence to Aristotle in the *Biographia* amounted to an assertion of the claims of the world on poetic language. Poetry was essentially ideal; it dealt in the general condition, not the particular instance. For it was the common fabric of experience that was of interest. Empirical language as promoted by Locke approached the condition of the image, and Coleridge suspected that something like this was Wordsworth's idea as well. The "best part of language" was derived by him from "the best objects," with all that implied of poetry as a sort of painting from nature. Against the idolatry of the image lurking in the empirical outlook, Coleridge would insist on the essential office of thinking in language, and on the way that the forms of language reflected its active mediation. The defense of the general (or supersensible) against the merely particular in poetic representation lay down this line.

For what were images but nature in its particularity? — as opposed to ideas, generalized from sensation, worked through to something human, and associated with experience at large. Coleridge could hardly defend the "idea" as an alternative to the image because he did not believe in it himself, as the Leibnitzian argument of the philosophical lectures shows.[38] Yet he continued to feel uneasy with Wordsworth's errant particularism. The "*radical* Difference in [their] Opinions" that Coleridge suspected in 1802 was associated at the time with the very different grasp of language which he identified in the "Preface." In time this difference took shape as a coherent critique of Wordsworth's poetic practice based on the claims which his associate had made for a new poetry and for the value of common language. The terms proposed by Wordsworth proving inadequate, Coleridge turned to Aristotle for support of his notion that poetry was more than the expression of a private condition even if it emerged with an individual signature. Abrupt as the transition is, it can hardly be considered as reneging on radical commitments. Aristotle is apt in context and true in a limited way to Coleridge's poetics — in about the same degree as Plato can be said to be to Wordsworth's. The symbolic function of language meant that poetry was a way of thinking. Where it seemed to become something else for Wordsworth, as in "The Thorn" or "The Idiot Boy," Coleridge would recall it to its high vocation.

The obsessive image of the thorn exemplifies the fate of poetry when it gives way to the language of things. The image was a Siren, fixing the poet by its powerful lure. He could not think about it, he could only stand in thrall. Such is, at least, a hypothetical epitome of

Coleridge's argument from principle as applied to his quarrel with Wordsworth in the *Biographia*. It is perhaps worth asking why he did not put it this way himself; why he fell back on Aristotle instead of making the case from first premises. Answers to this question must remain equally hypothetical, but they might at least intimate a different order of cogency in his thinking about poetry from what the *Biographia* offers. In context Aristotle does indeed appear a deus ex machina. Against the background of an expressive language of "arbitrary symbols in Imagination," with all that the symbol includes, his presence makes better sense. He is an entirely natural figure for a defense of poetry as a form of engagement. As I have already suggested, the argument from language to poetics would not have been at home here in any case. Operating from the critical philosophy, as Coleridge had done in the *Biographia*, precluded such an argument for other reasons. Herder's fragmentary *Metakritik* had charged Kant with missing language in his "Transcendental Aesthetic."[39] Following in Kant's footsteps, Coleridge might be said to have missed an opportunity here to make his idea of language the foundation of his poetics.

Such a charge betrays the modern interest in making Coleridge over in the image of its incipient formalist idea. This was his fate at the hands of Richards, and where recent versions of Coleridge on language have paid more scrupulous attention to the archive, they have not escaped a similar bias. Thus, Hamilton's assimilation of Coleridge to the positions of Kant and Schelling takes the high road to his poetics via a revisionist account of his aesthetics. Some cautionary observations are called for in considering his conclusions. It was Kant's first critique, with its distinction of reason and understanding, that attracted Coleridge's attention. The third, beginning from the "Analytic of the Beautiful," was of more limited use to him. Notes in a volume of Herder show that he had looked into the "Analytic" sufficiently to defend it, but he drew on it mainly in the aesthetic essays, which are marginal to his reading as it appears in the *Biographia* and elsewhere.[40] It is significant in this connection that Coleridge had nothing to say of Burke's *Philosophical Inquiry into the Origin of Our Ideas of the Sublime and Beautiful* (1756), that English standard on the subject.[41] It was Burke's political writings which consumed him in the notebooks and elsewhere. The aesthetic occupied a rather isolated zone of Coleridge's thinking, as of Kant's. Its bearing on his poetics—in theory and practice—is as doubtful as that of Burke's aesthetics on his politics.

Not that Coleridge did not make the effort of expanding on its possibilities. Schiller on the aesthetic education of man he followed some way and seems to have recalled in preparing the lectures of 1811–1812, though to little distinct effect (*CN* III, 4111n., 4112n.). Schelling was an altogether more potent informant, of course, yet Coleridge's debt to his specifically aesthetic ideas is again of limited significance for his thinking about literature, despite the aspiration of the *Biographia* to settle imagination in this idealist context. The place of Schelling in Coleridge's thinking has a long and difficult history; it remains, for current versions of his poetics, a force to reckon with. Without recapitulating the issues in detail, I would emphasize Coleridge's deep ambivalence about the *System of Transcendental Idealism*; his regret at the form of the first volume of the *Biographia*; and especially the difficulty of applying the critically elaborated idea of imagination to poetry.[42] Rene Wellek goes so far as to discount the formulation of primary and secondary imagination derived from Schelling on the ground that Coleridge did not return to it.

Wellek's litany of Coleridge's sources for the aesthetic, and of their inconsequence for his critical development, remains just and conclusive: "But all these speculations on beauty in Coleridge are undigested and uncorrelated: they do not lead to a theory of literature and play no role in it . . . His specific theory of poetry is far more important, for in it he made a genuine attempt at synthesis."[43] The poetics cannot be said to repose on an aesthetic idea—not even on the cardinal idea of imagination. A fundamental question of orientation thus arises in considering him as an English outpost of German idealist aesthetics. Where Hamilton observes that "Coleridge almost always thinks of poetry in the way that Kant thinks of aesthetic experience" (*CP*, 61), he would appear to have abandoned the record of reading and response. *Zweckmässigkeit ohne Zweck*, Kant's purposiveness without purpose, cannot be said to characterize the quality of Coleridge's engagement with poetry. The original proposal of an "Essay on the Elements of Poetry," to reiterate, "would in reality be a *disguised* System of Morals and Politics" (*CL* I, 623, 632). Such was his commitment in the beginning, and as it remained in his practice as poet, reader, and critic. To treat his poetics as aesthetic in inspiration, by direct influence or by analogy, is I believe to misapprehend the burden of his thinking about literature.

The categorical division of the language of poetry and prose entailed by Hamilton's hypothesis is one sign of how far it takes him from Coleridge's real commitments. Poetry had, on this reckoning, to be defended as sui generis; or as he puts it at this crucial pass, "For Coleridge, the difference between the poetic and the prosaic uses of language corresponds to the difference between aesthetic experience and knowledge in Kant's philosophy. In other words, Coleridge describes our prosaic uses of language as though they reveal the conditions under which it is possible to have knowledge. And he describes poetry as giving us a special awareness of these conditions" (*CP*, 60–61). Such an understanding is difficult given the long record of Coleridge's pronouncements on the subject. It is a distinction between poetry and science—not prose—that is correlated with the distinction between pleasure and truth by Coleridge: "Final Definition of a Poem & of Poetry—A Poem is that species of composition which being with some others opposed to Science, as having for its immediate object the communication of Pleasure, not of Truth, is distinguished from all others by proposing to itself such Delight from the Whole as is compatible with a distinct Gratification from each component part" (*CN* III, 4112). Even here, it is a distinction without a difference: the ratio of pleasure to truth, and the priority of the one or the other, defines the *relative* difference of two kinds of discourse. The distinction is nearly obliterated in modern writing:

> Where there are a few literary men, and the vast [majority] of the population are ignorant, as was the case of Italy from Dante to Metastasio, there will be a *poetical* Language—from causes, I need not here put down—but that a poet ever uses a word as *poetical*, i.e. formally—which he—in the same mood & thought—would not use, in prose or conversation, Milton's Prose Works will assist me in disproving—But as soon as literature becomes common, & critics numerous in any Country, and a large body of men seek to express themselves habitually in the most precise, sensuous, & impassioned words, the difference as to mere *words* ceases . . . The sole difference, *in style*, is that poetry demands a *severer keeping*—it admits nothing that Prose may not often admit; but it *oftener* rejects. In other words, it presupposes a more continuous state of Passion.   (*CN* III, 3611)

Far from sui generis, poetry was very much like prose in Coleridge's definition—and in his practice as a reader. "Equal and continuous attention" was a matter of degree, not of kind. The relation was, moreover, historically variable, not settled in advance in aesthetic principle. Understanding of this kind was historical as much as critical.

What German aesthetics could bring to bear on poetry was problematic in any case, fixated as it was—and as Hume had been before it—on the image as the source of response. English versions of the image in a philosophical setting are evoked, promisingly but in passing, by Hamilton as background to Coleridge's poetics. It is worth noticing, in this connection, the projected work "Concerning Poetry & the nature of the Pleasures derived from it" (*CL* II, 671). The aesthetic does seem close at hand here, at least as a possible avenue of approach. Yet the pleasures of poetry were not like those of images—"the sense of beauty in forms and sounds" (*BL* I, 10)—for reasons he was already taking into the investigation of language. Poetry partook of the pleasures of language in general, where language was grasped as an organ of thought. Hamilton is diverted from this orienting connection by his commitment to Coleridge's German informants and his investment in a "radical poetics" which came to grief in the *Biographia*. What transpired in the second volume, through the discussion of Wordsworth, was not a failure of nerve, rather a living recognition of the limits of imagination as a criterion of poetic value. Under pressure of his original doubts about Wordsworth's idea of language—doubts which constitute, in a public form, the main argument of Chapter XVII—Coleridge's critique proceeded on other grounds. Expressive language was defended against the rustic language theorem and "matter-of-factness," and vindicated in Wordsworth's own best practice.

The commitment of poetry to expressive language, and to a broadly symbolic function, converges at points with the promotion of imagination, and might even be thought to inform Coleridge's energetic pursuit of it. But imagination hardly subsumed expressive language in his thinking about poetry. The turn into the discussion of Wordsworth shows that Coleridge recurred to this resource when imagination proved limiting for questions of style and expression. An ideal of imagination is vital, certainly, in the *Biographia* and elsewhere, but it is not an exclusive one, nor does it adequately define Coleridge's poetics. When he postulated, in Chapter XVII, that "the best part of human language, properly so called, is derived from reflection on the acts of the mind itself" (*BL* II, 39–40), he was evoking a principle of long standing. Such a dialect was a rarified product, "formed by a voluntary appropriation of fixed symbols to internal acts, to processes and results of imagination, the greater part of which have no place in the consciousness of uneducated man." The force of the early investigation was realized here in the explicit contrast between rustic speech and the conscious exercise of a language of mind.

The value of Coleridge's idea extends beyond the originating context, as Richards sensed in promoting a symbolic order of language against the scientific criterion of fact. But his informant's allegiance to the language of mind did not represent a break with fact, only with the language of fact as a value in its own right in the poetic setting. Language was symbolic in a real world to which it referred obliquely, linking image and idea in a process of active mediation. Coleridge's conception of poetry, and his practice of the art, reflect his commitment to such a process, against those forces in modern experience that would segregate subject and object, mind and matter. Language as the dynamic middle term, an essential means in a divided world, has much to say to current institutional assumptions: to those which like Leavis's would hold words to a documentary standard as much as to those of Richards and his inheritors. In this living context, Coleridge's understanding represents both an indispensable point of reference and a preliminary step in the direction of integrated critical awareness.

5

Image and Idea in Coleridge's Poetics

At four o'clock I observed a wild duck swimming on the waves, a single solitary wild duck. It is not easy to conceive, how interesting a thing it looked in that round objectless desert of waters. I had associated such a feeling of immensity with the ocean, that I felt exceedingly disappointed, when I was out of sight of all land, at the narrowness and *nearness*, as it were, of the circle of the horizon. So little are images capable of satisfying the obscure feelings connected with words.   (*BL* II, 142; cf. *CL* I, 426)

"Frost at Midnight," the most psychodramatic of Coleridge's conversation poems, opens on the spectacle of a winter night seen from within a dark cottage. An unquiet voice renders the view in monologue, scanning the horizon for signs of life. There is little to report. Turning back to the "low-burnt fire" inside, the voice flickers but it does not fail. Uncertainty is in the air; the poem is adrift. Formally, there is the question of how to proceed when there is nothing left to describe. What is there to say? Reduced to a reflex of his hushed surroundings, Coleridge veers into that equatorial stasis which afflicts the Mariner— his own notorious abyss. He starts to repeat himself, straining to tease something from images which have failed him once already. He seizes on anything that moves. But it is not by grace of the objects around him that he finds his way out, though his poem concludes in praise of a nature so full it includes places of emptiness. What saves him is the word "stranger." With it the spell is broken, he recovers his voice and finishes the poem. On this encounter everything depends.

The language of "Frost at Midnight," as in much of Coleridge's earlier verse, is broadly descriptive, fitted with flourishes left over from a moribund poetry of sensibility. But it bears the marks of his search for a more satisfying idiom, one in which the descriptive and expressive functions would be integrated in a new rhetorical structure. His is a prototype of that characteristically romantic style which "favors implication rather than overt statement," while intensifying "directness of sensory presentation."[1] Implication takes some of the air out of the afflatus of Augustan rhetoric; the soritic gives way to the conversational tone and strategy. Attention to detail stays the plunge into aimless chatter while providing a steady locus of interest. These features characterize not only a new discursive structure but a new kind of metaphor. Tenor and vehicle no longer stand worlds apart, but "are wrought in a parallel process out of the same material."[2] The result is a means of expression seemingly less contrived, more spontaneous than what had been customary.

The rhetoric of the new style dissimulates the rhetorical function, as though figurative language had become a noisy embarrassment. As much is suggested early on in the phrases Coleridge excerpts from Young's essay "On Lyric Poetry" for his earliest notebook (1795): "— peculiar, not far-fetched — natural, but not obvious; delicate, not affected; dignified, not swelling; fiery but not mad; rich in Imagery, but not loaded with it" (*CN* I, 36). "Natural" in this context looks forward to Coleridge's appreciation of Bowles and Cowper as the poets who "combined natural thoughts with natural diction" (*BL* I, 16) — a predicate that compresses a program. These terms stand in Coleridge's critical vocabulary for a reformation of poetic possibility. Yet reform did not mean abandoning traditional poetic means, only modulating them in response to altered circumstances. The shape of an idiom committed to quiet force comes clear in Coleridge's meditative verse as it evolves.

In "Frost at Midnight" it appears in its maturity. A cool and precise diction renders the moment in fine strokes. This voice is patient about its anxiety, free for the most part of the rhetorical point which characterizes "The Eolian Harp" and "This Lime-Tree Bower My Prison," among its antecedents. Like the latter, "Frost at Midnight" begins in metaphor:

> The Frost performs its secret ministry,
> Unhelped by any wind.

And like the lime-tree bower prison, this figure dominates the poem from high ground. For it is oddly detached from the drama which follows. The frost envelopes the cottage and its surroundings, but it remains a world apart. The image confers on it the quality of sacral process. In the lines that follow little enough seems to come of it, yet it remains subliminally present:

> The owlet's cry
> Came loud — and hark, again! loud as before.
> The inmates of my cottage, all at rest,
> Have left me to that solitude, which suits
> Abstruser musings: save that at my side
> My cradled infant slumbers peacefully.
> 'Tis calm indeed! so calm, that it disturbs
> And vexes meditation with its strange
> And extreme silentness. Sea, hill, and wood,
> This populous village! Sea, and hill, and wood,
> With all the numberless goings-on of life,
> Inaudible as dreams! the thin blue flame
> Lies on my low-burnt fire, and quivers not . . .

The sacral process, the metaphor itself, lies latent in this landscape. Contrived for opening effect, it drops out of earshot as soon as enunciated. Its traces are submerged in the pregnant silence of the winter night. The shared context of ministry and frost is not immediately apparent even if the informing idea is familiar. No strain sounds through their conjunction but the terms are not obviously related. The metaphor is not "natural," and this colors what follows. The suspended animation of the frost becomes a general suspension of activity — a moment of suspense in the drama. As Abrams observes, "the images in the initial description are already suffused with an unstated significance which . . . is merely 'elicited' and expanded by subsequent reflection."[3] This undercurrent of unspoken significance follows from the unsettled metaphor. What is the secret mission of the frost, and what is its destination?

The metaphor is conspicuous, then, despite the understatement. It is not actually descriptive, though carefully joined to its material setting, dissimulating the idea: a good example of the new type. Its function is not stage-setting, it is orienting in a larger way. It seems designed to allay in advance the anxiety which the poem will excite and quell. The frost's ministry represents an assurance as much as assertion. Through it "Nature" is authorized to perform, to bear sacramental witness. Yet it will prove resistant in the testing. The "secret ministry of frost" which graces the poem's ending is achieved rather than granted, the product of strenuous effort to verify the inaugurating metaphor, to make it signify. In the wake of an erratic beginning this becomes a trial of strength and a program for what follows. Coleridge's stutters and starts record the stations of the way. Conceptually, resistance to the metaphor may be related to difficulties attending a sacramental vision of nature. Isolated by his sleeping family and the awful hush, the poet invokes the mediating powers of the natural world, but finds them elusive. Rhetorically, this resistance can be described as a problem of language. Here it is a question of how he performs the invocation that commands the frost's performance.

Coleridge's sense of anomie, as it develops in the wake of this invocation, is more than a psychological phenomenon; it has poetic implications. As a forceful step beyond descriptive discourse, his opening might be thought to represent a search for an expressive alternative. What comes of it is not immediately apparent. For he is unable to extend his ministry of frost in a productive direction, to make it drive his vision. It stands as a problematic origin, a potential but unrealized source of imaginative power. What follows develops the vehicle rather than the metaphor. The speaker's restless eyes move from the middle distance into the cottage, then out to the horizon before returning to what is at hand. There are signs of effort to get beyond surfaces. The double cry of the owl contributes a second sense, but inspires as little elaboration as the first. When the speaker tries to envision the far-off world of "sea, hill, and wood," it is not only ominously bare, it is "inaudible as dreams."

This abortive flight into a vision of the invisible is a mark of the uncertainty which haunts the passage. It speaks eloquently of the difficulty of moving from sensation to imagination. That is its real claim on power. And it associates the problem with the moralizing idiom practiced by Bowles and perpetuated by Coleridge in his early poetry:

> Only that film, which fluttered on the grate,
> Still flutters there, the sole unquiet thing.
> Methinks, its motion in his hush of nature
> Gives it dim sympathies with me who live,
> Making it a companionable form,
> Whose puny flaps and freaks the idling Spirit

> By its own moods interprets, every where
> Echo or mirror seeking of itself,
> And makes a toy of Thought.

The trouble, as enunciated by Coleridge himself and discussed often since by commentators, is the odd sorting of tenor and vehicle, which persists even where there is a common locus of reference in experience. If the object (any object) provides occasion and language to expatiate on anything at all, is it not as limiting as the tale of Alexander and Clytus, "which was equally good and apt, whatever might be the theme?" (*BL* I, 5). The originating ministry of frost, subtle as it is, can be seen to descend in this way from the affable apostrophes of Bowles to myriad rivers and streams. The rhetoric has been refined beyond recognition, but the forced marriage of elements endures.

What distinguishes "Frost at Midnight" in this company is not sudden success, but a growing awareness of the problematics of expressive discourse in the emergent romantic idiom. The dissolution of mind and matter unleashes a crisis of rhetoric. Insofar as the speaker's language remains bound to particulars, it stands to sacrifice imaginative penetration to unprincipled aggregation. When it remains true to the modifying impulse of imagination, it threatens to reduce its referential base to a "toy of Thought," something insubstantial in its plastic motility. Coleridge's retreat to the confines of his cottage dramatizes the shift from the former to the latter stance within his language. In the opening movement potential vehicles outweigh realized metaphors as the bold characterization of frost remains unelaborated. Instead, the poet encompasses what lies around him, shifting fitfully from object to object in search of something to free him to the play of his spirit. When at last he lights on it a flood of thought overburdens a fragile vehicle. The homely grate-film, a kindred spirit by adoption, turns him back on himself, confirming his retreat from sensation. An image of identity, it provides no productive resistance to the force of his self-consciousness. It is a short circuit.

The first stanza does not elude the pitfalls it knows so well. It acts them out, exposing them in the dark. But the second stanza finds a fresh source of strength outside the futile opposition of descriptive and expressive discourse, serial objectivity and subjective vertigo. The grate-film, a spectral presence only half-visible, leads the speaking voice beyond the analogy to something deeper—a source of identity within. The inward turn is of course a way around dependence on sensation, but that way lie the terrors of the isolated self. The solution Coleridge tried out here amounted to a plunge into association not unlike the revery of "The Eolian Harp," where it is set off by the lute, also in the second stanza. There a figural analogy is involved, the lute as phallus enabling a symbolic mating. In "Frost at Midnight" the inward turn seems less contrived for effect, nearer a living process of fear and escape. The grate-film is an encounter, not a symbol—a trapdoor which rescues the speaker from the hateful polarity of his situation. The confrontation in the cottage is not resolved, it is evaded:

> But O! how oft,
> How oft, at school, with most believing mind,
> Presageful, have I gazed upon the bars,
> To watch that fluttering *stranger*!

A mere aggregation of imagery thus gives way to a metaphoric procedure in which substitutions for this "*stranger*" govern the unfolding of poetic vision. What the speaker realizes in recollection is a meditation on himself as a stranger—an outsider at Christ's Hospital, alone with his revery then as now, awaiting the intrusion of another outsider:

> And so I brooded all the following morn,
> Awed by the stern preceptor's face, mine eye
> Fixed with mock study on my swimming book:
> Save if the door half opened, and I snatched
> A hasty glance, and still my heart leaped up,
> For still I hoped to see the *stranger*'s face,
> Townsman, or aunt, or sister more beloved,
> My play-mate when we both were clothed alike!

Oblivion falls before these images. The derelict self acquires context, relation, presence beyond its dumb sensations. A flickering voice assumes volume.

In the wake of this energizing encounter, affirmation becomes possible. The speaker embraces his opening metaphor, secure in its truth. A garden arises in the darkness as he envisions a world filled with the natural language of the Godhead—

> The lovely shapes and sounds intelligible
> Of that eternal language, which thy God
> Utters, who from eternity doth teach
> Himself in all, and all things in himself.

The grate-film is behind it all. But in moving to this conclusion the speaker has missed a step. It is not the grate-film that has freed him, it is the word "*stranger:*" not the language of nature but his own language. Coleridge confuses word and thing, attributing to "shapes and sounds" an agency which belongs, on the evidence of the poem, to his own imagination.

The confusion is not a lapse; it is consistent with the determination of his opening metaphor. Only by missing this step could he arrive at a conclusion confirming the pantheist idea at work there. The dominating metaphor effectively suppresses the truth of the associative process. For this delirious regression is shaped not by the image, but by the peculiar name attaching to the phenomenon: "*stranger,*" twice set off in italics—a word apart. It intrudes as though from outside the cottage, outside the monologue. Coleridge's note confirms its special status: "In all parts of the kingdom these films are called *strangers* and supposed to portend the arrival of some absent friend." Not so much the name of a phenomenon as a complex of sound, concept, metaphor, and prophecy. "*Stranger*" does not signify "grate-film," it displaces it, fueling an imaginative conflagration. The stanza glosses the word.[4]

In the beginning the child at school is fixated on the film, investing it with his hopes, seeing in it his premonitions. It is already more than an image—an amulet against absence, the sign of *something else.* "*Stranger*" signifies this alien presence from its first appearance, turning image into symbol. The symbolic process begins from the naming of the grate-film and proceeds to an identification of the word with the form of the visitant, passing through a symbolically featured version of the absent home:

> and as oft
> With unclosed lids, already had I dreamt
> Of my sweet birth-place, and the old church-tower,
> Whose bells, the poor man's only music, rang
> From morn to evening, all the hot Fair-day,
> So sweetly, that they stirred and haunted me
> With a wild pleasure, falling on mine ears
> Most like articuate sounds of things to come!

The estranged child feeds on this ringing like the grown man, estranged in his cottage, who makes poetry of the tintinnabulation of a word. An axis of association, the word does not flicker like the image under pressure of imagination. It rings on and on, delivering in the end the solace of

> the *stranger's* face,
> Townsman, or aunt, or sister more beloved . . .

Stranger visits stranger by grace of the word, in a symbolic process committed to creative imagination. For the word is an active presence, vital to his imagination as the image is not. "So little are images capable of satisfying the obscure feelings connected with words." His endorsement of natural impulse in the conclusion of "Frost at Midnight" loses sight of this fundamental value. Yet the poem tells the deep truth of his condition—of the preeminently verbal sources of his poetic power.

What transpires in "Frost at Midnight" might be characterized then as an epiphany manqué. The sententious triumph of matter over mind conceals a genuine triumph of imagination over the disruptive forces of the self. For the word becomes a medium of self-presence, affirmative and therapeutic, so different from an inert "toy of Thought"—the image as reflex of a desperate subjectivity. "*Stranger*" bridges self and other, cottage and horizon, opening this uncertain voice to affirmation. Turning away from the lure of sensation, the poem finds its natural ground (and a derelict voice its native element) with the recovery of the word as primary agent of imagination. It is not a sacramental frost but a sacramental *stranger* that redeems imagination in the midnight of the spirit.

Verbal Imagination

The idealist affiliations of Coleridge's concept of imagination reach back from Schelling through Kant to Shaftesbury, and back again to Plotinus and Plato himself, as McFarland proposes in recasting its formulaic reliance on Schelling.[5] His situation in the specifically English development of the term is comparably implicated, as James Engell demonstrates in his careful study of its trajectory in the eighteenth century.[6] The idea was of course common coin; the novelty of Coleridge's treatment of it lay in the consciousness he brought to its workings rather than in a reformulation of the premises. Yet he had not simply adopted the term despite his habitual employment of it. He worked through imagination in the formative moment of his career as a critic, trying out its value for the idiom he was concerned to defend. And he began applying it to earlier writing on his way to the conspectus of tradition presented in the lectures as well as the *Biographia*. His idea of imagination was refined in the process. Its private prehistory has attracted less attention than the English precedents, and certainly less than the German sources of his critical definition of the term.[7] With the notebooks integrally available, and the letters and marginalia in support, it is possible to expand on Coleridge's thinking on the subject at the moment when his poetic practice was being turned to poetic principle.

Verbal imagination, as he observes it in notes of 1802–3 on the mannered prose of Barrow, follows the early investigation of language through to a point about literary style. This context shows Coleridge thinking about image and idea in expressive language and coming to conclusions about the uses (and abuse) of the image for expressive purpose. His meditation reverts to earlier notes on the relative merits of languages for poetry. These notes have often been considered, notably by Richards and more recently by commentators concerned with recovering Coleridge's position on poetry as protoformalist.[8] Conclusions about their bearing on his poetics vary considerably. It is my contention that the early notes constitute incompletely formed reflections on language which look forward to the incipient investigation of 1801–2; and that they are further linked, in ways I shall be exploring, with the subsequent discussion of verbal imagination. They attest an insistence on style as a vital reflex of thinking—a corollary of Coleridge's promotion of expressive language. It is characteristic that language is seen here not in connection with stylistic norms, but as an organ of original thought.

The first of these notes, dating to 1799 and published in an abridged form in E. H. Coleridge's anthology, *Anima Poetae* (London, 1895), was once celebrated as a defense of obscurity in poetry. Richards was responsible for restoring the emphasis on poetic thinking:

> The elder Languages fitter for Poetry because they expressed only prominent ideas with clearness, others but darkly—Therefore the French wholly unfit for Poetry; because is *clear* in their Language—i.e.—Feelings created by obscure ideas associate themselves with the one *clear* idea. When no criticism is pretended to, & the Mind in its simplicity gives itself

up to a Poem as to a work of nature, Poetry gives most pleasure when only generally & not perfectly understood. It was so by me with Gray's *Bard*, & Collins' odes— *The Bard* once intoxicated me, & now I read it without pleasure. From this cause it is that what *I* call metaphysical Poetry gives me so much delight.   (*CN* I, 383)

Richards took the elder languages to refer to Elizabethan English and made Shakespeare's "structure of meaning" the exemplar against which the deficiencies of later poetry would be measured by Coleridge. He went on to draw a parallel, in modern verse, with Yeats, Eliot, Hopkins, Auden, and Empson, who stood for poetry with an "inside" against the Georgian idiom of Rupert Brooke, with its "Exhibition of Poetic Products" (*CI*, 215). Insofar as the analogy would promote a thinking poetry, it is consonant with Coleridge's idea. Yet Richards went on to defend obscurity in modern poetry on this basis. Thinking poetry would be obscure practically by definition.

The authority for this defense of poetic difficulty he found in a construction of Coleridge's jottings which lay stress on dark subordinate ideas. These were a part of the best poetic experience, as Richards understood the note, and while the elder languages left them in darkness, the modern (with French the significant instance) had brought them out of the shadows. Yet it seems most unlikely, in the first place, that Coleridge's contrast was actually between Elizabethan and modern English; and unlikely again that he was defending poetic difficulty of the sort Richards had in mind. At the time the note was entered he was involved in learning German, not in reading Shakespeare. The elder languages more likely refer to the early Germanic dialects whose literature he was browsing in Göttingen. Perhaps that explains why he thought they expressed "only prominent ideas with clearness;" languages half-understood typically gain in clarity what they lose in meaning. The point appears to be that by limiting their depth of field, such languages focussed sharply on a few ideas, leaving subsidiary ideas appropriately dim. Hardly a defense of poetic obscurity—nor of poetic difficulty. The contrast with French reflects badly on Richards's assumptions, as well; for why should Elizabethan English be contrasted with French? If Coleridge's point was that the "Anglo-Gallican fashion" (as he called it elsewhere) had captured modern poetry, he cannot be said to have chosen suitable examples in Gray and Collins.

Coleridge's argument is then for clarity, not for philosophical density. His idea of clarity was, however, confused by a distinction

which has misled his readers. Control of a limited number of prominent ideas, uncluttered by constant subordination, produced an exemplary "clearness," and understanding proceeded naturally. The clarity
of French was of a different order. It provided high resolution everywhere, with the result that everything appeared related and important.
Understanding was impeded by the proliferation of "obscure ideas"
associated with "the one clear idea." As applied to the modern idiom
that Richards was defending, Coleridge's distinction is thus of doubtful value, quite apart from its impressionism. But the conclusion arrived at in the original setting remains of interest for tracing the formation of Coleridge's poetics. For *"metaphysical Solution,"* as he would
soon call it (CN, 673)—the dispersal of poetic energies through an
indiscriminate clarity—involved a lack of ideal resolution. The pleasures of poetry of this kind he identified with the uncritical pleasures
of perception. Such poetry appeared to the reader as "a work of nature." The sublimity of "Gray's *Bard* & Collins' odes" was the sublimity of nature itself:

> On the rock, whose haughty brow
> Frowns o'er old Conway's foaming flood,
>   Robed in the sable garb of woe,
> With haggard eyes the poet stood;
> (Loose his beard, and hoary hair
> Stream'd like a meteor, to the troubled air)
> And with a master's hand, and prophet's fire,
> Struck the deep sorrows of his lyre.

Metaphysical solution was "a great Vice" (CN, 673) in poetry because
it turned a thinking art into a pictorial one. It presumed the mindless
sort of reading which debased poetry to a display of images, delightful
but vapid.

   The tortuous shorthand of Coleridge's note evidences a deep
struggle for understanding—a struggle only gradually turned to a clear
recognition of principle. It might be considered as a cognate of the
struggle within "Frost at Midnight" between the allure of nature and
the will to self-realization. In the beginning these seemed compatible,
and the poem's conclusion would affirm as much. But in practice,
images led only to images, as the opening of the poem attests. It was
the word that stood at the origin of the process by which a sense of
relation was achieved. Language was the essential medium of thinking,

as he would soon see it, and expressive language the cardinal resource of a poetry which would give voice to something more than the pleasures of nature. A year or so later, he would be working out the poetic consequences, distinguishing between a poetry of prominent ideas and one committed to particulars. The contrast is rough-hewn, and the notes on the "metaphysical" in poetry should be considered with this in mind—they are indicative rather than definitive. But they do point, as Richards recognized, to a primary commitment to a poetry of mind against the "metaphysical" particularity of the poetry of sensibility.

Such a commitment is prominently displayed in the opening metaphor of "Frost at Midnight," where the idea is carefully worked into the image. But the bond could not be sustained. Image and idea lived separate lives: the one led to the horizon, the other to the active engagement of imagination. The language of the poem kept the seam from splitting, but could hardly prevent it showing. The great problem for a thinking poetry—for Coleridge's poetry and often Wordsworth's as well—would be to find a way into the imagery that was the lumber of poetic construction without sacrificing expressive language and the meaning it conferred. At times this would appear as a problem endemic to the enterprise: "I cannot write without a *body* of *thought*—hence my *Poetry* is crowded and sweats beneath a heavy burthen of Ideas and Imagery" (*CL* I, 137). His early letters are full of similar complaints, and of defensive retreats to the rationale that the thinking justifies the tortuous phrasing. To Thelwall, writing in 1796, he defended a sonnet on grounds of "obscurity residing in the uncommonness of the thought"—as against "that which proceeds from thoughts unconnected & language not adapted to the expression of them" (*CL* I, 277). Expressive language might admit difficulty, but never confusion. Yet "Frost at Midnight" would tell on the troubles of a thinking poetry even where the idea was clear and the expression fitting.

Coleridge's note on the elder languages treats the problem of poetic expression as peculiar to modern language. In so explicit a medium, images would dominate ideas as they did in "metaphysical" poetry—and occasionally in his own practice. It was in this direction that he developed what might be called his critique of modern language: "Whether or no the too great definiteness of Terms in any language may not consume too much of the vital & idea-creating force in distinct, clear, full made Images & so prevent originality—*original* thought as distinguished from positive thought—Germans in general—" (*CN* I, 1016). What stands out here against the background of the earlier notes is the conflict of interest between image and idea. Images did not just distract from "originality," they actually prevented it. The definite terms of modern language gave rise to "distinct, clear, full made Images." Expressive language would have to fight an inside battle against the tendency of modern language to the condition of things, and its collaboration with the "positive thought" which he deplored in Locke and his inheritors. The trouble with modern poetry began with a language which distracted it from high philosophical vocation, reducing it to the thrall of nature. This was the substance of his initial turn against the Wordsworth of the "Preface," as I have proposed. A poetic diction committed to "the best objects" went Locke's way: the way of modern language in general.

Despite the admission that metaphysical diffusion in poetry had once given him pleasure, Coleridge's suspicion of the image actually reverts to his earlier notebook entries: "Dr Darwin's Poetry, a succession of Landscapes or Paintings—it arrests the attention too often, and so prevents the rapidity necessary to pathos.—it makes the great little.—seems to have written his poem as Painters who of beautiful objects—take—Studies" (CN I, 132). Against poetic painting, he had always promoted the poet himself as the vital subject of the art: "Poetry without egotism comparatively uninteresting" (CN I, 62). So long as things came down to the opposition of self and nature, as such a principle did, the practice of poetry was bound to prove difficult. These terms were never far from his thinking on the subject, but the introduction of language into the question of poetic means reformed the way he considered it. The notes on language (and on languages) had the effect of introducing a third term into an inadequately formed opposition. The investigation of how words signify, tested by publication of the "Preface" and extended by related concerns, led him in turn to a consideration of style as an immanent expression of a way of thinking.

The starting point was the issue of rhetoric, perhaps in the setting of his discussions with Wordsworth in the period—a context of the first importance for the new poetics. Wordsworth's inquisition of rhetorical means in the "Preface" was a landmark. Coleridge's response to it was an inquisition of his own, leading in a quite different direction. An early citation from Marvell's attack on Bramhall's *Vindication* (1672) set the tone if not the agenda: "impertinent Efflorescence of Rhetoric" (CN I, 703). It was on Isaac Barrow, another theologian of the Restoration, that Coleridge would try out this line. "Verbal imagination," as he observes it in notes on Barrow's writing, is excessive: "When our Lord was apprehended by the Soldiers, presently *up* was his Spirit, & *out* went his Sword in defence of him." And, "he fell to propose about making an abode there" (*CN* I, 1655). Each example features an egregious display of prepositions. Verbal imagination apparently designated such embroidery, but Coleridge's interest in the phenomenon suggests that more was at stake than a parochial point of style: "Examine minutely the nature, cause, birth & growth of the *verbal* Imagination of which Barrow is almost the ideal/" (*CN* I, 1275). Barrow's excesses took expression to the limits of decorum: "It is strange/the very men, such as Barrow & *Sa Theoria* Burnet, who wrote with more than ancient majesty in Latin, should in English be as pert as their subjects & ideas would permit their words to be" (*CN* I, 1655). Their words responded to their thought, but expressed in addition "a desire in all innocent ways to affect *liveliness*." Such innocence was provocative. It said more by its style than by its message. Barrow was apparently conforming to the prevailing decadence of the church in the period. He would become for Coleridge the concluding figure of "the first great period of the English language" (*TT*, 294).

Barrow's adverbial prepositions are striking in this context for the way they set the idea (of Christ's force, of settlement) in motion, illustrating it in the process. "Verbal imagination" expresses this debasement of thinking to a sort of cartoon. The term was aimed not at stylistic embroidery in general (for Coleridge does not appear to have extended it) but at an illustrative manner of working the idea into the world. His own manner, in the earlier conversation poems, had presumed that it was immanently present in the sounds and shapes of nature, and that it found a voice through the poet's mediation. Metaphor asserted the copresence of image and idea in this setting. But the difficulty of Coleridge's secret ministry of frost looked forward to his doubts about the "loose solution" of the simile, even to his dramatic renunciation of poetic vocation. Unless a sustaining bond could be formed, the simile only epitomized the hopeless difference of the self and its language from the condition of things. In such circumstances (linguistic first of all, as his notes would imply) poetry could only witness the tragic isolation of the speaking subject in an indifferent world. That would be the valedictory burden of "Dejection."

Verbal imagination designates a singular case, yet it too is indicative: of the decline of expression in the period to which it refers, of the general struggle of image and idea for primacy in literary discourse. Coleridge's difficulty with the image certainly reflects no failure of his "natural faculties"; only a primary allegiance to the idea, and to the expressive language which gave voice to it. If he was peculiarly sensitive to the ascendancy of the image in the poetry of sensibility and elsewhere, it was because it threatened to stifle the expressive idiom to which he was committed: "In the present age the poet . . . seems to propose to himself as his main object, and as that which is the most characteristic of his art, new and striking images . . . In his diction and metre, on the other hand, he is comparatively careless." Modern poetry sacrificed the passion of the inspired subject to "the glare and glitter of a perpetual, yet broken and heterogeneous imagery, or rather to an amphibious something made up, half of image, and half of abstract meaning."[9] The imagination that Coleridge would soon be deriving from the critical philosophy provided an alternative to the idolatry of verbal imagination and an answer to the problem of how to resolve image and idea. Its esemplastic power would forge a "broken and heterogeneous imagery" into something whole. Proceeding as it did from the faculties of the subject himself, this higher imagination would transform the things of the world in an act of appropriation. The image would then become truly integral to thinking instead of its rival for attention.

For examples of such imagery we need only look at the lines of Wordsworth singled out for praise in the *Biographia*—without detailed commentary on imagination, for the most part. It is striking, indeed, how little Coleridge devoted to elaborating on the idea of imagination outside its philosophical context. It would become, as McFarland concludes, a linchpin of his system more than an instrument of observation,[10] though it would remain evaluative as applied to writing in general. Against the background of verbal imagination, the term can be seen to identify particular poetic values nevertheless. In Chapter XXII Coleridge distinguishes between creation and painting (*BL* II, 103) in poetry, on grounds identical with those suggested by the early attack on verbal imagination. Wordsworth's "*matter-of-factness*," his "minute accuracy in the painting of local imagery" (101–2), is there castigated, while his "IMAGINATION in the highest and strictest sense of the word" (124) is extolled as his consummate virtue. The context is too well-known to need rehearsing, but it is perhaps worth dwelling on the continuity of concern to which it testifies. The critical formulation of imagination changed nothing in Coleridge's evaluation of poetic power; it only formalized his original doubts about impressions and about the language of fact in poetry. Kant's (and Schelling's) terms added important features to the argument for imagination of the higher kind, to be sure, raising the level of argument and the philosophical stakes. Yet their impact on Coleridge's response counts for less than his attention to their aesthetic ideas would perhaps lead us to expect.

Coleridge on poetic imagination has more to do, in a reactive way, with Locke's version of words, with the fate of modern language, and with "metaphysical Solution" in poetry. The subterranean river that is Coleridge on language nourished his thinking at a moment when the conversational idiom had grown problematic while the conflict with Wordsworth was driving him to first principles. Signification, broadly grasped, proved a resource of the first magnitude in addressing the problems and leading him on to a new phase of his career. It remains more than merely formative in his poetics through the emphasis on expressive language which lurks in his defense of poetic imagination at its best.

Coleridge on imagination makes the plainest sense, on this reading, against the background of a verbal imagination which in expressing the image distracted from the idea. Despite the salience of de-synonymy in his thinking about language in general, it was the comparatively latent meditation on how words mean that counted decisively for the development of his version of poetic value. Restoring the prehistory of his critical formulation of imagination means understanding the values which the term was supposed to defend. This involves a certain reorientation of the idea: away from the German sources, toward the integrity of Coleridge the reader and critical respondent. This is hardly a radical proposition. It has been current for at least a generation,[11] and despite McFarland's interesting effort to put the critical formulation to work, it is consonant with the conclusions to which his long study of Coleridge—nearly definitive, I believe, on the German informants—has led him.[12] If Richards's account of Coleridge on language proved too threadbare to make the case, it can still be said to have opened the dossier for consideration on premises more comprehensive than the German influence. For it was true to the living origin of an idea of imagination which turned its back on the images of nature as the model of the poet's art.

Graven Images

The concluding lines of "Frost at Midnight" have been praised as "one of the finest pieces of short descriptive writing in the language,"[13] and the poem has attained distinction in the conversational idiom largely on the basis of its powerfully realized images—in the opening and conclusion in particular. Coleridge's revision from the original text of 1798 shows that he chose to finish with a significantly expanded version of his first image:

> Therefore all seasons shall be sweet to thee,
> Whether the summer clothe the general earth
> With greenness, or the redbreast sit and sing
> Betwixt the tufts of snow on the bare branch
> Of mossy apple-tree, while the nigh thatch
> Smokes in the sun-thaw; whether the eave-drops fall
> Heard only in the trances of the blast,
> Or if the secret ministry of frost
> Shall hang them up in silent icicles,
> Quietly shining to the quiet Moon.

For control of means in rendering the idea, this is surely as successful as anything in his verse. The frost's ministry can be felt in the graceful delivery and traced in the development of the imagery toward a dynamic presence. The process which was "unheard" before is made sensible, something to be witnessed in the robin's song or the dew-fall. The growth of the image affirms the claim of the opening metaphor, certifying a natural agency which seemed for a moment to have failed its supplicant. That is of course the burden of "trances of the blast."

Humphry House makes an illuminating point about the conclusion in considering how Coleridge had originally gone on from this carefully crafted image, as follows:

> Quietly shining to the quiet moon,
> Like those, my babe! which ere tomorrow's warmth
> Have capp'd their sharp keen points with pendulous drops,
> Will catch thine eye, and with their novelty
> Suspend thy little soul; then make thee shout,
> And stretch and flutter from thy mother's arms
> As thou wouldst fly for very eagerness.

In the revision, instead of following the conversation through this ending, he had foreshortened it, bringing the poem full circle with the image—"intricate and yet sparsely clear, compressing so much of the moods of various weather," as House puts it.[14] What he gave up when he eliminated the original ending was more than an interminable conversational flux, however. The child Hartley's fixation on the dripping icicles of the morning to come speaks eloquently to the difficulty of the opening, where the speaker's eye found nothing to hold him. The child is father to the man here in the suspension of his "little soul," from which he will emerge to fly like a bird at the confirmation of a presence beyond himself. Such a conclusion is rounded in its own way, if not in the satisfying manner of the "silent icicles." For it takes the errant spirit as the point of the crisis, rather than the hypothetical ministry of frost. What matters in the end is not that the icicle is shining but that the imagination (of child as of father) has come alive.

The difference is more than one of emphasis, and it provides a way of raising within the text the question of the poetic image as Coleridge would soon be considering it. "Frost at Midnight" in its final form might indeed be regarded as a poem enclosed in an image: dominated by its opening metaphor, concluded in its realization. When the secret ministry of frost could be *seen*, and settled into definite lineaments, the poem had done its work. It had subdued natural impulse and proved, as it were, that ministry was in it. The struggle of the idea for mastery is the real story of "Frost at Midnight," on such a reading. The poem is indeed the most compelling of its type, though not I think because it realizes the image: rather because it dwells on the process by which the image is tried and confirmed. Here Coleridge brought to consciousness, or near it, the fears exposed by his naturalist assumptions, encouraged by the pantheist tendency of his thinking at the time. The dominance of natural impulse for the process of imagination meant a dangerous dependence on sensation. The implications could be suppressed by an act of faith, but they could not be evaded. The confrontation enacted in the poem showed how precarious imagination really was on such assumptions, and how threatening to those who lived by it. And it confirmed the poetic image as a fabrication, contrived rather than borrowed out of a natural setting: a matter of arduous working through, altogether different from the impression of the poetry of sensibility.

Romantic imagery, as it emerges in the conversation poems and in

Coleridge's related reflections on poetics, would have to become an instrument of expressive language. Otherwise it would lapse into the pointlessness of metaphysical solution, where the impression was the entire effect. Avoiding this meant beginning from the word and every-thing associated with it—not from natural impulse. After "Frost at Midnight," the conversation poems do in fact typically begin from words, from a line of Milton or a poem of Wordsworth's or an odd bit of "Sir Patrick Spence." For the word was the agent of thinking as sensation could not be, leading to a discourse of the self in its integral relations, and not only in relation to objects seen, or unseen.

The discovery of the word as primary agent of poetic imagination, as rehearsed in "Frost at Midnight" and confirmed in practice and occasional observation, was of the largest significance for the develop-ment of romantic poetics. The phenomenon has been recognized in passing under other auspices, but never adequately treated. It is per-haps most familiar in a negative form, in Frank Kermode's influential study of romantic imagism, where later attitudes are traced to the critique of mathematic form in Blake as well as to Coleridge's doubts about the image in the poetic setting.[15] Romantic language does not enter into the discussion. Yet it should be clear that the poetic image as it figures in Coleridge's thinking is indissociable from an incipient idea of language. In his notes he gets at the problematic matter of the image in poetry through the words of the mother tongue. What the image lost, the word gained in power for a poetry that would be committed to the vocation of thinking.

Kermode's recuperation of Coleridge's meditation on the image suggests the potential of this line of inquiry without restoring its origi-nal context. Leading up to Yeats's handling of the image, he required a romantic precedent, and he located it not in Coleridge alone but in a range of romantic practice. The image "as a radiant truth out of space and time" (RI, 2) was to be found preeminently in Shelley and Keats. It was enshrined by their Victorian inheritors as poetry's distinctive mark and assimilated in different ways by Yeats and Pound. Romantic im-agism was an idolatry of sorts, obsessive and enervating, yet there were signs of resistance in Blake and Coleridge, and the resistance too was accommodated, in Yeats's hypostasis of the artifice of the image as Byzantium, and in Pound's turn away from the stasis of Imagism (RI, 85). Coleridge's role as iconoclast was clearly indicated by Kermode, but it remained largely symbolic in part perhaps because important issues had not been resolved. With the role of language in his pursuit of poetic principle in mind, it is possible to appreciate how fundamental to his poetics were his reservations about the image.

For as his notes would imply, the image was the natural enemy of the idea even if their collaboration was a first premise for poetry. "Distinct, clear, full-made images" prevented originality, distracting attention and dissipating energy. Modern poetry was subverted by the tendency of modern language to a stifling clarity. Such is the language of the opening stanza of "Frost at Midnight," or rather the speaker's relation to his language, which might be described as documentary in assumption. But painting the horizon proves an exercise in self-obliteration. The speaker's voice attenuates as its internal sources are turned back in favor of a straining act of composition. Something like a conflict between painting and thinking is involved in this struggle for expression.

Another version of the speaker's trouble is reflected in the poem's original ending, as cited, where the infant's eye is caught and his soul suspended—an image of fixation. The icicle which he watches descends directly of course from the scenery of the opening, and so does his expectant hush. Suspense characterizes this moment of exposure, when everything hangs on the frost's performance. It proves a prelude to joy—a wishful version of the influence of sensation, surely, authorized by a happy resolution of the crisis. Yet the suspended spirit is seldom a happy phenomenon in Coleridge's imagination: rather the opposite. Fixation on the image is properly a sort of bondage, something which would find vivid expression in *Christabel*, and in the narrative introduction to "Kubla Khan," with its disappointment in the idle "curiosity" of the train of imagery which follows. The terror of this condition is both revealed and concealed by "Frost at Midnight," in defense of a naturalism that Coleridge entertained before turning against it.

The dominant idea appears, in such a perspective, defensive in relation to the threat posed by natural impressions. The secret ministry of frost which inaugurates the poem affirms in advance an agency which is then put deliberately to the test. It is as though sensation could only be approached as potential material under protection of such an idea. Poetic discourse on the model of painting led not just to idolatry but to an elemental fear, a sense of self-absence. The commitment of poetry on Coleridge's terms would be to self-presence, manifested in the idea through the agency of expressive language. The intensity of so much of his verse dramatizes this commitment, trying out a discourse of the self against the snares of the world, and a discourse of the other against the snares of personality. "Frost at Midnight" takes the first line halfway to critical awareness in its uneasy approach to a poetics of the speaking subject. The momentary blockage of this approach is as temperamental as it is conceptual, a product of underlying uncertainty about how to proceed. The conviction which Coleridge won in the testing contributed both to the development of the conversational idiom and to the formation of critical principle.

By way of expanding on this claim, I want to show how the defensive idealism of "Frost at Midnight" looks forward to Coleridge's important observations on the characters of Hamlet and Macbeth—the one a figure of "predominant idealism" (*SC* I, 25), the other of imperious imagination. Hamlet is practically an alter ego in the "ratiocinative meditativeness of his character," and the way Coleridge evokes his trouble mirrors his own condition as it appears in "Frost at Midnight" and elsewhere:

> Shakespeare's mode of conceiving characters out of his own intellectual and moral faculties, by conceiving any one intellectual or moral faculty in morbid excess and then placing himself, thus mutilated and diseased, under given circumstances. This we shall have repeated occasion to restate and enforce. In Hamlet I conceive him to have wished to exemplify the moral necessity of a due balance between our attention to outward objects and our meditation on inward thoughts—a due balance between the real and the imaginary world. In Hamlet this balance does not exist—his thoughts, images, and fancy [being] far more vivid than his perceptions, and his very perceptions instantly passing thro' the medium of his contemplations, and acquiring as they pass a form and color not naturally their own. Hence great, enormous, intellectual activity, and a consequent proportionate aversion to real action, with all its symptoms and accompanying qualities.   (*SC* I, 37)

As a portrait of the poet as a young man in extremis, this can hardly be surpassed. Coleridge showed himself acutely aware here of the excesses of a "predominant idealism" recognizably his own. With "Frost at Midnight" in mind, what stands out is Hamlet's isolation from natural response. Such is the posture of the subject in his polar alterity in a world of objects. "Sea, hill, and wood" are already more than percepts, they render an *idea* of the world outside. The bondage of the image is the confinement of the self, as the poem's opening testifies. The speaker's fixation is identical with his abstraction, and with his fear. The escape into "*stranger*" is an escape from the obsessive image, from isolation and the terror associated with it. The word restores the sense of relation to a larger world. For the context of language is always social by implication. The image remains private, exclusive, even fetishistic by comparison.

Hamlet's "play on words" (*SC* I, 22f., 38) is associated with his "activity of mind." This is not pointless paronomastics, nor even wit in the usual sense, as Coleridge's commentary insists in contradicting Warburton's doubtful analogy to Donne's sermons. Hamlet's is the discourse of the self in its social confinement:

> [*Pol.* Do you know me, my lord?
> *Ham.* Excellent well; you are a fishmonger.]

i.e. you are sent to *fish* out the secret. This is Hamlet's meaning. The purposely obscure lines —

> For if the sun [breed maggots in a dead dog, being a god kissing carrion — Have you a daughter?]

I rather think refer to some thought in Hamlet's mind contrasting the lovely daughter with such a tedious old fool, her father, as *he* represents Polonius to himself   (*SC* I, 26).

Speech in such a situation could only be ambiguous, yet it remained fully social in intention. There was nothing private about Hamlet's language, as Shakespeare made his audience understand. The character played on the assumption of his madness, all the while making sound (if difficult) sense. Language was the instrument of this "activity of thought," a way through limits imposed on other kinds of activity. Coleridge's defense of Hamlet here represents a defense of expressive language against those who would understand it conventionally — as "witty" or otherwise mannered when it was always, in the voice of the expressive subject, a means of making sense.

The public uses of language might confuse a Polonius (or a Warburton), yet its "outness" — a significant echo of the early note — took nothing away from its vital interiority for the reflective mind: "And note how the character develops itself in the next speech — the aversion to externals, the betrayed habit of brooding over the world within him, and the prodigality of beautiful words, which are, as it were, the half embodyings of thoughts, that make them more than thoughts, give them an outness, a reality *sui generis*, and yet retain their correspondence and shadowy approach to the images and movements within" (*SC* I, 38). Expressive language acquired an important precedent in this discussion, as compact an account of its workings as Coleridge would ever arrive at. Expression of this sort presumed indeed a predominant idealism, a sense of self which can be called self-conscious, in response to compelling social circumstances: isolation, marginality, perceived threat. These were Coleridge's circumstances as much as Hamlet's, and what he was describing here of a character remote from himself in place and time was something profoundly true to his own life in language. An isolated cottage on the road out of Nether Stowey and a late winter night alone among family provided an occasion for his own soliloquy from Elsinore. "Frost at Midnight" plumbs the possibilities of expression in this emblematic environment.

Macbeth is not Hamlet, nor so obviously an antecedent of the expressive language developed by Coleridge in the new discourse that would be called romantic. Yet he too is understood from within this achieved idiom, in what is perhaps the most distinctively Coleridgean line of observation in the body of his Shakespeare criticism. The contrast with Hamlet proceeds through a dramatic difference of self-expression: in *Macbeth* there is not "a single pun or play on words" (*SC* I, 78). Yet in the protagonist Coleridge identifies "an active and combining intellect, and an imagination of just that degree of vividness which disquiets and impels the soul to try to realize its images. Greatly increase this creative power, and the images become a satisfying world of themselves; *i.e.* we have the poet, or original philosopher" (*SC* I, 81). Macbeth is Hamlet in a worldlier key, not far from the condition of poet or philosopher. Where Hamlet lives by words, Macbeth is driven to realize his images in an act of will. The conjunction (and contrast) is significant in the context I have been elaborating. Both represent potential versions of the poet. The image realized in an act of will has affiliations with Schelling's secondary imagination, "co-existing" as it does "with the conscious will" in Coleridge's rendition (*BL* I, 202). This is perhaps how he conceived the poetic act under the influence of Schelling's idea. He had already tried it out in practice: "realiz-[ing] the image" aptly characterizes the enterprise of "Frost at Midnight," with its wilful (or wishful) metaphor of ministry. The failure of the premise in the living world of sense experience diverted the speaker into the very different associative process of the second stanza. Hamlet's "activity of thought in the play of words" characterizes the diversion, underwriting the primacy of language for poetic imagination as Coleridge would pursue it.

Poet as imagist, poet as idealist: the real poet was both, yet the contrast of the two types in Coleridge's discussion shows how conflicted he felt the relation to be. Macbeth the imagist was not yet a poet or original philosopher. Hamlet the idealist was endued with Shakespeare's own powers in an excessive degree. Each exemplifies the fate of a certain kind of poetry. The distinction reverts to a much earlier stage of Coleridge's critical formation. Thus, in an early letter, he can be observed playing Hamlet to Southey's Macbeth: "I *think* too much for a *Poet*; he too little for a *great* Poet" (*CL* I, 294). Southey was the poet of local beauties and realized images, and he never grew beyond it to something more substantial. "A great poet must be a profound Metaphysician" (*CL* II, 810), as he would put it in a celebrated letter. But, as he added there, verging on paradox, "He may not have it in logical coherence, in his Brain & Tongue; but he must have it by *Tact*/for all sounds, & forms of human nature he must have the *ear* of a wild Arab listening in the silent Desert, the eye of a North American Indian tracing the footsteps of an enemy upon the leaves that strew the Forest —; the *Touch* of a Blind Man feeling the face of a darling Child —. . . ." Such instinctive powers could not be explained, only imagined. They had nothing to do with thinking, or "logical coherence." Far from the rational equipment of the "profound Metaphysician," they were nearly primitive qualities. An exceptional power of perception made the great poet capable of effects "simple, sensuous, impassioned": Milton's terms as transmitted by Coleridge and "the ineradicable *nisus* of poetry," in the words of a commentator.[16]

This "original power" Coleridge felt himself lacking, in comparison with Wordsworth especially, at the moment when he abandoned the art (*CL* I, 656; see also 714). More than a creature of instinctive sense, the great poet found means to join his perceptions to something far more deeply interfused. For despite the occasional lapses into "matter-of-factness," Wordsworth had shown himself philosophical in the way that Coleridge prescribed. His example witnessed what meditative poetry might aspire to if it could control the image:

> Would any but a poet — at least could any one without being conscious
> that he had expressed himself with noticeable vivacity — have described a

bird singing loud by, "the thrush is *busy* in the wood?" — or have spoken of boys with a string of club-moss round their rusty hats, as the boys "*with their green coronal?*" — or have brought all the different marks and circumstances of a sea-loch before the mind, as the actions of a living and acting power? Or have represented the reflection of the sky in the water as "*That uncertain heaven received into the bosom of the steady lake?*" (*BL* II, 83–84)

The emphasis in Coleridge's commentary falls on the idea realized within the image, and so naturally conceived in this setting as to be irretrievable as an "idea" in the odious, neo-Lockean sense of the word. Such imagery actually contradicted the corpuscular "idea" by making it always a product of "the mind thinking in such a situation." Expressive imagery, as it might be called, managed the difficult balancing act, yielding neither to the idolatry of the image nor to predominant idealism. Wordsworth's images, as cited, stand out for their simple clarity. They are not overdrawn to a "laborious anatomy of description;" they include detail sufficient to render the thought, and no more. Yet they are always more than an idea dressed up as a "formal simile" for effect.

Image and idea are the habitual currency of Coleridge's observations on the style of poetry and prose, bringing the philosophical context of his resistance to an ascendant empiricism with them. Expressive language aspired to the condition of philosophy through the informing process to which it gave voice. The conversation poems show Coleridge trying out an idiom that would be responsive to the fluctuations of his thinking — "the images and movements within," as he put it of Hamlet's lucubrations. This was not thinking in a narrowly rationalist sense; it included all the phenomena of subjective awareness, from fear to subliminal imagery. It would be misleading to consider his poetics under the title of rationalist despite his adoption of a sympathetic point of view in dismantling the positions of Locke and his inheritors. Rendering the shadowy self intelligible meant including more than reason could initially accommodate. The discourse of poetry remained accountable nevertheless to rational understanding. It would be the vocation of criticism to bridge the gap, defending poetry as fully rational and singularly valuable. Image and idea were the basic instruments of this enterprise, responding as they did to familiar notions of literary expression.

Yet Coleridge's deep-seated reservations about both words in their ordinary applications remained in force. The idea could hardly be said to exist apart from a process of thinking, while the image was readily confused with the forms of nature, to bad poetic effect. His criticism would have to make shift with these problematic terms and the unsatisfactory epistemology which they presumed. As his recognition of their limitations grew through practice, he became cautious about their uses in critical argumentation. Criticism served him in this way as a propaedeutic to the enlarged understanding which he would present on other grounds in the Philosophical Lectures of 1818–19. After this date (after the publication of the *Biographia* in fact) he turned his attention to other issues — related, certainly, to the vocation of poetry, but distinct from it. His criticism stands between poetry and philosophy in the development of his thinking, looking forward to the largest questions of the time from a background of poetic self-realization. What appears as a problem of expression in "Frost at Midnight" thus recurs as a critical problem in his early reactions to the "Preface," and as a philosophical problem in the account of Locke in the later lectures.

His pursuit of language cannot be entirely abstracted from this context, for it assumed its distinctive shape through the formation of his response to Hartley, Tooke, and Locke himself. A reformed notion of language involved very different conceptions of image and idea from what was current in their dominant way of thinking. The idea in its perfection was indeed simply an image for Locke. Against his example, Coleridge would dwell on the difference, and on the subsisting tension between image and idea in the poetic setting. Poetry broke up the wilful solidarity of nature and mind which lay at the bottom of empirical understanding. The mind could no more be considered as, ideally, a mirror of nature than the idea could be imagined as the reflected form of the natural phenomenon. The human place in nature was not so simple. The language of poetry, in practice and in theory, provided means to this recognition and a way beyond the limitations of so tendentious an understanding.

Poetry at its best produced not a simulacrum of nature but a second nature of the imagination. The likeness was twice mediated: the poetic image, constructed in language, was of a cognitive order entirely different from the natural image, or impression. Yet it aspired to the "sweetness and easy movement of nature" (*SC* I, 214), and if it was not actually a reflection of the sights and sounds of the world, it constituted a reflection on them. Poetry was an "imitative art" in its constant recourse to familiar types of human activity and response. An imitative art of this kind might be descriptive at times, but a copy was not the point. What the best poetry got at was the ideal, in its integral relations with the various faculties of a comprehensive reason: with perception and memory, and with imagination in all its degrees and qualities. Poetic discourse might approach the condition of the impression, in its simplicity and sensuousness:

> [S]implicity, while it distinguishes Poetry from the arduous processes of Science, laboring towards an end not yet arrived at, & supposes a smooth and finished Road on which the reader is to walk onward easily, with streams murmuring by his side, & Trees & Flowers, & human dwellings to make his journey as delightful as the object of it is desirable, instead of having to toil with the Pioneers, & painfully make the road, on which others are to travel, precludes every affectation . . . The second condition, sensuousness, insures that framework of objectivity, that definiteness and articulation of imagery, and that modification of the images themselves, without which poetry becomes flattened into mere didactics of practice, or evaporated into a hazy, unthoughtful day-dreaming; and the third condition, passion, provides that neither thought nor imagery shall be simply objective, but that the *passio vera* of humanity shall warm and animate both.   (CSC, 547)

But good poetry rose above the contrary dominions of image and idea to constitute a world of its own, a familiar landscape at one remove. Such a passage attests the force of a traditional literary decorum on Coleridge's conception of poetic value. And it shows his employment of image and idea in a critically refined form, as "imagery" and "thought," to express this decorum in a way consistent with his developed understanding. Coleridgean poetics would be committed to the ideal in the context of a living tradition whose values it promoted and defended under modern conditions. Science stands for these conditions here as it would in Cambridge English, with differences appropriate to circumstances. With Locke in the background, Coleridge drew a provisional line, dividing the ground in a familiar way. The difference was real even if science was informed by the same reason as imagination.

The balancing of the claims of thought and imagery in this passage has deep roots, yet Coleridge can be said I think to have put the case against the image as the model of poetic discourse into a canonical form for modern readers. His suspicion of "the too great definiteness of Terms" and of the "distinct, clear, full made Images" to which they gave rise identified a conspicuous tendency of modern writing if not of modern language. It is a tendency observed elsewhere by Henry James of Tennyson's vividly pictorial "Tithonus": "It is poised and stationary, like a bird whose wings have borne him high, but the beauty of whose movement is less in great ethereal sweeps and circles than in the way he hangs motionless in the blue air, with only a vague tremor of his pinions. Even if the idea with Tennyson were more largely dramatic than it usually is, the immobility, as we must call it, of his phrase would always defeat the dramatic intention."[17] The conflict of image and idea underwrites this act of recognition, the vividness of the one subverting the dynamic forces of the other through the inert phrase. The author of "The Coxon Fund" relied here on a way of thinking about poetry which Coleridge had observed, refined, and consolidated from traditional sources. It was not an original, but a modification, on ground which he surveyed with clear eyes, of traditional practices. Coleridge's enduring contribution to critical tradition lay in this revitalizing act — in defining a way of reading and writing for himself and his contemporaries at a moment of uncertainty about the future of poetry.

III

COLERIDGE'S POETICS
OF RESPONSE

6

Poet as Critic in the Conversation Poems

The poet-critic is a fixture of the modernist imagination, a privileged source whose authority derives from a double commitment: to the practice of the art and to its defense against devaluation. Only a sage tried by the fire could stand strong against the disruptive forces at work in an emergent industrial order.[1] Theory and practice, act and explanation were aligned by this sacerdotal figure to make the case for poetry.[2] Coleridge, Arnold and Eliot have filled the role variously for posterity, each bringing something characteristic to it. In Cambridge English, the institutional locomotive of the new criticism, cultural arbitrage devolved on a clerisy which presided over poetry's last alternatives while concerting its energies on reading and education in the shadow of science.[3] Richards set the pattern, taking Coleridge as the model reader, Eliot as the modern oracle, poetry as a pastime, and criticism as a professional vocation, with Basic English at the utilitarian cutting edge. This program was reproduced by his followers with changing emphases. Empson proved a fine poet as well as a penetrating reader. Tate and Ransom, too, defended the art in a more than theoretic way. Leavis consolidated the professional core around moral argumentation, leaving poetry to the poets while subverting their influence through a high-handed attack on Eliot and modernism generally. With the romantics and their inheritors effectively dispatched, only criticism was left to keep up the ancestral standard: Arnold's tale writ modern. The poet-critic remains an authoritative figure, but the institutional splitting of the role has done damage both to critical conviction and to the poetic voice.

Coleridge has been the conspicuous victim of this development — more than Eliot, certainly, if only because Eliot was on hand to answer his critics.[4] He was in a position to respond to Richards as Coleridge was not, and he did so to good effect. What institutional criticism knows of Coleridge it knows largely from Richards's promotion of the degrees of imagination, in one form or another, and from Leavis's dismissal of the idea as metaphysical brainstorming. Coleridge's poetry survived the clash of wills, but the record of his reading and response was fatally compromised. For it was made to appear forbiddingly hypothetical and limited in concern by both parties. In fact, as the notebooks and marginalia testify, it was expansive and eclectic to a fault—a salutary corrective to the aridity of formalist reading of the sort promoted by the new criticism in its institutional versions. It is commonly regarded now as a matter of historical importance, grist for surveys of English criticism with no living significance: a triumph for Leavis, but a loss for poetry as a modern art.

For Coleridge's conception of poetry, formed by practice at a transitional moment in its history, tested by deep and diverse reading, is a monument of enduring value. Not only as a way back to the premises of English versification but as a guide to good reading at a time when readers have trouble grasping what is involved in writing of this unpractical kind. He was not the first poet of stature to articulate his principles, but he was the first to have recognized the fate of writing under modern circumstances, and to have sought a place for it in the utilitarian utopia, against dominant empirical values. The lasting significance of Coleridge's long philosophical investigation lies not in his assimilation of German ideas for their own sake, but in his employment of them against Locke, Hartley, and the Gradgrinds of the brave new world of scientific understanding. Insofar as his critical response is seen as an outpost of Kant's (and Schelling's) version of imagination, it is bound to be regarded as an imported product, fundamentally alien. So it has come to seem despite thoughtful efforts of rehabilitation. When restored to the originating context—to his doubts about the "Preface" and his disaffection with Hartley—the philosophical investigation assumes a natural place in his work, as a demonstration of the poverty of empirical understanding. Poetry had quickened his sense of the activity of mind in understanding. Philosophy confirmed the recognition, providing rational foundation for the promotion of creative imagination in a world that included more than nature.

Coleridge's poetry has long been read in the philosophical spirit which he intended, as mental enactment. The conversation poems in particular have come to stand for the possibility of a thinking verse, looking back on Cowper and the poetry of sensibility, and forward to Wordsworth and the meditative blank-verse idiom which owes so much to their example.[5] Appreciating these poems does not require a developed sense of their canonical value, but they can hardly be read at this remove without consciousness of an originality and importance exceeding their limited occasions. They are a phenomenon of modern reading, as the record of commentary witnesses: a crossroads of tradition where ways part, a future opens up, and a past disappears abruptly over the horizon.[6]

The comparison with Cowper is a suggestive one, for it shows how Coleridge relied on his meditative procedure and diction while trying for something of a different discursive cast: less disjointed and aimlessly reflective, more integrated and thoughtful. Yet it is not for its modification of Cowper's voice that Coleridge's conversational poetry matters in the way that it does. The poetic voice which he developed between 1795 and the "Dejection" ode of 1802 coincides with that of his earliest notebooks, of his formative correspondence with Wordsworth, Southey, Poole, and Wedgwood, and of his early lectures and journalism on subjects religious and political. It acquired fluidity and assurance from his Hartleyan enthusiasm, taking the process of association as its element.[7] It is not just a reflective voice but a searching one, actively in pursuit of ground and bearing in a world at once familiar and unknown. This voice expresses the uncertainties of more than an individual mind. It evokes a kingdom where political foundations had been shaken, religious conviction had fallen foul of the established church, and conventional explanations surrounding both no longer answered anything. Doubt and fear sound unmistakably through it.

The context of Coleridge's innovative line was broadly social rather than narrowly philosophical. A general crisis of values was its element. The immediate antecedents of the conversation poems show the aspiring poet exercising (and exorcising) "the fear of death" while trying to envision the meaning of freedom for human society at large.[8] The association of private anxiety with public concern in this monodic mode is a distinctive one, even if it is not always effective. At Chattertons's imagined grave Coleridge rants, presumably at death:

> Away, Grim Phantom! Scorpion King, away!
> Reserve they terrors and thy stings display
> For coward Wealth and Guilt in robes of State!

The effort of displacement is transparent. Death is reserved for the socially culpable instead of the heroic outcast, a figure of identity. Anxiety is thus turned to wishful ends.

In "Religious Musings," begun Christmas Eve, 1794, Christ is made to stand for a social ideal while palliating the same fear. The "Man of Woes," "Despised Gallilean" is portrayed not only as Saviour but as the permanent source of a communitarian self:

> Toy-bewitched,
> Made blind by lusts, disherited of soul,
> No common centre Man, no common sire
> Knoweth! A sordid solitary thing,
> Mid countless brethren with a lonely heart
> Through courts and cities the smooth savage roams
> Feeling himself, his own low self the whole;
> When he by sacred sympathy might make
> The whole one Self! Self, that no alien knows!
> Self, far diffused as Fancy's wing can travel!
> Self, spreading still! Oblivious of its own,
> Yet of all possessing!

The reconstruction of this fallen self was as much Coleridge's project as it was Blake's, with the difference that energetic social engagement made. Such a passage, buried in a remote early poem, should make clear how fully social was his idea of personal identity, and how much a product of large social thinking. The point, here as in his "Destiny of Nations," was to begin from first principles in order to arrive at tenable social ideals. Selfhood "disherited of soul," that self-consciousness which was an intense selfishness, was the common enemy of Christian precept and the earthly paradise. What appeared as a social question in the early monodies would recur in the conversation poems as a problem of private situation. What was the poet's place among family and friends, and in nature seen under a peculiarly personal aspect?[9]

The processive approach of these rambling, disjointed versifications looks forward to the conversation poems as well. Their commitment to something more inclusive than a well-made statement of the articles of faith was important for the future of Coleridge's voice, and of romantic poetics generally. In his *Conciones ad Populum* of early 1795 he spoke of "that small but glorious band of thinking and disinterested Patriots, accustomed to regard all the affairs of man as a process" (CC 1:40, ellipses deleted). The context has nothing to do with poetry, yet the judgment expresses more than a political viewpoint: the quiet strength of attention to method. *How* the thinking man attained his ends was his constant occupation. Laborious attention to the process of ideation makes Coleridge's monodies the overwrought, turgid productions they are. The stentorian style strains to throw every point into high relief. As poems they are less than uneven, but the burden of writing personally about collective experience was an honorable one, and the attention to process proved productive for the future of their author's voice. Their Miltonic originals show what he was trying for under altered circumstances of language and culture.

His search for a socially potent voice in this formative period is in fact practically definitive of his enterprise as a writer. As House observes, against the grain of modern reading, neither Wordsworth nor Coleridge "had made any formal decision to be 'poets,' or at least to be poets only or mainly. They felt primarily the need for action" (*CCL*, 63). Poetry had always served political expression, and in their hands it was fitted to the needs of a new audience. The fitting was far from graceful at first—a sign of the strain involved. In the *Conciones*, delivered at Bristol, Coleridge worked bits of verse into his argument for figurative effect. In the "Introductory Address" in particular, political discourse took poetic means as a suitable complement. Speaking of the French revolution, he compared the people to Samson, strong but blind, citing *Samson Agonistes* to draw the consequences (*CC* 1:34). Later citations to Akenside, among others, are counted among what appear to be his own productions, some of them apparently concocted for the occasion. The poetic diversions thin out as the lectures proceed and his voice grows stronger and more directed to particular abuses. Perhaps the change reflects a growing awareness of his audience, and of his responsibility to speak not vatically but pragmatically. John Colmer contrasts the Bristol Lectures unfavorably with Burke and Paine in their different ways, noticing Coleridge's failure to command "a consistently powerful style."[10] They bear witness all the same to their author's aspiration to an effective public voice.

The continuity of concern across the range of his writing is attested by Colmer's observation that he relied entirely on verse for the public expression of his political views between the last issue of *The Watchman* (May 13, 1796) and his engagement with *The Morning Post* (from November 1799).[11] This span of three and a half years includes most of his significant poetic production, a coincidence worth considering. Can subliminal imagery surrounding an oriental potentate be devoid of political dreamwork when its author is constantly preoccupied with political questions? Probably not, for whatever it might yield, even if it can hardly be made to yield an exclusively political meaning. Yet this profound commitment of poetry to public discourse in an expanding public sphere has usually been discounted. Coleridge on imagination has roots in the same soil. The faculty is identified at the outset of his attack on the slave trade (*The Watchman*, March 25, 1796) as the source of venal social desire:

> WHENCE arise our Miseries? Whence arise our Vices? From *imaginary* Wants. No man is wicked without temptation, no man is wretched without a cause. But if each among us confined his wishes to the actual necessaries and real comforts of Life, we should preclude all the causes of Complaint and all the motives to Iniquity. What Nature demands, she will supply, asking for it that portion only of *Toil*, which would otherwise have been necessary as *Exercise*. But Providence, which has distinguished Man from lower orders of Being by the progressiveness of his nature, forbids him to be contented. It has given us the restless faculty of *Imagination*. (*CC* 2:130–31)

Against this animal hunger for possession Coleridge posed the "intellectual activity" awakened in reaction to it: "and from such enlargement of mind benevolence will necessarily follow" (*CC* 2:139). Here is the original context of his enduring counterpoint of image and idea, a setting of the first importance for his long investigation of imagination. Far from the disembodied, transcendental operation posited by Kant, imagination took its place in the organic life of the fallen self.

The necessitarian argument underwriting such a conception was indebted to Hartley, but as Lewis Patton notices of this passage, Coleridge took the case beyond his informant.[12] The subsequent disavowal of the Hartleyan agenda changed the ordonnance but not the orientation of his own position. Association remained fundamental to Coleridge's understanding of mental process, including imagination, and of language, as I have suggested. Imagination might be exalted as the poetic faculty par excellence, but it remained bound to this idea of rational function and this sense of human possibility. Poetry figured accordingly among the attainments of a counteractive reason, even if it descended from imagination's progeny:

> From Avarice thus, from Luxury and War
> Sprang heavenly Science; and from Science Freedom.

> O'er waken'd realms Philosophers and Bards
> Spread in concentric circles: they whose souls,
> Conscious of their high dignities from God,
> Brook not Wealth's rivalry!

Imagination followed Love in this latter-day theogony, as a disruptive principle giving rise to the antagonistic forces of reason. The participation of imagination in poetry was primordial, but as an incitement to improvement—not a featherbed for adepts. The passage from "Religious Musings" cited by Coleridge in his article on the slave trade shows that this was what poetry reacted against—

> the soft Couch, and many-colour'd Robe,
> The Timbrel and arch'd Dome and costly Feast,
> With all th'inventive Arts that nurse the Soul
> To Forms of Beauty . . .   (CC 2:131)

Poetry as he would conceive it was a recoil from the featherbed, not a form of indulgence in it.

The theogonic trappings of this part of "Religious Musings" are peculiarly apt to the purpose of such an argument, relying on sources which witnessed the ubiquitous activity of an originating principle. In the prototypical Hesiod, Chaos was followed by Gaia, the great mother, and then Eros, through whose agency the contrary generation of Titans came into being. The dynamic setting of the theogonic machinery provided means for the expression of a human condition characterized by the working of antithetical forces—an attractive framework even if the Hellenic inspiration violated the affinities of the decidedly Hebraic poet. Later allegorical deployments of the mode had made it the vehicle of a self-conscious poetic display. In Coleridge's hands, the choice of means imposed form on the process of thinking at the heart of poetry while providing anchorage for his vatic persuasion. The poetic voice was suited by venerable precedent to public expression of the largest kind.

Coleridge's early monodies make difficult reading at this distance, yet they are essential to understanding the philosophical vocation of his meditative line in a way that the sonnets are not. For these lead to a pictorial appreciation of the conversation poems even where, as in Wimsatt's influential essay, emphasis is laid on their thoughtfulness. The sonnets belong to the sentimental world of Bowles, as Coleridge himself recognized. They stand in his poetic formation for the possibilities of the image, as the monodies stand for the possibilities of the idea. The split exemplifies the dissociation between "natural faculties" and the life of reason in Coleridge's constitution: a dissociation which would lead him, in a moment of crisis, to doubt his poetic vocation. Bowles restored him to "my fancy, and the love of nature, and the sense of beauty in forms and sounds," as he would put it later in the *Biographia* (*BL* I, 10), providing entree to the images that were the lumber of poetic construction. What he made of them was something quite different from his model's effusions. Even in the sonnets he can hardly keep his social muse at bay. "To the River Otter," the best known among them on the basis of his recasting of Bowles's technique, is uncharacteristic, little more than an exercise.

The conversational idiom emerges in the midst of these divided allegiances, sublating both voices in a vigorous, personal presentation of the speaker in his homely environs. With Cowper in the background, he proposed simply to talk, with himself more than with a presumptive audience. The Horatian epigram of "Reflections on Having Left a Place of Retirement" (1796) suggests as much: "Sermoni propriora." Not a conversation poem, it is nevertheless counted among the meditative poems in blank verse where they are mostly to be found in *Sibylline Leaves*. The conversational premise is seldom more than a pretext for lucubrations of this kind, even where his audience has a name and assumes a dramatic agency. Monody accedes to monologue in the new form. Yet Coleridge presumes from the beginning to speak for more than himself alone—

> Low was our pretty Cot: our tallest Rose
> Peep'd at the chamber-window. We could hear
> At silent noon, and eve, and early morn,
> The Sea's faint murmur. In the open air
> Our Myrtles blossom'd; and across the porch
> Thick Jasmins twined: the little landscape round
> Was green and woody, and refresh'd the eye.
> It was a spot which you might aptly call
> The Valley of Seclusion!

The inclusive voice is a constant feature of his verse in this vein, in part because of the community forming around him through friendship and marriage, and what they appeared to offer him in his role as *vates*. It was a moment of rare promise, sustaining his aspiration to make "the whole one Self . . . that no alien knows!" This is the living context of the conversation poems. When the communal ideal failed along with the optimistic naturalism that was its expression, Coleridge found himself indeed "a sordid solitary thing/'Mid countless brethren with a lonely heart," and he disowned the naturalism in response. His newly integrated discourse, as it developed through these years, celebrated the integral self in its extended relations with others and with a nature which mirrored, like the twining jasmine, the human condition in its optimal state. The Edenic bower would be its home until the fall turned him out.

The pattern of reclusion and expulsion is already implicit in "Reflections," where the speaker is driven to recognize the artifice of his position and to choose the thorny path of history. The appealing images of the poem's opening acquire moral significance through the contrast with commerce in the eye of "Bristowa's citizen" sauntering by. Nature as an alternative to conventional social affiliation yields a vision of the world from on high:

> But the time, when first
> From that low Dell, steep up the stony Mount
> I climb'd with perilous toil and reach'd the top,
> Oh! what a goodly scene! *Here* the bleak mount,
> The bare bleak mountain speckled thin with sheep;
> Grey clouds, that shadowing spot the sunny fields;
> And river, now with bushy rocks o'erbrow'd,
> Now winding bright and full, with naked banks;
> And seats, and lawns, the Abbey and the wood,
> And cots, and hamlets, and faint city-spire;
> The Channel *there*, the Islands with white sails,
> Dim coasts, and cloud-like hills, and shoreless Ocean—
> It seemed like Omnipresence! God, methought,
> Had built him there a Temple: the whole World
> Seemed imag'd in its vast circumference:
> No *wish* profan'd my overwhelméd heart.
> Blest hour! It was a luxury,—to be!

Yet it is unreal, as the conclusion suggests, when seen from a human vantage point. As a privileged act of vision it provides an image of earthly paradise, satisfying to imagination, evacuating all desire. The image is perfect, but inadequate to real human need as it appears from the valley below. The principled turn away from an alluring but static perfection is paradigmatic of Coleridge's forthright commitment to a progressive social process and of his commitment to thinking through the contradictions in his own experience.

The prime contradiction, as it appears in "Reflections," is between the world as image and as idea. This context provides an early version of his doubts about the image as they emerge in his notebooks at the end of the decade. The very fulness of the impression from the mountain, its "omnipresence," is immobilizing. It fixes the speaker in his spot, at the center of a "vast circumference" where he stands alone in solitary ecstasy. His voice shifts from the collective to the subjective self here, as if the image were of a private condition. This cannot be considered an incidental correlation, even if the view is open to the public and the voice means to speak personally for all.

The symbolic dimension of the ascent is indicated in several ways; it evokes the prophet, solitary in his quest for revelation. What he finds is not the Heavenly City but the fallen world in its consuming beauty. Consuming because absorbing, complete, self-valorizing: a world of its own. The passage is particularly effective in drawing us into an imaginary plenum of this kind before the speaker turns his back on it. When Coleridge noticed the tendency of modern language to "distinct, clear, full made Images" (*CN* I, 1016) he was pondering the effect of such stunning impressions in verse, and he came down against them. In "Reflections" the turn away from the image is dramatized and made to bear a particular meaning, against "the coward heart" and social disengagement. In the fallen world the consuming image was a snare, drawing in, isolating, and charming its spectator. Vision of this self-centered kind was implicated as a beautiful illusion, split off from collective experience.

The poem is concerned with something more than its stated conclusion. It exhibits, in its central movement, reflection in a root sense—the subject as a reflector, transmitting the impressions of the world. The poet as maker of images is celebrated and surpassed in turn, in response to an insistent moral imperative. As a reflection of (and on) the image, it witnesses that attention to process which characterizes all of Coleridge's thinking, including his poetic thinking. For his modern readers especially, this sustained act of attention is important, and not only for keeping his poetic flame burning. Following Kermode, it can be said to anticipate the Yeats of "Byzantium," of the dancer and the dance,[13] and to express that deep romantic ambivalence to the image so evident in modern practice—in Pound and Stevens, conspicuously. The conversation poems hardly invented it, but they do constitute the most penetrating treatment of its consequences in the period, Blake's visionary allegory apart. For in consolidating his discourse of the self, Coleridge was drawn constantly to the question of the resources of nature observed under the auspices of his social ideal: a world of companionable forms. The question arose, and was resolved in the poetry, through the image as what nature presented to the fallen senses.

Against this background, what stands out in "The Eolian Harp" (1795) is the equation of the natural impulse with the imagery to which it gives rise. The poem, usually accounted the first of the conversational type, reenacts the drama of "Reflections" from another cottage, digressing into private vision and recovering its social direction in the end. The conclusion, with its sententious wife and rather wooden phrasing, has never commanded the conviction which Coleridge evidently intended, yet it is plausible enough given his commitments and the similar return to first principles in "Reflections."[14] What makes this conclusion distinctive, and altogether more interesting, is the obvious strain of its resolution. The descent from the mount in the earlier poem was made to seem entirely natural, as though the lure of the image were no match for the will to carry on the good fight. The conflicting claims are dramatized in "The Eolian Harp" as an imagistic presentation of the pantheist thesis followed by an abrupt recanting. There is no middle ground here, only two exclusive ideas. The choice of commitment to Sara and her God entails a summary dismissal not just of the pantheist vision of "all of animated nature" as "organic harps diversely framed" but—as it would seem—of the process which authorized its expression. No wonder the choice has proved difficult for readers to accept.

For it is just this process, and Coleridge's attention to it, that animates the poem. Here the central movement dominates as it does not in "Reflections," diminishing the rest to a setting of the virtuoso performance—little more than a framing device. The images which lay at a safe elevation in the earlier poem now cast a shadow across the poet's world, threatening his conviction and disrupting the marriage at the heart of his community. The tone of contrition in the end sounds distinctly pro forma even if the commitment is real. For there is no real resignation of the claim on imaginative power—

> These shapings of the unregenerate mind;
> Bubbles that glitter as they rise and break
> On vain Philosophy's aye-babbling spring.

— only a recognition of the conflict with larger values. A weakening of resolution or an expansion of perspective? Inspired by these seething images, the poet concedes the force of natural impulse through its influence on the mind, making for a potent sense of "the one Life within us and abroad." Yet the immediate doubt with which the proposition is met musters an equal and opposite show of force. The realized ambivalence of this encounter, far from unsatisfactory, gives voice to the living conflict between the claims of mind and matter on the one hand, of spirit on the other.

Mind and matter are indeed virtually identified in the central passage, which yields more to empirical understanding than anything in Coleridge's poetic production. It was this identification that lay at the bottom of Locke's empiricism, as he would come to it in the letters to Wedgwood of 1801. In a clear state, the mind was simply a reflector. Like the Eolian harp, it was moved by the wind to sing, and what it sang was what it was moved *to*:

> And now, its strings
> Boldlier swept, the long sequacious notes
> Over delicious surges sink and rise,
> Such a soft floating witchery of sound
> As twilight Elfins make, when they at eve
> Voyage on gentle gales from Fairy-Land,
> Where Melodies round honey-dropping flowers,
> Footless and wild, like birds of Paradise,
> Nor pause, nor perch, hovering on untam'd wing!

The translation of impulse into image by analogy is naturalized in the passage which follows — inserted by the poet only later, at a time when his understanding of Locke was completely formed. Sound was thus converted to something visible not by an act of will but by instinct, as it were. Images were only impressions from sensation, the spontaneous product of an active nature. Imagination was itself only a branch of passive perception:

> O! the one Life within us and abroad,
> Which meets all motion and becomes its soul,

A light in sound, a sound-like power in light,
Rhythm in all thought, and joyance every where—
. . . .
Where the breeze warbles, and the mute still air
Is Music slumbering on her instrument.

Music was not more than the impression of the breeze, an allegorical figure of repose—a far cry from the Terpsichorean Muses, traditional figures of inspiration. It was all one life, the "indolent and passive brain" of the poet, recumbent on the hill, just one harp "diversely fram'd" among others.

If this portrait of the artist as nature's instrument bears rehearsing in the present context, it is for its subliminal reflection on the poet's imagery, and how it exercises Coleridge's ambivalence. The passivity of imagination on the empirical model was a luxurious yielding to sensation, as the plainly sexual crescendo of his fantasia intimates. Imagination of this kind is indeed virtually equated with a passive procreativity. The imagery it produces is pictorial, even if it does not reproduce a visible scene. For the impulse in this case is aural; it is in the music of the passage that the mimetic instinct is at work. The associated imagery follows the lead of a subtly modulated rhythmic. Its pictorial values are made to seem "natural," all the same, in keeping with the premise of the "one Life within us and abroad." The appealing lyricism of the passage expresses the pleasure of yielding to sensation—animal joy in the rhythm and form of natural experience. And the theoretic calculations after the fact provide a rationale. Nature really was the home of imagination, and by implication (through the marriage consummated in the passage) of human community.

Yet imagination of this kind could only appear fallen, its pleasures instinctive and profane, from the cottage where he had started. "These shapings of the unregenerate mind," as he calls them in the final stanza, led him away from his real home, making him the willing prisoner of a limited understanding. The merely generative position, beautifully illustrated in the central fantasia, is thus demoted to an illusion. As this resolution reflects on the image, it must be taken to involve a rejection of the enabling process. The assumption that the impulse produced the image spontaneously, without an intervening act of will, lay at the bottom of this "natural" sort of imagination. The subject could hardly be held accountable for his response on such a premise. Yet the product of his fancy appears in fact to be anything but automatic. Despite the justification of "one Life within us and abroad," what he voices in response to sensation is transparently subjective, peculiar to himself — "natural" by assumption more than by imitation. Pictorial imagery was an illusion, evidently enough but in an expanded sense now. The illusion lay in the presumption of the mind's passivity before a dominant natural impulse. The premise was false not just to the human condition, but to the poetic image as it was conjured from an imagination which answered to higher powers. The beautiful illusion was acted out, then left in abeyance, making the ascent and descent of "Reflections" into an ambivalent expression of the condition of poetry in a fallen world.

This reflexive consciousness of means is, to be sure, only inferentially involved in the turn away from the "midway slope" of an empiric imagination. But to confine the content of the poem to its overt argument is to miss the impact of the conclusion in its full force. Or, more conventionally, it means ignoring the conclusion, settling for a fallen imagination and a comfortable illusion of "one Life within us and abroad" which Coleridge himself instantly recanted. The quality of his ambivalence invites the fuller reckoning accorded by McFarland in his treatment of the pantheist dilemma as Coleridge confronted it.[15] Such a reckoning would include much more than antithetical approaches to nature. For in his practice as a poet and writer at large, Coleridge was faced again and again with the consequences imposed by his ambivalent understanding — metaphysical, ethical, and broadly literary. He did not evade them, he engaged the alternatives prospectively, as in "The Eolian Harp," elaborating on the possibilities, weighing the implications. This is indeed a considerable part of the burden of the conversation poems, and what confers philosophical scope on the discursive method developed through them. They exemplify poetic thinking, as he promoted it from the beginning of his career, in the living context of the pantheist challenge to his convictions. The voice which he arrived at in the process included a great deal by implication. Reading from a limited idea of "text" as a closed unit violates the processive quality of his discourse: a quality indigenous to "The Eolian Harp" as we know it through the growth of the text over time in response to enlarged understanding.

The reflection on the image is "in the text," then, on the assumption that the text includes more than the sum of its variant readings. The main line of Coleridge's meditative verse can be approached as an integral sequence which resolves poetic questions in the process of considering the dilemma of the human situation between God and nature. The conversation poems might be regarded in this way as a propaedeutic to his reading and criticism — an active interrogation of image and idea in the poetic setting. The poetry then becomes something more than a brief burst of power at the beginning of a disjointed career. It becomes a basis for understanding the critical commitments of an important arbiter of poetic value.

Coleridge attained to his position as prime poet-critic of English tradition in part at least on the basis of his verse, yet he has too often been adjudged a failure on account of its inconsequence. The "failed" poet became a critic, then a doubtful acolyte of Kant's critical philosophy, never following through what he had begun. He clearly felt something like this himself, and his defensiveness has provoked those who would undermine his voice, beginning with Wordsworth. When his achievement is considered as an open text, its fits and starts the signs of a conflicted condition which was historical, not only pathological, it comes to more than meets the sceptical eye. Not, on a dispassionate reckoning, to the system to which he aspired in reaction to his own diffuseness, but to a record of struggle with forces which militate against all thinking in modern circumstances, reducing the will to passive submission.[16] To read the poetry in this way is not at all to diminish its impact as verse — only to describe its place in the long trajectory of its author's thinking. The pleasure of the parts cannot be abstracted from the effect of the whole without distorting the concerted achievement.

If the formative examples of Coleridge's meditative line are concerned with reconciling private imagination and public vocation, the mature examples witness the activity of imagination close up, as it were, in settings which try its power. They are, like "Frost at Midnight," reality tests, probing the sources of a presence beyond sensation. The image remains the sign of presence, its place between nature and the speaking self a constant preoccupation. In "This Lime-Tree Bower My Prison" (1797), Coleridge exercises his imagination as a substitute for a walk in the hills with friends which he missed when Sara dropped boiling milk on his foot. The experiment works: the poem compensates for their absence and the loss of natural impression. Or rather, its images supply a vicarious experience of sensation, leading him to conclude, in the spirit of "Frost at Midnight,"

> That Nature ne'er deserts the wise and pure;
> No plot so narrow, be but Nature there,
> No waste so vacant, but may well employ
> Each faculty of sense, and keep the heart
> Awake to Love and Beauty!

The dominance of sensation remains overwhelming in this resolution, with its implication of a passive and perhaps empty self which must be entertained. Yet the process of imagination as it is pursued in the poem tells a different story. What Coleridge formulates as the adequacy of Nature to human need actually appears as the sufficiency of imagination in a world where he finds himself out of step and isolated.

As in "Frost at Midnight," the difference between what the poem states and what it suggests makes for difficulties. It is simple enough to follow the argument to its conclusion, yet the result is peculiarly flat given the interest of the process. For it is the process that counts: how a voice finds means to evoke its situation, how it makes a place for itself in its confinement. Nature has little enough to do with it, on the evidence of the text and from the longer perspective imposed by "Dejection," the ode of 1802 which brings the meditative line to crisis with a resounding endorsement of the priority of self:

> I may not hope from outward forms to win
> The passion and the life, whose fountains are within.

Coleridge would come to this pass in time, against his earlier vision of a companionable Nature, resolving his poetic conversation while dramatizing his understanding of Locke's (and Hartley's) position. Such a recognition hardly invalidates the natural theology of the conversation poems, but it does implicate it in a process reaching beyond the conclusions of individual poems. "Dejection" provides, as I shall be arguing, a collective conclusion which modifies the sense of the earlier poems after the fact. These can be seen, from its clairvoyant altitude, as steps in the direction of an achieved understanding.

In the case of "This Lime-Tree Bower My Prison," such an approach yields a nearly deconstructive sense of the poem's working against its own conclusion. For what it discloses is the originality of an impulse resigned, in the voice of its author, to an omnipotent Nature. Coleridge gives the impression of denying his own power by subordinating it to an external ideal, and of defending this ideal in the argument against the living instance of his poem. For these images are products of an imagination whose agency is clearly indicated:

> They, meanwhile,
> Friends, whom I never more may meet again,
> On springy heath, along the hill-top edge,
> Wander in gladness, and wind down, perchance,
> To that still roaring dell, of which I told . . .

Far from a simple reflection of the impression, the poetic image has its source in a telling self. The picture it paints is hardly a reproduction, though the voice adopted for the purpose dissimulates this effect:

> The roaring dell, o'erwooded, narrow, deep,
> And only speckled by the mid-day sun;
> Where its slim trunk the ash from rock to rock
> Flings arching like a bridge; — that branchless ash,
> Unsunn'd and damp, whose few poor yellow leaves
> N'er tremble in the gale, yet tremble still,
> Fann'd by the water-fall! and there my friends
> Behold the dark green file of long lank weeds,
> That all at once (a most fantastic sight!)
> Still nod and drip beneath the dripping edge
> Of the blue clay-stone.

Here is Coleridge's pictorial power on the wing, at once true to a recognizable world and peculiar to his imagination of it. The dell is figured as a sort of deep romantic chasm; the dappled light and bridge of ash evoke a world of opposing qualities, of dispersion and mediation. All are features which recur in "Kubla Khan." The apparition of *asplenium scolopendrium*, or Adder's Tongue, as his note informs us, is orchestrated for an effect both ordinary and dramatic. Nature contributes the flora, but imagination provides the formative power of this act of poetic construction. What it is made to exemplify in the poem's conclusion hardly satisfies the sense of accomplishment.

The poet thus appears at odds with his own understanding when seen from the hindsight of "Dejection," where the initial feeling of likeness to the brewing storm — the incipient pathetic fallacy — is met by the recognition that

> we receive but what we give,
> And in our life alone does Nature live. . .

The recourse to Nature is depicted there in its essential relation to the poet's condition: his estrangement from others, his fear and self-consciousness. This configuration is constant in the conversation poems, but it is only gradually recognized and confronted. Consciousness is enabled at every stage by the commitment to a symbolic process which underwrites Coleridge's discourse of the self—a commitment to active imagination operating under guise of a benevolent Nature. Only tentatively exposed at first, under protection of an idea of secure dependence, this imagination appears in the margins, as it were, of the argument for Nature. In "This Lime-Tree Bower My Prison," the collusion is apparent in the passage where the poet's isolated bower is identified with the community from which he has been excluded. For he can make himself at home here in the absence of his friends only by grace of a ubiquitous, personal Nature of this kind. The pleasures of imagination are made to appear dependent on it, and an expression of collective vision:

> My gentle-hearted Charles! when the last rook
> Beat its straight path along the dusky air
> Homewards, I blest it! deeming its black wing
> (Now a dim speck, now vanishing in light)
> Had cross'd the mighty Orb's dilated glory,
> While thou stood'st gazing . . .

Active imagination is thus hitched to the lead of an all-providing Nature which binds up the tribe as it ministers to the individual in his need. The idea of Nature provides a refuge for imagination, and the poetic image is made to confirm its primordial power.

Control is the point of this arrangement, as it is evidently the point of Coleridge's approach to the image in his notes on the metaphysical in poetry. Only under influence of the idea did the image signify. The opening proposition of "Frost at Midnight" shows how this animating relation was expressed in a finer tone:

> The frost performs its secret ministry,
> Unhelped by any wind.

As I have proposed, the image amounts to a theorem which the poem tries out. The dominant idea proving difficult, the succeeding imagery loses its way as the poet's voice struggles for direction. In the effort to relax "the heavy burthen of Ideas and Imagery" under which he labored, he only seemed to be losing control of his means. Yet "Frost at Midnight" opened a horizon unrecognized before: the word as instrument of a dynamic inner consciousness, free of the shackles imposed by a governing idea. The word broke up the solidarity of image and idea, providing a way out of the congestion and forward to a fluid, "natural" voice. This solution was indebted to the process pursued in the earlier poems, relying for inspiration on the companionable forms of an ideal Nature. Yet it looked forward to "Dejection" in its realization of an imaginative agency free of the bondage of this Nature.

In "The Nightingale" (April, 1798), written not long after, the shift is pronounced. The opening imagery is not committed immediately to a sacramental Nature. It appears at first as an imaginary product — a negation rather than a reflection:

> No cloud, no relique of the sunken day
> Distinguishes the West, no long thin slip
> Of sullen light, no obscure trembling hues.
> Come, we will rest on this old mossy bridge!
> You see the glimmer of the stream beneath,
> But hear no murmuring: it flows silently,
> O'er its soft bed of verdure. All is still,
> A balmy night! And though the stars be dim,
> Yet let us think upon the vernal showers
> That gladden the green earth, and we shall find
> A pleasure in the dimness of the stars.

A change of air is perceptible in these lines, and not only through the Wordsworthian modulation of an established voice.[17] Compared with the cottage openings of "Reflections" and "The Eolian Harp," the sense of situation is deeply realized, by evocation instead of exposition. The speaker settles easily into his surroundings, enveloped in the forms of a familiar world. The drama is much the same as in "Frost at Midnight": isolation, malaise, the impulse to establish a dependable presence as a way of allaying fear. The silent spring and dim stars take the place of the secret ministry of frost, without dwelling on the idea. Distraction from the terrors of a still night follows the pattern of the earlier poem. Thinking through isolation, Coleridge finds his way to a source of identity outside sensation. The lulling timbre of his voice attests the influence of an active imagination akin to the one disclosed in "Frost at Midnight" as a resource against emptiness.

The abrupt announcement of the nightingale's song interjects, like the fluttering grate-film, a pregnant word and the reflections occasioned by it:

> And hark! The Nightingale begins its song,
> 'Most musical, most melancholy' bird!

The association sounds entirely natural: the displacement of the bird's song by Milton's evocative line follows the Wordsworthian cadence through before interrupting it in the next lines —

> A melancholy bird? Oh! idle thought!
> In Nature there is nothing melancholy.

The change of pace is subsequently imaged as the bird's fitful warble. The poet's suddenly tremulous voice is justified in this way by Nature's example:

> 'Tis the merry Nightingale
> That crowds, and hurries, and precipitates
> With fast thick warble his delicious notes,
> As he were fearful that an April night
> Would be too short for him to utter forth
> His love-chant, and disburthen his full soul
> Of all its music!

For in the intervening lines, he has gone off uncertainly in the direction of "some night-wandering man," a transparent image of identity and of his immediate poetic predicament. The nightingale comes to stand, in this context, for the anxiety of expression. Nature is confirmed, through the example of its song, as a deep reservoir of influence for the poet's act and identity. Playing to Wordsworth and his sister, his intended conversants, Coleridge thus evades the real import of the nightingale's intrusion into his Wordsworthian melody. For it is the word, not the song — "melancholy" and not the music of Nature — that he is trying to come to terms with here, though he manages to counteract the one with the other in deference to the faith of his friend.

To put it this way is to admit that the poem is conflicted. Its fealty to Wordsworth interferes with its psychological attentiveness, while its emphasis on the adequacy of Nature barely conceals the underlying doubts. Its peculiarity in the group is defined by its inclusion in *Lyrical Ballads* (1798), where it mimics Wordsworth's natural theology:

> A melancholy bird? Oh! idle thought!
> In Nature there is nothing melancholy.
> But some night-wandering man whose heart was pierced
> . . . .
> First named these notes a melancholy strain.
> And many a poet echoes the conceit;
> Poet who hath been building up the rhyme
> When he had better far have stretched his limbs
> Beside a brook in mossy forest-dell,
> By sun or moon-light, to the influxes
> Of shapes and sounds and shifting elements
> Surrendering his whole spirit . . .

The evasion of the Miltonic theme is indicated in the lines elided here, which identify the "night-wandering man" with the pathetic fallacy. This figure is conjured only to be dismissed, rather theoretically. The split in Coleridge's voice between the stream and the nightingale—a mellifluous Wordsworthian naturalism and a bright Miltonic melody—could hardly be more dramatic.[18] The triumph of the one over the other in this night scene is the most interesting feature of an obviously distracted performance.

For the critic in the poem, the nightingale's intrusive music intimates that the rhythm of the opening could not long contain the speaker's sense of purpose. Coleridge might mimic Wordsworth's pacific murmur, but another song too striking to ignore rang in his ear and inhabited his voice. It was immediately associated with the problem of pathetic fallacy confronted in "Frost at Midnight"—a sign of ambivalence in response to the Miltonic interjection. In the earlier poem, the "puny flaps and freaks" of the grate-film provided an image of the "idling Spirit." A stronger voice emerged only after the analogic dependence on sensation was exposed as a circular trick.

Here, the powerful allure of Milton's voice is implicated in the pathetic fallacy, effectively preserving a dominant reliance on Wordsworth. Yet what was the Wordsworthian voice but the pathetic fallacy writ smooth? Like the "night-wandering man" who first named the nightingale melancholy, Wordsworth indeed

> filled all things with himself,
> And made all gentle sounds tell back the tale
> Of his own sorrow . . .

An effort of disaffiliation is involved in Coleridge's treatment of the "night-wandering man," his weak and mimic self. But Milton may only be standing in for Wordsworth here, absorbing the blow sacrificially as it were, and so securing the elective affinity with the friend of choice. The speaker's difficulty in handling both voices is evident in the vacillations of the long opening stanza, which alternates without conviction between exalted Wordsworthian pronouncement and "Philomela's pity-pleading strains."

Milton's "melancholy" was the occasion of this uncertain *valse hésitation*, confirming what the word offered imagination. Sensation only led Coleridge out of himself, into a Wordsworthian naturalism which he could not sustain. The word led him back to his native powers of observation and association. Criticism assumed the character of poetic dreamwork here, imaging the poet's condition in its living relation with the voices of his principal models. The triumph of Wordsworth's example is dictated by circumstances and limited in advance by Coleridge's commitment of poetry to the ideal in a responsive social setting. The solution proposed in "The Nightingale" to the conflict of interest is a romantic voice, in a root sense—a modern version of romance, poised between a settled moral orientation and the significant detail observed under its auspices. Romance offered Coleridge an approach that was eminently "simple, sensuous, impassioned," in the Miltonic formula which he never tired of rehearsing. It was an approach readily adapted to that rendering of the extraordinary in human experience undertaken programmatically for the *Lyrical Ballads* volume. "The Nightingale" provides an inside account of the genesis of romance in Coleridge's poetic voice, against the background of his struggle with contending alternatives.

The tale of the Maid and the Nightingales, as it might be called, has evident similarities with *Christabel*, which Coleridge had been working on for some time. The figure of innocence unprotected in the forest by night, threatened by obscure danger, is here turned to a parable of Nature's plenum reminiscent of the conclusion of "Frost at Midnight":

> A most gentle Maid,
> Who dwelleth in her hospitable home
> Hard by the castle, and at latest eve
> (Even like a Lady vowed and dedicate
> To something more than Nature in the grove)
> Glides through the pathways; she knows all their notes,
> That gentle Maid! and oft, a moment's space,
> What time the moon was lost behind a cloud,
> Hath heard a pause of silence; till the moon
> Emerging, hath awakened earth and sky
> With one sensation, and these wakeful birds
> Have all burst forth in choral minstrelsy,
> As if some sudden gale had swept at once
> A hundred airy harps! And she hath watched
> Many a nightingale perched giddily
> On blossomy twig still swinging from the breeze,
> And to that motion tune his wanton song
> Like tipsy Joy that reels with tossing head.

The shift in the end from the Maid to the nightingales moves the poem toward its finale, where the infant Hartley serves again to affirm the instinctive bond with Nature, settling the poet's uncertainty. The recourse to romance thus proves transitional, transfiguring the bird's "most musical, most melancholy" strain into something acceptable to the poem's Wordsworthian dominant. The nightingale is made to celebrate

> With skirmish and capricious passagings,
> And murmurs musical and swift jug jug,
> And one low piping sound more sweet than all—

Yet this is hardly a Wordsworthian air. It represents rather a distinctive Coleridgean rendition of the sonorous Milton, his melancholy tune sublated as plangent piping. The romance disguised the metamorphosis, and Coleridge emerged with conviction in his voice, singing a song of his own in a way that Wordsworth was bound to approve.

The conversational idiom was confirmed in the process as fundamentally Miltonic, like the poetry of sensibility before it, reproducing the moral concern of its original in conjunction with the musical score reviled by modernist readers, Eliot foremost among them.[19] Its dramatic rhythmic effects and percussive consonance extended the past of English poetry in the face of Wordsworth's challenge. Coleridge would not abandon the traditional devices, though he would make every effort to submit them to a larger idea of poetic organization. On the basis of such an idea and of his own practice, he would resist the implications of Wordsworth's recurrence to a model of speech. Poetic diction had its justification in the history of the art, and as a refined instrument of argumentation. Overcome by Wordsworth's voice, he would have to seek for his own while struggling against its tidal drawing power. For this voice was as a second nature to him. Working free of it meant making a break with the idea of Nature vividly expressed along its fluid line.

For the Nature of the conversation poems is not only Wordsworth's companionable element tried by his friend's philosophical awareness, it is Wordsworth's voice, at least as Coleridge heard it. He cast himself as a harp to Wordsworth's wind—

> In silence listening, like a devout child,
> My soul lay passive, by thy various strain
> Driven as in surges now beneath the stars,
> With momentary stars of my own birth . . .

The tribute responds to the reading of the "poem to Coleridge" which would become *The Prelude*. The interdependence of their voices in the formation of the meditative verse usually identified with Wordsworth alone is one of the important demonstrations of recent scholarship, though it had long been recognized.[20] But it was an uneven relation, as Coleridge's image would suggest, with Wordsworth playing the dominant role. Yielding to this force of nature became an uncomfortable habit, and he resisted even as he affirmed the Nature which inspired it. His loss of poetic confidence coincides with his effort to identify the empirical mind at the bottom, as it seemed to him, of Wordsworth's naturalist creed. In renouncing vocation he yielded to a superior force. But he lost no time breaking with the passive mind and the instrumental Nature which it presumed.

The definitive expression of the break is "Dejection: An Ode" (1802), long regarded as his finest achievement in the conversational line — a culmination which was also a conclusion. In origin a verse epistle to Sara Hutchinson, the poem expresses a failure of relation which was deeply personal. Yet it is not as a confessional exercise that it has usually been appreciated. In finished (and familiar) form it became, as Reeve Parker puts it, an "epithalamic gesture" on the occasion of Wordsworth's marriage.[21] "Dejection" was addressed to Wordsworth via Sara Hutchinson, as the poem constantly recalls in its paraphrastic response to the "Intimations" ode. An answer to Wordsworth's naturalism, it takes advantage of the doubts developed there to make a graceful exit from illusions which Coleridge could no longer admit. The failure of the Nature celebrated in "Frost at Midnight" and "The Nightingale" cannot be separated, in this context, from the failure of relation in the social sphere of which Wordsworth had become the center. The awkward reality was dissimulated, for public consumption, by Coleridge's formulaic compliance with Wordsworth's terms. "Dejection" remains a testament of fealty even as it declares independence. Its reliance on the phrasing and cadence of "Intimations" is unmistakable:

> It were a vain endeavour,
> Though I should gaze for ever
> On that green light that lingers in the west:
> I may not hope from outward forms to win
> The passion and the life, whose fountains are within.

Wordsworth's aggravated reply to it in "The Leech-Gatherer" (later "Resolution and Independence") exhibits disgust with the dependency which it effectively continues.

Yet there is more to "Dejection" than acquiescence; more even than a companionable difference of understanding in place of the restless compliance of the earlier verse. Despite its Wordsworthian echoes, the ode fulfills the strong associative voice which emerged in "Frost at Midnight." The word which set it off rose here to the head of the text, appearing in the form of an epigram, and the opening stanza proceeded as a commentary on it. Dependence on Nature, and on the voice that transmitted it, was displaced in this way by an exegetical relation: a paradigm of the critic as poet. The prophecy of Sir Patrick Spence, like the prophecy of "stranger," became the point of entry for an associative treatment of estrangement:

> Well! If the Bard was weather-wise, who made
>   The grand old ballad of Sir Patrick Spence,
>   This night, so tranquil now, will not go hence
> Unroused by winds, that ply a busier trade
> Than those which mould yon cloud in lazy flakes,
> Or the dull sobbing draft, that moans and rakes
> Upon the strings of this Aeolian lute,
>   Which better far were mute.

Coleridge's effort to speak with a voice of his own is pronounced in these lines, which look consciously back on the achievement of the night pieces as well as "The Eolian Harp." The poem addresses the common situation of the conversational line in a tempestuous setting which plays counterpoint to its agonized threnody.

Counterpoint rather than correspondence, since the indifference of the elements is a part of the poet's complaint. Their alterity is acknowledged from the beginning—an advance on the enactment of its prototypes:

> And oh! that even now the gust were swelling,
>   And the slant night-shower driving loud and fast!
> Those sounds which oft have raised me, whilst they awed,
>   And sent my soul abroad,
> Might now perhaps their wonted impulse give,
> Might startle this dull pain, and make it move and live!

In the absence of some such impulse, poetry on the conversational model would be impossible. For its premise was the companionable Nature whose benevolence was affirmed against all the difficulties entailed in the demonstration. In "The Nightingale" the act of negation sustained the idiom. The presumption of a motivating agency was there to be refuted, but at least it was available for consideration. What would poetry be without Nature—without a steady source of impressions and what they offered discursive possibility? Once the trick of analogy was exposed, the exercise drifted from its bearings.

This problem haunts "Dejection" as it expands from negation toward other sources of inspiration. Originality, the self as source of a voice of its own, provided an answer but hardly an idea of how to go on:

> Ah! from the soul itself must issue forth
> A light, a glory, a fair luminous cloud
>   Enveloping the Earth —
> And from the soul itself must there be sent
> A sweet and potent voice, of its own birth,
> Of all sweet sounds the life and element!

For the joy which animated it was a thing of the past, as the speaker went on to tell. And so he was driven back on Wordsworth's example:

> There was a time when, though my path was rough,
>   This joy within me dallied with distress

The sense of impulse lost was forbidding. Only recourse to something known could allay the uncertainty and enable him to go on. Wordsworth's "Intimations" served as a guideline, returning him to a past which could be recapitulated, though only as an explanation of present failure. In the end he went back to the storm, whose raving gave resonance to his own. His rendering of it as a human voice extracted the last wine from the analogic press:

> Thou Actor, perfect in all tragic sounds!
> Thou mighty Poet, e'en to frenzy bold!
>   What tell'st thou now about?
>   'Tis of the rushing of an host in rout,
>   With groans of trampled men, with smarting wounds —
> At once they groan with pain, and shudder with the cold!
> But hush! there is a pause of deepest silence!
>   And all that noise, as of a rushing crowd,
>   With groans, and tremulous shudderings — all is over —
> It tells another tale, with sounds less deep and loud!

What the storm was finally made to tell was the terror of a human condition reduced to its essential state of suffering and isolation:

> 'Tis of a little child
> Upon a lonesome wild,
> Not far from home but she hath lost her way:
> And now moans low in bitter grief and fear,
> And now screams loud, and hopes to make her mother hear.

An act of poetic ventriloquism, this "scream/Of agony by torture lengthened out" emerges nevertheless as the expression of a more than private despair. The effort to situate suffering in the lineaments of history was true to the legacy of his meditative verse, which had concerned itself from the beginning with the social horizon of the individual experience.

Wordsworth's naturalism, and his emphasis on the nuclear group in isolation, can be said on the evidence of the poetry to have distracted Coleridge from this social horizon. The return to the domestic fold in the resolution of all of the conversation poems until "Dejection" follows a course which is basically Wordsworthian, as against the descent into the fallen world at the end of the "Reflections." The loss of the broadly social scope of some of the earlier (and concurrent) meditative verse is nearly definitive of the conversational line. Coleridge was successful for a period in writing on its more personal premises, but the strain shows nearly everywhere, and the effort exhausted his poetic faith. Achieved as they are, the conversation poems seem less resolved and convincing than commentators have usually insisted. As a record of struggle with an appealing idea of Nature they have a permanent value. As a search for a satisfying poetic idiom they show what was involved in the development of the romantic voice. As poems of a particular moment and place, they participate memorably in Coleridge's construction of the intelligibility of a difficult time. But only "Dejection" among them manages to include enough to escape a limiting interiority. Redeemed by attention to process—by the consciousness which they bring to bear—they remain deeply conflicted and problematic, for better and worse.

The discursive instincts revealed by the conversation poems show Coleridge to have been responsive in a special sense of the word. He wrote against a background, to an established context, and he lost his sense of direction where the background receded, as it did with his uncertainty about Nature. Conversation as a discursive convention provided a context, but it too often served as a pretext for monologic encounter with an elusive idea. His associative voice might be thought to epitomize his monologue at its best. But even here, he was typically responding to a word, or a line of verse or a poem. His poetics of response, as it might be called then, began from the language of the other: from Wordsworth or Milton, or just "stranger" as it evoked his own situation. It was an art of private commentary. Like his lectures on poetry, philosophy, and the fine arts, it responded to an existing discourse, often echoing its sources, straying in places into plagiarism. Wordsworth saw the poetics of response as an expression of compulsive dependency, and so in the conversation poems it occasionally appears. Yet it is just this responsiveness that gives Coleridge's writing its peculiar sense of relation: what confers range and interest on his concerns. He proved his own best critic, in the poems and outside them. He listened to his voice and learned its ways. In resigning poetic aspiration he was responding to the critical reflection mounting in a line of meditative verse which underwrites his developed thinking on the art of poetry.

7

The Metaphysical Solution

Coleridge's poems of the supernatural, as they are usually called, challenged every expectation yet survived the doubts of Southey and Wordsworth to be celebrated as the epitome of the romantic idiom.[1] Their strange symbolic procedure, mixing romance and a species of realism, confused readers from the start; it is through defining the procedure that criticism has long sought to justify "The Rime of the Ancient Mariner," in particular, and *Christabel* and "Kubla Khan" as well. Justification remains, at the distance of nearly two centuries now, the order of the day. Empson's observation late in his career that the "Ancient Mariner" "really does need rescuing if possible" is indicative. In the age of psycholinguistic reading it had come to "reek of false sentiment and cranky self-righteousness and a deceitful pretence of infantilism."[2] Richards lay behind the renewed scepticism, at close remove. Writing in 1929, he had made the poem an exemplum of the belief problem which confronted modern readers. Coleridge's great white bird flew in the face of reason, but it hardly mattered since "the question of belief or disbelief, in the intellectual sense, never arises when we are reading well."[3] Intellectual disengagement was his version of "that willing suspension of disbelief for the moment, which constitutes poetic faith" (*BL* II, 6). In effect, Richards exonerated Coleridge of any belief at all, freeing readers to make of the poem what they would.

What was made of it proved remarkable considering the liabilities of this approach. Warren's account of the imagination at work in a sacramental nature, with sun and moon providing symbolic support, was a classic of the new criticism. It built on the naturalism of the conversation poems while extending Richards on Coleridge on imagination. Meaning was displaced from the Mariner to his author, where it belonged, but the essential message was preserved.[4] Empson's effort to connect the text with Coleridge's images of the slave trade, and his identification of neurotic guilt as its virtual theme, aimed to save the "Ancient Mariner" for the psychologically minded audience cultivated by his teacher (*CV*, 25–81). Jerome McGann, writing from a related sense of past dispensation and present possibility, has recently proposed to save it for an audience of a different mind.[5] The poem's form is seen to shadow the Higher Criticism; its marginalia and critical apparatus were meant to be recognized as a secular equivalent of the new Biblical exegesis, with the implication that traditional ballads amounted to native scripture. Coleridge invited his readers to participate actively in the construction of the poem's meaning, which was indeterminate by design. It thus becomes a parable of interpretive relativity in an uncertain world: teachable material. Cardinal Newman is produced to damn Coleridge's heathenish "liberty of speculation," disposing of his awkward religious convictions as the brave new world of perspectivism comes into view.

There are slippery slopes at every turn in this self-regarding itinerary. It is of interest in the present context mainly for its unwitting reflection of Richards's agenda after two critical generations. The metric features which recall the balladic imitation at every stop are long gone; such was the way of meter as the motion of meaning. The seeming incongruity of a sixteenth-century exploration narrative (as McGann regards it) in this popular idiom goes unremarked as a result.[6] Exegetical imitation displaces poetic imitation as the obvious formal reference of the "Ancient Mariner" is sacrificed to an arcane reorientation completed with the addition of glosses in *Sibylline Leaves* (1817). Neither Coleridge nor his readers ever imagined the poem as a commentary on commentary, on the available evidence at least. Justifying its procedure so hypothetically means defending old privileges on new grounds instead of accepting the thoroughgoing revaluation which the case would seem, by the lights of Ricardian reading, to require.

I would suggest that if reading has become as arbitrary (and as pointless) as McGann believes, it is high time to abandon the Ancient Mariner and his author altogether. For the understanding which both are concerned to transmit really would be, in that case, "only qualitatively less alien to ourselves than the ideology which supports the *Iliad* or the writings of Confucius" (*MAM*, 54). Poetry itself has no vital place in so deracinated a world. Richards had preserved it from corrosive scrutiny by stripping it of engaged intellectual aspiration, demeaning it to "attitudes." Coleridge's poetic faith became, in his hands, poetic free-play. The next step is only incrementally more isolating: the notion is consigned to the museum by McGann, for whom it is part of "Romantic ideology . . . a historical phenomenon of European culture, generated to save the 'traditional concepts, schemes, and values' of the Christian heritage" (*MAM*, 65). All that is now fortunately past, though it remains interesting for what can be made of it in support of "enlightened" understanding. If it is all a question of where one stands the instance of the past hardly matters of course, and readers enjoy a perfect freedom to interpret as they please. Which is, not quite coincidentally, just what Coleridge's ballad encourages them to believe under the auspices of the new historicism.

Freedom of this vacuous kind, akin to the familiar anomie of deconstruction, was perhaps the inevitable destination of psycholinguistic reading from the start. An historicism appropriated after the fact cannot save it; it is as instinctively antihistorical as the splitting of "emotive language" from the living tongue and its past. The canons of evidence employed in McGann's demonstration intimate as much.[7] As for the "social and historical resource" which he offers in place of the poem's testament, there are surely other texts more revealing for the purpose. What is left of the "Ancient Mariner" in the wake of Cambridge English is a heightened sense of a problem felt by readers from the start. "Belief" does not approach it, and poetic faith, though an idea of enduring value, appeals perhaps too openly to the modern retreat from judgment. I have considered its theoretical dimension under the heading of the problem of representation for an expressive poetics. The "Ancient Mariner" drives the conflict at the heart of Coleridge's poetics to bald contradiction. Against the background of his developing idea, it can be seen to mark a stage of trial and investigation.

What readers have responded to in the poem from its first version — what Wordsworth himself recognized, and what Lamb noticed in a letter deploring Southey's pseudonymous attack on it — is the power of Coleridge's imagery.[8] Through the general dismay about the character of the protagonist and the peregrinations of the narrative, this note rings clear. Commentators have occasionally missed it: the reviewer of *Lyrical Ballads* (1798) for the *British Critic* remarked on the "confusion of images, which loses all effect from not being quite intelligible," a complaint echoed in some later reviews.[9] But the poem's imagistic qualities continued to compel attention, as Richard Haven shows in his survey of its following in the century after. The praise is all for the inspiration of particular passages, despite the ill-sorting of means and ends:

> In spell poetry [Coleridge] is far more potent than any writer of the present age . . . In his "Ancient Mariner," the solemn helplessness of the narrator, condemned to live amidst supernatural horrors, is awfully expressed . . . How the image of the strange loneliness strikes upon the heart, when he with the fatal ship and her ghastly crew burst into the sea, "where God himself" scarcely seemed present! And with how pure a thrill of delight are we refreshed, in the midst of this terrible witchery, when the poor creature, whom superior power has enchanted, sees the water-snakes sporting in the sun, which at happier seasons would have filled him with disgust, bursts into a blessing of these "happy living things" . . . .   (*MNC*, 367)

The eloquence of such reports makes an exhilirating contrast to the prickly dismay of prosaic readers from Wordsworth to the present day. The scope of the poem's celebrity—its enduring appeal, the record of illustration and translation—tells the story of its real force.

The "Ancient Mariner" most resembles *Christabel* and "Kubla Khan" in this respect: it depends on striking images for its effect. Lowes led the way to recognizing that these images reflect an active, apparently unconscious working through of Coleridge's reading and observation.[10] In the poetic setting their intensity is consuming and the conflict with other poetic values pronounced. Thus, the character of the Mariner as Wandering Jew—something essential to the conception, on the author's later telling (*CN* I, 45n)—simply goes missing against the hallucinatory background of natural extremity and supernatural intervention. Since the protagonist counted for so much in the balladic line which the author was imitating, the conflict was felt by Wordsworth to be a fault. To put a point to his objection: if Coleridge's idea of the Mariner was so definitely conceived, why was it so obscure in the poem?

There is no satisfactory answer to such a question. The poem as it stands is conflicted: the same imagistic power which is the source of its appeal subverts the narrative realization, investing the detail at the expense of the larger pattern. The "Ancient Mariner" exemplifies, in short, the difficulty of striking a balance between image and idea, as Coleridge would soon be formulating the problem. Perhaps because the poem's texture, condensing a wealth of association, "consumed too much of the vital & idea-creating force in distinct, clear, full made images" (CN, 1016). Its associative delirium was at odds with thematic development in the traditional ballad. Two senses of poetic possibility met here without successful coordination. Two main lines of response witness the inner conflict from without.

Coleridge's poems of the supernatural are "metaphysical" in this sense: they confirm the triumph of image over idea in the reformed poetic discourse envisioned in the opening of "Frost at Midnight." Evidence is sparse, but it is a hypothesis worth entertaining at least that Coleridge had these poems in mind in his meditation on "metaphysical Solution," with all it brought to the issue of poetic value. Since they also represent, on most accounts, the distinctive line of his verse production, their limitations may be thought to have contributed to his renunciation of vocation. Certainly the discouragement about *Christabel* was important; the disclaimer of "any supposed *poetic* merit" for "Kubla Khan" lay down the same line. Coleridge attended to the image from the first entries of his notebooks, in opposition to the pictorial practice of Erasmus Darwin, then to the metaphysical particularity of Gray and Collins. Having tried out experimentally an idiom which took full advantage of the image, he abandoned the effort as unworthy. The chronology and course of his meditation on the elder languages, ideas, and poetry support an inferential association of theory and practice at the turning point of his career as poet-critic. Such an association goes far to explain the larger bearing of "metaphysical Solution" and "metaphysical poetry" in the important notes already discussed. If these are taken to refer by implication to his problems with the "Ancient Mariner" and then with *Christabel*, his struggle with the "metaphysical" can be seen to reflect a personal struggle for poetic direction.

The story of the image begins with Coleridge's response to Darwin's *Botanic Garden*, beginning from a note of 1795–96, when the conversational idiom was just underway: "Dr Darwin's Poetry, a succession of Landscapes or Paintings—it arrests the attention too often, and so prevents the rapidity necessary to pathos.—it makes the great little.—seems to have written his poem as Painters who of beautiful objects—take—Studies" (CN I, 132). In her commentary, Coburn introduces Darwin's distinction between poet and painter as a plausible source for the note: "The Poet is happier in describing successive scenes; the Painter in representing stationary ones" (*CN*, 132n). Against the grain of this proposition, Coleridge characterizes the pictorial approach of Darwin's verse as unpoetic. Darwin's distinction of the poet's act only added the element of time to the descriptive idea — *ut pictura poesis* remained his premise. The objection raised here is the more interesting as the problem he describes is one which would afflict the "Ancient Mariner" and *Christabel* as well. In both, narrative development is distracted. Fluidity and empathy are sacrificed to overpowering images: to polar ice and evil eye. These become the point of the exercise, and the detailed accounting of Lowes, Coburn, Beer, and others shows how much their author had invested in them. Considering his objection to Darwin's pictorialism, how did he come to this pass? For the images of the "Ancient Mariner" owe something to Darwin's example,[11] and *Christabel* and "Kubla Khan" follow suit, taking pictorial expression to exotic ends.

Coleridge's "Preface" to his early *Poems on Various Occasions* (1796) had laid stress on recognition and empathy in the sort of verse that he was writing. This was the basic statement of his expressive poetics. He was keenly aware of the snare of "querulous egotism," yet defended the display of himself as more forthright than the presumptuous modesty of more indirect forms of address, which only seemed to be impersonal. The monodic voice of his early effusions proceeded on the assumption, noted some time before, that "Poetry without egotism [was] comparatively uninteresting" (*CN* I, 62). Darwin violated this principle, and his retentive accumulation of detail exemplified the result. Such was the tendency of descriptive poetry which was not animated by the spirit of the speaker bringing himself to bear on everything he observed. The poet was indeed "a man speaking to men," and what he owed them first of all was a sense of himself.

Coleridge's earlier verse fails on this count, though not through a precocious tendency to overdraw the image. It is congested with disjointed imagery which leaves no clear impression, either of the speaker or of his object. Full of poetical "stereotype pieces" of the sort he would later condemn, it manages to be pictorial nevertheless, in an entirely conventional way. An incidental example: "Lines to a Beautiful Spring in a Village" portrays in passing the rustic lad and his water-bearing lass in a familiar attitude of parting. The image of the tumultuous stream in the poem's conclusion is pursued for what it yields as a reflection of the hard course of the speaker's experience — to no very good effect. Neither the picture nor the reflection comes clear. Already in the contrived analogy the disabling conflict of image and idea is apparent. A better-known instance of the same, in the sonnet "To the River Otter," included in *Poems* (1797), has since Wimsatt's essay served to show how Coleridge solved the conflict, surpassing the unsatisfactory example of Bowles.[12] It also shows how he improved the resolution of his own earlier efforts, achieving a clarity of impression apparent in both the speaker and his object. Here the image is plain enough, without distracting from the self-presentation at the heart of the enterprise.

Yet the conflict was enduring, as "Frost at Midnight" would soon testify. The collusion of the poet and the scene promoted by Wimsatt has a more limited bearing than usually conceded, representing only a temporary accommodation in a long struggle for poetic dominion. Even the conversation poems seldom find a balance that can be sustained. Descriptive and expressive functions do not often coincide successfully in them. If the point was to move easily from the one to the other, it turned out to be a difficult trick. Darwin's pictorial idiom would prove attractive after all—a refuge despite its abdication of higher poetic value. Beer has made a great deal of Darwin's influence on Coleridge's idea of nature;[13] his persistence in Coleridge's voice suggests something more. The imagery of vegetative reproduction in the second stanza of "The Eolian Harp" is derived from Darwin. Its particularity is absorbing, and quite different from the occasional imagery of the poem's opening. There is continuity of attention, yet this stanza leads Coleridge away from the familiar address and conversational tone which he had adopted. The pictorial approach might be unsatisfying in itself, but "distinct, clear, full made images" were compelling, and worth trying out in a setting which began by honoring "querulous egotism" and the priority of the ideal.

Some two years after, the "Ancient Mariner" would draw extensively on Darwin's arctic imagery and also, it seems, on his distinction of mania and delirium. "The excess of fancy is delirium, of imagination mania," as Beer cites Crabb Robinson quoting Coleridge viva voce.[14] Beer infers that this delirious fancy was an important premise of the poem, citing DeQuincey's story "that Coleridge, shortly before writing [it], had been thinking of writing a poem on delirium, confounding its own dream-scenery with external things, and connected with the imagery of high latitudes." Whatever the connection between the psychological idea and the program worked out with Wordsworth, the finished piece answers directly to this description. DeQuincey's is a compelling version of what was involved, accounting in a uniquely satisfying way for the poem's intensity. As a case study in delirium, Coleridge's experiment would represent a contribution to his picture of the life of the imagination at a time when he was already occupied with it elsewhere.

As a portrait of human extremity the "Ancient Mariner" answers to another, related agenda. Speaking of the drama and public taste in a vein recalling the argument of the "Preface," Coleridge would deplore the reliance of modern playwriting on conventional stage language. One cause of "the diseased disposition" of the drama he assigned to

> the security, the comparative equability, and ever increasing sameness of human life. Men are now so seldom thrown into wild circumstances, and violences of excitement, that the language of such states, the laws of association of feeling with thought, the starts and strange far-flights of the assimilative power on the slightest and least obvious likeness present-ed by thoughts, words or objects—these are all judged of by authority, not by actual experience—by what men have been accustomed to regard as symbols of these states, and not the natural symbols, or self-manifesta-tions of them. (*LR* II, 50)

Here is a context that would make sense of a display of delirium for poetic effect. With Shakespeare's drama as his case in point, Coleridge defended the display of "wild circumstances" and the "states" they excited on broadly cultural grounds. The extraordinary was only that part of the ordinary suppressed by modern life, to apply the terms he would soon be using to account for his own effort in this direction. Expanding the receding horizon of the real was Coleridge's assignment in *Lyrical Ballads* (1798), as Chapter XIV would summarize it (*BL* II, 5-6). The defense of Shakespeare's language underway in his lecture looks back on that early adventure, justifying long after the fact the wayward course of a far-fetched Mariner.

Coleridge had of course tried his hand at writing for the stage, and if the "Ancient Mariner" falls prey to problems of dramatic con-struction akin to those which afflict *Osorio*, it cannot be said to yield to a conventional idea of dramatic language. The peculiar voice of the poem might indeed be considered an attempt to find a modern equiva-lent of Shakespeare's language of extremity in *Lear*, *Hamlet* and *Mac-beth*. As his lecture develops the case, Shakespeare's tragic dialect combined "the language of men" with what he called "the language of nature," "not merely recalling the cold notion of the thing, but expressing the reality of it, being itself a part of that which it manifests." Drawing on the sense of language which he had subsequently formed, Coleridge's discussion of Shakespeare evokes the Mariner as protagonist of his own interior drama. Like Lear's, his voice is full of the language of nature. It takes the elements as the real world, and gives them a powerfully expressive presence in human terms:

> And through the drifts the snowy clifts
> Did send a dismal sheen:
> Nor shapes of men nor beasts we ken —
> The ice was all between.

The world outside assumes human dimension even where it appears utterly alien. Yet there is nothing artificial about the Mariner's approach to the elements. They are rendered in the language of men as it might have been rehearsed in the old ballads.

Darwin was one source among others for Coleridge's portrait of the language of nature; the leading source for his notion of a delirium confusing mind with matter. The "Ancient Mariner" explores Darwin's pictorial poetics for its author's own purposes, with a critical eye to the place of the image in human experience. The poem is not "about" this, nor does its imagism have much to do with the meaning pronounced by the protagonist and endorsed by his author. But it has something important to do with Coleridge's developing poetics, in practice and in theory. For here he gave real latitude to the image, identifying it with a delirious state in an effort to render the delusions of extremity actual to an audience used to melodrama and the artificial expression which went with it. Such an approach afforded him the opportunity to experiment with the image under cover, as it were—insulated from the Mariner's suffering, at one remove from his desperate attachment to natural impressions. The drama of the protagonist's salvation transpires through his sublation of a naturalism which the author was confronting elsewhere in his own person.

The poem is then of a piece with the conversation poems, whose meditation it may be thought to interrupt. It resumes their insistent position that "Nature ne'er deserts the wise and pure" even as it tells a horrific tale of man crucified by the elements. The displacement of author by narrator is prophylactic, sparing Coleridge the terrors of exposure. He might have made more of it, and could perhaps have done so a few years later, after working his way through a tentative naturalism to something deeper. Yet even the mature Coleridge would add a marginal summary to reify the supernatural machinations of his Mariner's tale, seeming to endorse the visions of delirium, adding to the confusion. His ambivalence is the root of the problem, but it is a genuine reflection of mixed feelings. As it stands, the poem gives narrative expression to his simultaneous sense of the truth of Nature and the horror of experience. The latter is interpreted sacramentally by the Mariner and his author, but the essential recognition is of the burden of life in the inhuman elements, in an unfathomed world.

The Mariner's psychodrama is invested from the beginning in a glittering eye which would become the serpent's eye of *Christabel*—an eye both fixing and fixated. It is the imaging eye of "Reflections" loosed on the world, free to pursue its private vision; the half-closed eye of "the Eolian Harp" uncorrected by intrusive others. The manic eye of a lime-tree bower prison, conjuring elaborate trains of connected imagery in compensation of lost beauties, turns delirious in this disjointed production of fancy on the run. The Mariner's eye is "bright" like the searing images of a tale of high noon, white cold, and waves "a-flame." His tale is flooded with lights of every description, and these shine with the menace of truth for the Wedding-Guest and his author.

The apparition of the Mariner, posited *ab nihilo* like Melville's Ishmael in line one, takes the Wedding-Guest off-guard, fixing him in his steps. Fixation is the main event for Mariner and Wedding-Guest alike. It is all in the eye, as the gloss would underline: "The Wedding-Guest is spell-bound by the eye of the old sea-faring man, and constrained to hear his tale." In the beginning, fixation means a child-like abdication of will, the inertia of sitting on a stone: the attitude of fancy as it appears on the "midway slope" of the "Eolian Harp." This is the stance of the Mariner as well, in the world he describes. Without character or intentional presence, he is a recorder of facts—Locke's passive intelligence or Gradgrind's mental automaton. Such is the real exposure of the experiencing subject in an instrumental Nature. Fixation means subjection.

The world of the Mariner is a clockwork where things happen mechanically, on their own:

> The sun came up upon the left,
> Out of the sea came he!

> And he shone bright, and on the right
> When down into the sea.

There is nothing to be done with it but record the fact. Yet the facts are strangely charged from the start, and not only by a kind of primitive animism. Dawn and dusk divide the sphere with Manichean intensity, while "up" and "down," "left" and "right" partition a continuum into conflicting terms. A world of luminous impressions is transmitted as dramatic images which fix the Wedding-Guest against his will, subjecting him to the delirium of a man obsessed. He becomes in his turn the "subject" or "I," vulnerable in its passivity, which succumbs to the power of images. Nature dominates his response through its human agent, the Mariner's eye. The tale of terror on the high seas, obviously driven, accentuated by a drumming meter, elicits a different response from witnesses at a certain distance. Its delirium is identified with the point of view, coloring the images which it relays. Passive perception is revealed in the process as far from neutral, or impersonal—much as in "The Eolian Harp" where

> through my half-clos'd eye-lids I behold
> The sunbeams dance, like diamonds, on the main,
> And tranquil muse upon tranquillity;
> Full many a thought uncall'd and undetain'd,
> And many idle flitting phantasies,
> Traverse my indolent and passive brain . . .

The fantasy does not stand inspection. Proceeding from passive perception, it turns out to be all in the "I." The image of the Eolian harp— the vision of Nature itself—proves a wilful delusion. In the "Ancient Mariner," the vision is spun out at length and the delusion committed to an extreme, yet still human point of view.

These poems have in common the memory of Darwin, and both answer his claim that "the Poet writes principally to the eye" with an instance.[15] Writing to the eye meant reproducing the lineaments of Nature under human auspices, with everything imported of human feeling and interest. Darwin's verse showed the consequences of so simple a theorem. The sublime creation myth of his *Botanic Garden* observed the vegetable kingdom through the lens of Greek cosmogony: the Goddess of Botany related the unfolding of the elements in a manner (and in a voice) which verged on unwitting parody. Poetic painting was defended in this context as an exclusive ideal. Writing in defense of it, Darwin charged that

> Mr. Pope has written a bad verse in the Windsor Forest, "And Kennet swift for silver Eels *renown'd*." The word renown'd does not present the idea of a visible object to the mind, and is thence prosaic. But change this line thus, "And Kennet swift, where silver Graylings *play*," and it becomes poetry, because the scenery is then brought before the eye. (*BG* II, Interlude i)

If Coleridge attended to this passage at all he found the poetic equivalent of Horne Tooke's harrowing of the tongue. The substitution of "Graylings" for Pope's "Eels" vividly displays the effort to include sensation immediately in words — to reduce language to a reproduction of sensation. The confusion of word and image reverts ultimately to Locke's empirical ideal. Darwin was pursuing the implications, defending *ut pictura poesis* on the original grounds that only the pictorial part of language was suitable for poetic purpose.

The "Ancient Mariner" looks back to the *Botanic Garden*, if we follow De Quincey's account of its beginnings, identifying delirium with poetic painting, turning Darwin's characterization of excessive fancy against his insipid versifying. Coleridge's experiment is further connected, I have supposed, with the metaphysical in poetry as the idea is developed in his notebooks. This line of observation would associate the poem, at a distance, with the subsequent move against Locke's epistemological naturalism. It can hardly be considered a critique of empiricism, but it is certainly involved through its exercise of Darwin's assumptions in a preliminary cleaving of image and idea. Coleridge's engagement with these matters is best approached through a passage from the same prose interlude of Darwin's poem that he relied on in an early note:

> It has been already observed, that the principal part of the language of poetry consists of those words, which are expressive of the ideas, which we originally received by the organ of sight; and in this it nearly indeed resembles painting; which can express itself in no other way, but by exciting the ideas or sensations belonging to the sense of vision. . . . The painter, to produce a strong effect, makes a few parts of his picture large, distinct, and luminous, and keeps the remainder in shadow, or even beneath its natural size and colour, to give eminence to the principal

figure. This is similar to the common manner of poetic composition, where the subordinate characters are kept down, to elevate and give consequence to the hero or heroine of the piece.   (*BG* II, Interlude iii)

Coburn's suggestion that he drew on this interlude (*CN*, 132n) would perhaps confirm it as his original source for the idea of the metaphysical in poetry. The sense of conflict between principal figure and detail, as reflected in his notes, is clearly expressed here in a passage which had attracted his consideration. The elder languages were fitter for poetry "because they expressed only prominent ideas with clearness, others but darkly" (*CN* I, 383). In contrast, the clarity of metaphysical poetry was the undifferentiated light of nature, and it gave "most pleasure when only generally & not perfectly understood." The pictorial idiom of "Gray's *Bard* & Collins's odes" invited unreflective browsing. Metaphysical solution of this kind would soon be accounted "a great Vice" (*CN* I, 673) and "distinct, clear, full made Images" the natural enemy of "*original* thought" (*CL* I, 1016).

Now the terms of these notes yield a penetrating reflection on Darwin's idiom. The pictorial hypothesis from which they are apparently developed actually exposes the shortcomings of Darwin's pictorial practice. Reading him is an ordeal, not least for the absence of leading ideas, despite the large premise of the work. The argument at the head of each canto effectively abstracts the ideal content; browsing is as much as the verse allows. The imagery is both "full made" and congested, as in late baroque painting, and if there are "principal figures" its profusion still manages to distract from them. The poem made a strong impression on Coleridge, galvanizing his critical imagination; it is possible that he is speculating in his notes from a lingering sense of Darwin's congestion, as well as from the pictorial pretence. "Metaphysical" occurs in the interlude just cited, in the conventional sense of "abstract" — "It is a metaphysical question, and requires more attention than Sir Joshua has bestowed upon it" — and in this sense the term certainly applies to the *Botanic Garden* as a whole. The disjunction of pictures and argument makes it a tedious exercise in fancy on the run. Something of the same abstraction afflicted Darwin's antecedents in the poetry of sensibility. If Coleridge had Darwin in mind in the notes, as seems likely, this sense of "metaphysical" is perhaps involved.

The abstract and the supernatural meet in the lexical history of the word and occasionally in the "Ancient Mariner" as well. The

Albatross appears in a fog, the ice splits and the wind blows up, the bird follows:

> In mist or cloud, on mast or shroud,
> It perched for vespers nine;
> Whiles all the night, through fog-smoke white,
> Glimmered the white moon-shine.

The apparition remains "metaphysical" to the end of its brief life, and beyond. It hovers uncertainly in the Mariner's delirium between nature and the supernatural. The details are clear enough but the image is significantly obscured. The trappings of the sublime evoke a numinous presence and speculation about the Albatross's influence on the ship's course extends the impression that it is more than a bird. The equivocation is important not only for the resolution of the drama but for the sense of the Mariner's delirium. The association of the killing with the subsequent dying might be regarded as a primitive superstition or an allegorical device. Or it might be regarded, in light of other features of the narrative, as a delirious symptom—a confusion of the *post hoc ergo propter hoc* variety, induced by a frantic imagination. The Mariner's search for meaning raises "metaphysical questions," in Darwin's sense: imponderables, or "abstractions" in the empiricist acceptation. His narrative is further metaphysical, in Coleridge's notational employment, by its solution of thinking, which incorporates echoes of the *Botanic Garden.*

The sacramental reading has every claim to authority but it does not effectively contain these inferences. The superstitious Mariner undergoes a conversion and the Albatross appears after the fact, a harbinger of the spiritual crucifixion or Death in Life which lies in store for him. Such is the tale as the Wedding-Guest hears it. What Coleridge emphasizes at the same time is the disjunction between event and interpretation, and the anxiety attendant on perception in extremis. Obsessive images expose the excessive fancy of the Mariner for what it is, and there is no mistaking the cause. Parched to a furious pitch, he strains to make out his approaching destiny:

> At first it seemed a little speck,
> And then it seemed a mist;
> It moved and moved, and took at last
> A certain shape, I wist.

> A speck, a mist, a shape, I wist!
> And still it neared and neared:

The uncertainty and mounting apprehension are perhaps the poem's most powerful strokes. For here the drama converges in the fevered mind of the narrator, and his author's horror of isolation and estrangement is relayed in a convincing voice. The crescendo of repetition is particularly effective.

What the Mariner sees is only gradually resolved into a settled form. His helplessness in the face of an alien nature is translated by what might be called the drama of the image. Is this the ship that will rescue him from certain death? Or is it Death come to wrench from him the vestiges of life? Annihilation lies at the root of this wild display of speculation; here Coleridge approached his own deepest fears. The infusion of the deranged victim's wondering keeps the impression vividly before us as the image is clarified:

> Alas! (thought I, and my heart beat loud)
> How fast she nears and nears!
> Are those her sails that glance in the Sun,
> Like restless gossameres?
> Are those her ribs through which the Sun
> Did peer, as through a grate?
> And is that Woman all her crew?
> Is that a Death? and are there two?
> Is Death that woman's mate?

In this passage Coleridge answers Darwin's arid pictorialism with the image as seen from a dramatic point of view. It is never dissociated from an animating way of seeing, nor from the question of what is being seen. For it was the process of perception that brought poetry to life, not a gallery of pictures. The image was valuable as it revealed (and was revealed by) the reflecting subject.

In his terror, the Mariner's eye is overcome by the impressions of a nature with which he would identify his destiny in the end. He becomes a figure of submission with some kinship to the Coleridge of "Frost at Midnight." His endurance is obviously inspirational as the Wedding-Guest sees it and as his author apparently meant it. Yet the fixation of this gaze is a sign of his condition, and it is associated along the way with a discredited poetic model. The Mariner intuits with the empirical eyes of Darwin, taking the world for a series of snapshots.

Indeed, he sometimes sees what Darwin had taught him to see — the floating ice, the mists and winds refer to the *Botanic Garden* as well as to Shelvocke. What Coleridge shows us is something more, however, than an album of the weather at sea. His poem explores seeing, the process as well as the product of the Mariner's ordeal. This emphasis is especially pronounced in the central sequence, with its pointed attention to the eye:

> I looked upon the rotting sea,
> And drew my eyes away;
> I looked upon the rotting deck,
> And there the dead men lay.
>
> I looked to heaven, and tried to pray;
> . . . .
> I closed my lids, and kept them close,
> And the balls like pulses beat;
> For the sky and the sea, and the sea and the sky
> Lay like a load on my weary eye,
> And the dead were at my feet.

Looking everywhere for refuge, the Mariner's eye lights at last on the lowly water-snakes, and in their seething motion he finds something which responds to his feeling. The deep significance of this is obscure, but the animation is clearly the point, against a background of stasis. It is when the Mariner begins to see in a more than merely passive way that he is released from his bondage — from a world of predatory forms.

As a meditation on the image, this speaks cryptically of the hazards of "single vision and Newton's sleep." The Mariner's isolation and estrangement are associated with his fixation, while his release commits him to a sacramental view of nature that would save the image, under other auspices, for human discovery and expression. He is "refreshed with rain" as the world comes dramatically alive. *Natura naturans* displaces the *natura naturata* of fixed perspective and particular objects. The ship is transported by supernatural machinery and the Mariner lapses into trance. The conclusion of agents and motives in this part of the poem is disconcerting, but it does not diminish the force of his escape from the oppressive stasis of the line. Identified with his transgression, the doldrums remain a state of seeing as much as a state of being. The cathartic tempest which blows up to free him from his bondage of vision dissolves the boundaries. What he sees now is an animated Nature whose fury recalls him to participation—to life itself:

> The upper air burst into life!
> And a hundred fire-flags sheen,
> To and fro they were hurried about!
> And to and fro, and in and out,
> The wan stars danced between.
>
> And the coming wind did roar more loud,
> And the sails did sigh like sedge;
> And the rain poured down from one black cloud;
> The Moon was at its edge.

The animation of the Mariner's voice contributes to a spectacle which images his condition. No longer alien, this nature expresses something essential in his response. The reintegrated world displays a more than mechanical motion; its element is fluid kinesis and interactivity.

It is not necessary for my purposes to follow the Mariner to his conclusion. It is only important to notice that the change of air in the wake of his release makes him an altogether different painter of the world of things, one who sees with an inner eye. Of the spirits of the dead companions ascending he observes:

> Around, around, flew each sweet sound,
> Then darted to the Sun;
> Slowly the sounds came back again,
> Now mixed, now one by one.
>
> Sometimes a-dropping from the sky
> I heard the sky-lark sing;
> Sometimes all little birds that are,
> How they seemed to fill the sea and air
> With their sweet jargoning!
>
> And now 'twas like all instruments,
> Now like a lonely flute;
> And now it is an angel's song,
> That makes the heavens be mute.

The change of voice is perhaps less striking because of the narrative confusion, but it may be thought to express the joy of discovery, as against the passive submission of eye to object. Poetic painting as

Coleridge pursued it here was not a matter of "fixities and definities," of the "distinct, clear, full made Images" of "metaphysical Solution." It descended to no "laborious anatomy of description," as he would later put it in a related context. His treatment of poetic painting recognized the priority of the observing subject for an art which would excite empathy and recognition.

In the destiny of his Mariner, Coleridge showed empirical vision to be a sort of death in life: a way of viewing a merely mechanical nature, of losing touch with the vital forces of human feeling. He did this without sacrificing the dramatic interest of the narrative—without making the delirious Mariner as tedious, in the opening parts, as Darwin. Considered as a critique of Darwin's pictorialism, the poem contrasts two approaches to the image, and if both occur in the voice of a single narrator, the sense of difference is only the more pronounced. This difference has long been recognized by commentators, and usually accounted a part of the poem's thematic structure. Restoring it to the Mariner's point of view recovers its psychological force; the association with delirium is plausible enough on the evidence, I believe, even if Coleridge makes the case study into an exemplum of a more philosophic kind. The mixture of motives is characteristic, in fact. So is the poetic elaboration of a way of thinking which was fundamentally critical. Like the conversation poems, and in a comparably complex way, the "Ancient Mariner" raises questions of poetic value as it ponders the human place in a nature where Coleridge still hoped to find a home.

Is this reflection on the poetic image, at sea in a problematic text, so intramural that it has nothing meaningful to say to modern circumstances? What is the social and historical value of Coleridge's experiment, considered in this way? The evidence is elusive but leading when taken in connection with related concerns in the notebooks and the subsequent record of reading and response. The poet-critic was reacting against the pictorial practice of Darwin and his antecedents— against a certain conception of the image, though not against the image itself. The note on Mackintosh (*CN* I, 634) shows that he soon came to suspect the identification of image and idea, the cornerstone of Locke's system. The "Ancient Mariner" makes the case against the image-as-idea in a dramatic setting, showing how vulnerable life in a world conceived in this way would be. If man were really only a recorder of the impressions of nature, he was in the situation of the Mariner at the line—fixed immutably in place, a cog in the infernal round of an indifferent machine. To view things in this way was to be already caught up in the horror of the naturalist mill. Such was the Mariner's situation. Yet it was not a fate ordained entirely by alien forces. He was compliant, his imagination willingly committed to turning the wheel. The will that bound him to this rack was fortunately free, as his spontaneous act of sympathy with the water-snakes showed. When he chose to see the elements as live instead of inert, he himself returned to life. What he now saw was a nature transformed, through the lens of eyes which recognized something larger than his own finite sensation. The disjointed imagery of his narrative assumed a corresponding vitality. He had been living in Darwin's blinders; he could choose to attend to the living process of the world around him instead. As an exposé of the empirical mill of particulars, this is vivid if not very explicit. It remains a potent reminder of the implications of life conceived in the mechanist manner of Locke and his followers, and of the will which, by an act of sympathetic imagination, is free to expand the horizon of the real. In a world grown ever more subject to images—a world increasingly known only through images at multiple remove—such reminders are invaluable. The rising empiricism of Coleridge's time is the confirmed ideology of our own, full of political resonance. His resistance to it is perhaps his most compelling claim on modern attention.

Coleridge's incipient critique of empiricism was intimately associated with his defense of poetry, as this context would suggest. It would soon give impetus to his pursuit of the idealism of Kant and Schelling, which defended the integrity of the experiencing subject without effectively reintegrating the foreclosed world of society and history. This connection has never been adequately developed, but it goes far to explaining the grip of the new German thinking on an imagination which had once cultivated the world of things. The reaction against the hypothesis that McFarland calls "it is" became the story of Coleridge's philosophical career. His poetry had made the effort of saving the appearances, while moving him ever closer to the recognition that "we receive but what we give/And in our life alone does nature live." When he resigned his aspiration to poetry he turned his back on the elements, which he had tried to salvage for purposes more than merely utilitarian. The "Ancient Mariner" became an exhibit to be arranged for inspection under modified convictions. Its latent meditation on the image would be consigned to the argument with Locke and assimilated to Leibnitz's rationalism.

Conclusion: After the Language Revolution

"With Coleridge we step across the threshold of a general theoretical study of language capable of opening to us new powers over our minds comparable to those which systematic physical inquiries are giving us over our environment. The step across was of the same type as that which took Galileo into the modern world" (*CI*, 232). Richards's conclusion of 1935 is worth recalling fifty years after, at a moment when the quandaries of linguistic scientism invite revaluation of our idea of language, and of critical practice in the institutional setting as it relies on a hypothesis of this kind. The symbolic idea promoted by Richards in Coleridge's name underwrote a new criticism and a way of reading which bore little resemblance, in their institutional employments, to his interested, culturally alert practice. For many professionals who learned to read in Richards's wake, the new criticism amounted to a literary logical positivism. For students it typically meant the end of reading as an extensive activity, the end of literature as a resource for self-reflection and cultural pathfinding. The momentous expansion of higher education at the same time magnified the effect. Close reading became a belated sort of scholasticism just where larger commitments were supposed to prevail. English as a forum of classical and modern culture, a place where the older world might mix with the newer, gave way to disciplinary aspirations based on competing conceptions of the common tongue.

So general a development cannot be attributed entirely to Richards's example, of course. His assumptions were resisted from the start, and there are interesting if rather dispersed elements of cultural commentary and critique in the work of literary critics associated with the new developments. Kenneth Burke provided a model of wider response in the American grain, while Leavis continued to play this role in England for the generation of students trained in the sixties. Richards's own claim to authority as a moral critic was compromised by the direction envisioned in *Coleridge on Imagination*, as reactions to the book show. Yet his vague linguistic idea has remained a subterranean force in the academy, nourishing a belated episode of the structural revolution inaugurated by Jakobson and living on, under other auspices, in its aftermath. Currently influential ideas of language as indeterminate, fundamentally equivocal, a mug's game in a mug's world, mark the moment of negation in a quest which began from the proposition that poetry was capable of saving us from chaos.

The search for stable ground in language did not begin with Coleridge, and his reliance on the symbolic of a transcendental Logos makes him an improbable source for modern jousting at the windmill of language. His conviction that signification was ordained in advance spared him the arid brainstorming of so much subsequent thinking on the subject. For natural language, that materialist rock of ages, has proved as transcendental as its suppressed original. The story extends beyond the horizon of Cambridge English; it includes the development of modern analytical thinking insofar as this takes its bearings from first questions about signification and significance. The obsessive idealization at work in the imagination of language since Coleridge's time represents a powerful sublation of the transcendental assumptions for which his name has come to stand.

Bracketing the transcendental Coleridge is one way of evading such a recognition. It has been the usual way since Richards's time — another sign of the persistence of his approach. Yet what Coleridge has to tell us about language now has everything to do with his central assumptions. Words as "living Things" look forward to language as presence in phenomenology and its derivatives, and to the cult of the poem in the new criticism. Observing the continuity means taking responsibility for premises which usually go unconsidered. It might indeed mean reconsidering a habitual way of thinking about writing. Coleridge's determined effort to save words from naming — from a mere identity with natural impressions — should invite resistance to other forms of idolatry. For those who have reacted against current idealizations of language have often fallen back on empirical mirages as fraught with unexamined baggage. Their appeal in an empirical climate remains a strong one, as Leavis's career demonstrates, and as recent accounts of critical history further suggest. Between the Word and the name a gulf has long since opened. In English studies it has flared into a gulf war.

Coleridge's attempt to ford these embattled straits was an early and distinctive one, and his approach is still worth following far enough to grasp the implications for the warring parties. Too baldly transcendental for both, his speculative intelligence remains a touchstone for the language question among his inheritors. Empson preceded Williams in making the most of it for modern purposes. Both lay stress on the central value of particular words for literary understanding. The lexicon as a broadly ideological matrix comes close, perhaps, to summarizing their working idea. The mode of etymologic argumentation which they developed represents a native version of a widespread modern recognition. The order of meaning introduced by thinking about signification as more than individual expression, as something informed by a comprehensive code, involves a conception of language as a collective organ, if not quite as a complete system. The tongue precedes speech, the long history of words all poetic statement. The artificially self-enclosed text brings all of this with it—in the margins, as it were—and finds its meaning and value within the larger horizon of the common language. Writing is always writing in society from the start, not least because natural language lies at the crossroads of human polity.

Language and mind, a leitmotif of Coleridge's mature reflection, was as important to his critical enterprise as the more celebrated search for the wellsprings of imagination, and it has proved nearly as influential for modern thinking. Yet his wayward observations on language have usually been conceived as a narrowly logical quest for rational or aesthetic premises, when their association with issues of broadly social value shows his employments to have been instrumental in a developing critique of English enlightenment culture. The distortion is symptomatic, a sign of what we have made of him. Writing in society with a full sense of social bearing was his habit from the beginning of his career—from *Conciones ad Populum* and *The Watchman*. The philosophical Coleridge should more often be read as the dreamwork of the author of *The Friend*, of *Aids to Reflection* and *On the Constitution of Church and State*. That he has been read the other way around for so long says more about the modern sense of the literary than about his real bearings. Coleridge's scouring of the grounds of signification should make sense to us now, after the language revolution, mainly as an example of original thinking against the grain of dominant scientific assumptions, and against habits of reading which are still with us.

Notes

Introduction

    1. See Excursus Note XIII, "Coleridge's Theory of the Imagination," *Coleridge and the Pantheist Tradition* (Oxford, 1969), 306–10; and *Originality and Imagination* (Baltimore, Md., 1985), 96.

    2. "Mr. Coleridge," in *The Spirit of the Age* (1825); rpt. in *Selected Essays of William Hazlitt*, ed. Geoffrey Keynes (London, 1930), 727.

Chapter 1

    1. For a discussion of language and the modern mind in a literary perspective, see George Steiner, *Extraterritorial* (London, 1972), esp. 72f. Dedicated to Richards, this book makes the case for "a linguistically educated literary criticism" (92) against the background of what the author calls the language revolution, with Coleridge's "linguistic poetics" (134) as antecedent. The former argument expands the scope of Cambridge English through related developments in the period. The latter makes explicit what Richards clearly had in mind but never argued forthrightly. As I shall be suggesting, "linguistic poetics" is a problematic characterization of Coleridge's position.

    For a historically alert account of Richards's enterprise see Chris Baldick, *The Social Mission of English Criticism, 1848-1932* (Oxford, 1983), 134–61 and passim. With Arnold behind him, Richards appears here as an ethical thinker; contemporary developments abroad are out of bounds and the language question is marginalized. Yet Richards's obsession with language was fundamental to his social vision, as the Basic English program shows. Coleridge's virtual absence from the discussion is notable in this connection. As Steiner indicates, his example was crucial not just for Richards but for others working in a broadly linguistic vein. This is the English line of the formalism that consumed critical response in the period elsewhere, and to miss its linguistic orientation is to miss its period flavor.

George Watson is more representative in recognizing the connection to Coleridge while missing the central importance of the linguistic emphasis. His remarks on the difference of Richards's approach remain valuable nevertheless. See *The Literary Critics* (London, 1964), 177–82. Also see Basil Willey, "I. A. Richards and Coleridge" and Kathleen Coburn, "I.A.R. and S.T.C.," in *I. A. Richards: Essays in his Honor*, ed. Reuben Brower, Helen Vendler, and John Hollander (New York, 1973), 227–44. Willey defends Richards's role as "the Coleridge of our time." Coburn sees him as a revisionist for whom "the key" is "Coleridge's attention to words." Both underscore the essential relation from a personal sense of Richards's vocation.

2. See I. A. Richards, *Coleridge on Imagination* (New York, 1935). Subsequent references in the text cite *CI*. All emphasis is in original unless otherwise noted. For a sense of the setting, see the recent discussion of the "English way of life" by Martin J. Wiener, *English Culture and the Decline of the Industrial Spirit* (Cambridge, Eng., 1981), 41f. As a characterization of a state of mind, his observation of "rest as a social ideal to so many in the English middle classes, whether they professed conservatism or radicalism," rings true to the writing of the period and to habits of reading which Richards was concerned to reform. Coleridge's remarks about habits of a century earlier bear comparison; see *BL* I, 34n.

3. Thus Evan Watkins cites "the almost religious awe" with which Richards described poetic unity as the occasion of a deconstructive reaction which further alienates the critical act from its object. See *The Critical Act: Criticism and Community* (New Haven, Conn., 1978), 9. And of the formation of another way of reading, Frank Lentricchia, in *After the New Criticism* (Chicago, 1980), observes that

> the first step is Richards's view of the poet as a supreme juggler, whose vastly inclusive consciousness can contain and balance a welter of opposed attitudes and impulses, with none subordinated or sacrificed to another for purposes of coherent action. The complex consciousness, the suppression of action in the contemplative . . . is sustained primarily by the ironic attitude; in Richards and his New-Critical inheritors, what is meant by irony is not an indirect way of saying something but a tactic which apparently allows one to escape all saying, all stance-taking. Irony, after Richards, becomes a synonym for complex awareness. (234–35)

Lentricchia associates Coleridge with a symbolist aesthetic, Kantian in inspiration, which nurtured Richards's psychologistic relativism and contributed to defeating "the referential for literary language" (60). The symbolic Coleridge has a long pedigree, certainly, but this version of his position rests on a Ricardian reduction. For Coleridge retreated from Schellings's promotion of the work of art to cult status, and his symbolic view of language includes central referential assumptions. Coleridge on language, and on literature, was committed from the outset to the social horizon which Lentricchia would recuperate for critical purpose. Against such egregious simplification, see James McKusick, *Coleridge's Philosophy of Language* (New Haven, Conn., 1986), 88–91.

4. McKusick's study provides a useful survey of the German background (53–86), with important qualifications as noted in my n. 8 and elsewhere. See also Paul Hamilton, *Coleridge's Poetics* (Stanford, Calif., 1983), 42–43, on Coleridge's employment of poetry to break the grip of empirical habits of thinking; and Owen Barfield, *What Coleridge Thought* (Middletown, Conn., 1971), 99–101, on language and understanding. Their approaches to Coleridge on language are considered in chapter 4 of this book.

5. For the term in the context of a treatment of the cultural crisis of the 1790s, see Thomas McFarland, *Romanticism and the Forms of Ruin: Wordsworth, Coleridge and the Modalities of Fragmentation* (Princeton, N.J., 1981), 4f.

6. The elaboration of Eliot's formula is my own. For an overview of the last point, see Emerson Marks, *Coleridge on the Language of Verse* (Princeton, N.J., 1981).

An idea of Eliot's sense of his bearing may be gathered from "Shakespearian Criticism: From Dryden to Coleridge," in *A Companion to Shakespeare Studies*, ed. H. Granville-Barker and G. B. Harrison (Cambridge, Eng., 1934):

> The writings of Coleridge upon Shakespeare must be read entire; for it is impossible to understand Shakespeare criticism to this day, without a familiar acquaintance with Coleridge's lectures and notes. Coleridge is an authority of the kind whose influence extends equally towards good and bad. It would be unjust to father upon him, without further ceremony, the psycho-analytic school of Shakespeare criticism; the study of individual characters which was begun by Morgann, to the neglect of the pattern and meaning of the whole play, was bound to lead to some such terminus, and we do not blame Morgann for that. But when Coleridge released the truth that Shakespeare already in *Venus and Adonis* and *Lucrece* gave proof of a "most profound, energetic and *philosophic* mind" he was perfectly right, if we use these adjectives rightly, but he supplied a dangerous stimulant to the more adventurous. "Philosophic" is of course not the right word . . . The sense of the profundity of Shakespeare's "thought," or of his thinking-in-images, has so oppressed some critics that they have been forced to explain themselves by unintelligibles. (298–99)

This last observation is an apt characterization of Richards following Coleridge on language as well.

7. On Tooke, see my discussion in "Coleridge on Language: A Poetic Paradigm," *Philological Quarterly* 62 (1983), 52f. and chapter 4 of this book. For a different view see McKusick, *Coleridge's Philosophy of Language*, 33–52. On desynonymy, see Hamilton, *Coleridge's Poetics*, esp. 62–88. On the

influence of Hartley, see Jerome Christensen, *Coleridge's Blessed Machine of Language* (Ithaca, N.Y., 1981), 33–95, and chapter 4 of this book.

8. McKusick makes Berkeley the key figure for the early formation of Coleridge's idea of language (4–32). With Plato's *Cratylus* in the background and a theory of natural signs in view, Coleridge relapses on the association of word and thing, against Locke's arbitrary sign and the linguistic relativism of both Hartley and Berkeley. Evidence presented in my chapter 4 suggests Coleridge's debt to Hartley's account of language as a conventional bond, and his endorsement of the arbitrary sign. The one limits the scope of the analogy of Berkeley's language of nature and natural language. The other implies that it is Hartley, not Berkeley, who counts fundamentally for Coleridge's developing idea. McKusick's pursuit of a theory of natural signs leads him to exaggerate the importance of Berkeley's example, real as it undoubtedly was, and to miss the importance of Hartley's. This emphasis inflects his discussion of Coleridge on language throughout the book.

9. Richards, *The Philosophy of Rhetoric* (New York, 1936), 17–19.

10. Croce, *European Literature in the Nineteenth Century* (London, 1924).

11. For a summary account, see Roman Jakobson, "Linguistics and Poetics," in *Style in Language*, ed. Thomas A. Sebeok (Cambridge, Mass., 1960), 350–77.

12. See D. W. Harding, "I. A. Richards," *Scrutiny* 1 (1933); cited in *The Importance of Scrutiny*, ed. Eric Bentley (New York, 1964), 350.

13. See Jerome P. Schiller, *I. A. Richards's Theory of Literature* (New Haven, Conn., 1969).

14. "Coleridge in Criticism," *Scrutiny* 9 (1940), 69.

15. Schiller, 18f.

16. *The New Criticism* (Norfolk, Conn., 1941), 7. Subsequent references in the text cite NC.

17. Hugh Kenner, *The Pound Era* (Berkeley, Calif., 1971), 67–69.

18. Empson, *Seven Types of Ambiguity*, 2nd. ed. (New York, 1947), 51.

19. See Owen Barfield, "Coleridge's Enjoyment of Words," in *Coleridge's Variety*, ed. John Beer (London, 1974), 212. For a discussion, see *PL*, 49; and Barfield, *What Coleridge Thought* (Middletown, Conn., 1971), 20–21.

20. For Eliot, see n. 21. Cf. Valéry: "Quant au *Cimitière marin*, cette intention ne fut d'abord qu'une figure rhythmique vide, ou remplie de syllabes vaines, qui me vint obséder quelque temps." From "Au sujet du *Cimitière marin*," cited by G. D. Martin, *Le Cimitière marin* (Austin, Tex., 1971), 86.

21. See Eliot, *The Use of Poetry and the Use of Criticism* (London, 1933), 155. Subsequent references in the text cite UP. These, the Charles Eliot Norton Lectures, address Richards and his position directly. For the sake of emphasis, I have avoided qualifying Eliot's statements with his later reservations.

22. For discussion, see George Whalley, "Coleridge's Poetic Sensibility," in *Coleridge's Variety*, 23. For related commentary see below, p. 143f.

23. On Eliot's cryptoromanticism, see George Bornstein, *Transformations of Romanticism in Yeats, Eliot, and Stevens* (Chicago, 1976), 94–162. The historical roots of Eliot's critical position are worked out by Edward Lobb, *T. S. Eliot and the Romantic Critical Tradition* (London, 1981).

24. F. R. Leavis, *New Bearings in English Poetry* (London, 1932; rpt. Harmondsworth, Eng., 1982). Subsequent references in the text cite *NB*.

25. See Francis Mulhern, *The Moment of "Scrutiny,"* (London, 1979), 26–27. Cf. Eliot, *UP* 124f.

26. Personal communication, Tübingen, 1979.

Chapter 2

1. Leavis, "Revaluations (VIII): Shelley," *Scrutiny* 4, no. 2 (1935), 159. René Wellek ("Literary Criticism and Philosophy," *Scrutiny* 5, no. 4 [1937]), responded in defense of the metaphor without challenging Leavis's assumptions directly:

> The comparison of loose clouds with earth's decaying leaves does not seem to me merely vague and general. A defence could suggest that the parallel can be made plausible by imagining Shelley lying in his boat and seeing in the loose clouds the counterpart of the leaves swimming in the stream or even seeing clouds mirrored in the water together with leaves. These are the "tangled boughs of Heaven and Ocean," which I don't think could have been suggested merely by leaves, but rather allude to the old mystical conception of the two trees of Heaven and Earth intertwining. (380)

Leavis's testy dismissal of these propositions ("quite unacceptable," without further commentary) shows his commitment to the documentary standard and his suspicion of claims for the familiar sort of figurative derivation invoked by Wellek. See Leavis, "Literary Criticism and Philosophy: A Reply," *Scrutiny* 6, no. 1 (1937), 68. This exchange is indicative, I think, not only of a peculiarly straitened literalism, but of Leavis's defensive rejection of "foreign" ideas. Wellek stands by implication for "philosophy," with all it implies of continental thinking and the idealist imagination.

"The poem as thought" has been identified by one commentator as Leavis's key contribution, but the formula is undermined by the bias evident here and elsewhere in Leavis's work. See Robert Boyers, *F. R. Leavis: Judgment and the Discipline of Thought* (Columbia, Mo., 1978), 20f.

2. Leavis, "The Latest Yeats," *Scrutiny* 2, no. 3 (1933), 294. The comparison with the earlier poem is explicit on this count: "The world of sense, the pride and beauty of life, so potently present in "Sailing to Byzantium," are

now merely (though there is a 'dolphin') 'complexities of mire and blood.'" (293).

3. Leavis, "The Great Yeats, and the Latest," *Scrutiny* 8, no. 4 (1940), 439. The terms of his disappointment in Yeats's later work are characteristic: "poems that, whatever they were for Yeats, are not poems for other readers: things in which the poet has handed over his job to Crazy Jane, and others in which allusiveness, oracular spareness, esoteric suggestion and familiar types of 'images' and symbols don't produce organization" (437).

4. Eagleton, *Literary Theory: An Introduction* (Minneapolis, Minn., 1983), 37.

5. Leavis, "Criticism and Literary History," *Scrutiny* 4, no. 1 (1935), 96–100.

6. Mulhern shows how this idea, developed from Richards, became the basis of a critical morality at odds with modern conditions. Culture was identified with "English," civilization with its debasement. See *The Moment of "Scrutiny,"* 36–37. For Williams's revision of these influential terms, see below, chapter 3.

7. Colin MacCabe, "Towards a Modern Trivium—English Studies Today," *Critical Quarterly* 26, nos. 1, 2 (1984), 75.

8. For an account of their relations see Bernard Bergonzi, "Leavis and Eliot: The Long Road to Rejection," *Critical Quarterly* 26, nos. 1, 2 (1984), 21–43: "What Leavis does to Eliot in *The Living Principle* looks like a mode of psychodrama, involving rituals of expulsion and exorcism and ultimate destruction. Striking the father dead may be a necessary part of achieving maturity and independence, but it usually occurs near the beginning rather than at the end of the son's career" (41).

9. Leavis, "Dr. Richards, Bentham, and Coleridge," *Scrutiny* 3, no. 4 (1935), 383.

10. Leavis, "What's Wrong With Criticism," *Scrutiny* 1, no. 2 (1932), 132–33.

11. See Eliot, "Shelley and Keats," *The Use of Poetry and the Use of Criticism*, 87–102.

12. See Heaney, "The Fire i' the Flint," in *Preoccupations* (New York, 1980), 79–97.

13. Leavis's problems at the end of his career with Eliot's *Quartets* show how exclusive (and how private) his sense of language would become: "*Four Quartets*, for the responsive reader, testifies that 'using words' is a misleading way of describing its author's relation to the English language . . . It is *in* the English language that he conceives, feels, refines, and achieves subtleties of definition . . . In the English language he is drawing on the creativity of numberless generations of mankind and profiting collaboratively . . . to say this is to dismiss his conception of reality" [*The Living Principle* (London, 1975),

214]. For discussion see Ronald Hayman, *F. R. Leavis* (London, 1976), 137–44.

14. Leavis, "Dr. Richards, Bentham, and Coleridge," 382–84.

15. Leavis, "Revaluations (XIII): Coleridge in Criticism," *Scrutiny* 9, no. 1 (1940), 57–69. For discussion see William Walsh, *F. R. Leavis* (London, 1980), 154–71. His case for a Coleridgean Leavis demonstrates how imposing Coleridge's example has been; how indispensible even for a critic who, like Leavis, explicitly disavows it. The observation that "Leavis's account of language seems . . . strikingly in harmony with Coleridge's" (164) is based on a cursory treatment of both. Yet it does suggest what Coleridge's thinking might have meant to a more receptive, and more reflective, intelligence.

16. In his important preface of 1879, Arnold put it that "Cambridge was a place where Coleridge's influence had great action, and where Wordsworth's poetry, therefore, flourished especially . . . the influence of Coleridge has waned, and Wordsworth's poetry can no longer draw succour from this ally." See "Wordsworth," in *The Complete Prose Works of Matthew Arnold*, ed. R. H. Super, 11 vols. (Ann Arbor, Mich., 1960–77), 9:36–37. Their real complicity, evident to readers from the start, is worth recalling at a moment when commentators are apt to insist on their differences and to write off Coleridge's critically balanced reading to personal motives. Would a less balanced reading have made a more effective case for Wordsworth's poetry? M. H. Abrams, in *The Mirror and the Lamp* (New York, 1953; rpt. 1971), emphasizes Coleridge's recourse to first principles as the basis of his claim "that Coleridge, more thoroughly than Wordsworth, was the innovative English critic of his time" (124). This understanding, current since Arnold, remains general despite resistance among some recent Wordsworthian apologists. For further discussion, see chapter 4.

17. Leavis, "Dr. Richards, Bentham, and Coleridge," 399.

18. Read, "Coleridge as Critic," in *Lectures in Criticism* (New York, 1949), 74–75. Subsequent references in the text cite *LC*.

19. For extended discussion, see R. K. Meiners, "Marginal Men and Centers of Learning: New Critical Rhetoric and Critical Politics," *New Literary History* 18 (1986–87), 129–50.

20. R. P. Blackmur, "A Critic's Job of Work," in *Language as Gesture* (New York, 1952), 389–90. References in the text to essays from this volume cite *LG*.

21. Babbitt, *Rousseau and Romanticism* (Boston, 1919), 296.

22. Babbitt, *On Being Creative* (Boston, 1932), 129.

23. Ransom, *The New Criticism*, 3–131. References in the text cite *NC*.

24. Thus Ransom in *The New Criticism*, 85: "I should feel disposed at the moment to argue for a logical propriety, a specific 'point of the analogy,' as the occasion for any given metaphor; and then for brilliance and importance in

the body of the vehicle in its own right. But it seems to me scarcely open to question that the vehicle must realize itself independently and go beyond its occasion. (And I think nowhere does Richards say the contrary.) In doing this the vehicle becomes irrelevant to the structure of the argument, and asserts the poetic undertaking to incorporate local texture."

25. Allen Tate argued at the time that "if there is an objective relation of part to whole, Coleridge does not say what it is; nor does he distinguish that relation in terms of any specific poetic work. It is strictly a quantitative analogy taken, perhaps, from geometry" ("Literature as Knowledge," in *Collected Essays* [Denver, 1959], 37). Subsequent references in the text cite *LK*.

This observation and what Tate makes it bear betray a limited exposure to Coleridge's critical corpus — a limitation evident in Richards, Leavis, Babbitt, and nearly every commentator of the period. We are faced with a general problem, then: in the absence of the philosophical lectures, notebooks, and marginalia, Coleridge appeared to promise more than he delivered. A fair judgment on the evidence, perhaps, and one which would justify the familiar conclusion that Coleridge's criticism amounts to little more than an account of his own taste. Yet the intense particularism of the new criticism might have made a virtue of Coleridge's bittiness. In the work of Kenneth Burke, it often did in fact.

26. Fraser, "The Man within the Name: William Empson as Poet, Critic, and Friend," in *William Empson, The Man and His Work* (London and Boston, 1974), 54.

27. Empson, *Seven Types of Ambiguity* (London, 1930), 39. Subsequent references in the text cite *ST*.

28. See *BL* II, 53:

Metre in itself is simply a stimulant of the attention, and therefore excites the question: Why is the attention to be thus stimulated? Now the question cannot be answered by the pleasure of the metre itself: for this we have shown to be *conditional*, and dependent on the appropriateness of the thoughts and expressions, to which the metrical form is superadded. Neither can I conceive any other answer that can be rationally given, short of this: I write in metre, because I am about to use a language different from that of prose.

29. For discussion of the limits of aphoristic reading, see Gary J. Handwerk, *Irony and Ethics in Narrative: From Schlegel to Lacan* (New Haven, 1985), 18f.

30. See Eliot, *To Criticize the Critic* (London, 1965), 13; and Fraser, "Man within the Name," 53–54.

31. *AR*, 223–24. For commentary, see Barfield, *What Coleridge Thought*, 99f.

32. See *PL*, 369; and "Idols of the Marketplace" in chapter 4 of this book.

33. Davis S. Ferris, "Coleridge's Ventriloquy: Abduction from the *Biographia*," *Studies in Romanticism* 24, no. 1 (Spring 1985), 62.

34. From Benjamin, *Einbahnstrasse* (Berlin, 1928), trans. as "One Way Street" in *Reflections*, trans. Edmund Jephcott (New York, 1978), 61.

35. Hugh Kenner, *The Invisible Poet: T. S. Eliot* (London, 1959: rpt. 1965), 4f. and 47f.

36. Hyman, *The Armed Vision* (New York, 1948), 288f. Subsequent references in the text cite *AV*.

37. See *Coleridge's Verse. A Selection*, ed. William Empson and David Pirie (London, 1972), 1–100.

38. Empson, *The Structure of Complex Words* (London, 1951). Subsequent references in the text cite *SCW*.

Chapter 3

1. Carlyle, *Critical and Miscellaneous Essays*, 5 vols. (London, 1899), 2:66.

2. See Leavis, "Mass Civilisation and Minority Culture," (Cambridge, Eng., 1930; rpt. in *For Continuity* [Cambridge, Eng., 1933], 13–46). Leavis takes his bearings from Arnold, who developed Carlyle's association of civilization with the mechanical while confirming culture as the significant antithetical term.

3. Williams, *Culture and Society* (London, 1958). See p. 62:

> This idea of Cultivation, or Culture, was affirmed, by Coleridge, as a *social* idea, which should be capable of embodying true ideas of value . . . it was Coleridge who first attempted to define, in terms of his changing society, the *social* conditions of man's perfection. Coleridge's emphasis in his writings is on *institutions*. The promptings to perfection came indeed from "the cultivated heart"—that is to say, from man's inward consciousness—but, as Burke before him, Coleridge insisted on man's need for institutions which should confirm and constitute his personal efforts. Cultivation, in fact, though an inward was never a merely individual process. What in the eighteenth century had been an ideal of personality—a personal qualification for participation in polite society—had now, in the face of radical change, to be redefined, as a condition on which society as a whole depended. In these circumstances, cultivation, or culture, became an explicit factor in society, and its recognition controlled the enquiry into institutions.

Subsequent references to *Culture and Society* cite *CS*.

4. See Leavis, *Mill on Bentham and Coleridge* (London, 1950).

5. See Williams, "The Romantic Artist," *CS*, 30–48.

6. Williams, *Writing in Society* (London, 1984), 73–74. References in the text cite *WS*.

7. For an extended discussion of his relations with Leavis and the institutional setting, see Williams, "Cambridge English, Past and Present," *Writing in Society*, 177–91.

8. See Williams, *The Country and the City* (London, 1973), 148–49; 127–141.

9. E. S. Dallas, "Popular Literature and the Periodical Press," *Blackwood's* 85 (January–February 1859), 86.

10. Terry Eagleton, *The Function of Criticism* (London, 1984), 110.

11. See Eagleton, *The Function of Criticism*, 20–21, for a discussion; on Williams see 108–15. John Gross, in *The Rise and Fall of the Man of Letters* (London, 1969), had made the case for Williams in these terms some fifteen years earlier, observing that "his influence will, I believe, prove much longer-lasting than that of Caudwell or any of the Marxist critics of the 1930s, because it is much more securely rooted in the realities of English culture and English tradition . . . One can easily imagine an entire school of revisionist literary history developing out of his work" (301–2).

12. Abel, *Linguistic Essays* (London, 1882), v.

13. See for instance *CN* III, 4247, where the interest lies in the intramural sense of language caught between image and idea:

> Homogeneous Languages favorable to Metaphysics—exemplified in the Greek and in the German. And why?—the Words, as *percipere*, i.e. *capere per sensus* . . . *Einbildung* i.e. *formatio in unum*—bedingt, bedingung, i.e. what presupposes some thing as the condition of its existence, i.e. *bethinged*—all are like a series of historical medals—the stamps remain—while in derivative Languages they are mere *Coins*, current for so much, by a *credit*, without any distinct knowledge or reference . . . Hence Indistinctness—& as the human mind still craves for distinctness, thence the turning to & resting wholly in *imagible* things/but as there must likewise be a sense of indefiniteness (or all activity would cease) this is wasted on what is called common sense. . . .

For a related discussion of the image, see "Verbal Imagination" in chapter 5.

14. H. J. Jackson, "Coleridge, Etymology and Etymologic," *Journal of the History of Ideas* 45, no. 1 (1983), 86–87, ellipses removed for continuity.

15. For discussion of Hartley and Tooke, see "Idols of the Marketplace" in chapter 4. For corroboration of their endurance in Coleridge's thinking, see Christensen, *Coleridge's Blessed Machine of Language*: "Hartley is as important as any other intellectual influence in Coleridge's career—both as proponent of a particular philosophy and as the emblem of a way of philosophizing" (75), and "Coleridge never *overthrows* Hartleian association, but he does continually interrupt it . . . Although that interruption displays the inconsistencies of association, it does not constitute a positive, philosophical, and moral refutation of the theory" (94).

16. Much has been made of Coleridge's notion of desynoymy as "the

progress of language," yet it distracted him from an emergent historical sense of the institution which was the real progress of language in the period. The analogy to Richards's situation is irresistable: his semasiology might be regarded as a sentimental regression to that transitional moment when the historical status of language could be recognized without incurring responsibility. The recent effort of Paul Hamilton to view the *Biographia* as "a protracted act of desynonymy" constitutes the most ambitious effort to date to identify it as the essential process of Coleridgean understanding. See Hamilton, *Coleridge's Poetics*, 73–81.

17. *AR*, vii.

18. Ms. Egerton 2825f29, from the "Sketch of the History of Logic." Printed in *CC* 13:17–18.

19. The immediate source of the formula is Herbert Read, *Coleridge as Critic* (London, 1949), 15.

20. Eliot, *Notes towards the Definition of Culture* (London, 1948), 31.

21. Williams, *Politics and Letters: Interviews with New Left Review* (London, 1979), 98. Subsequent references in the text cite *POL*.

22. See DeLaura, "Heroic Egotism: Goethe and the Fortunes of *Bildung* in Victorian England," in *Johann Wolfgang von Goethe: 150 Years of Continuing Vitality*, ed. U. Goebel and W. T. Zyla (Lubbock, Tex., 1984), 41–60, esp. 45.

23. For extended discussion, see Williams, "Crisis in English Studies," in *Writing in Society*, 192–211. Yet the destination of Williams's cultural analytic was the sociology of culture established in *Culture* (London, 1981). The scientism of this phase of his work evidences a deep ambivalence, which he shares with Richards. Criticism would turn its back on science, yet remain attached to the idea of scientific method—one sign among others of its conflicted condition.

24. Empson's discussion of the matter, a possible source of Williams's semasiology, exhibits a strong sense of the difference of word and concept. Williams's evasion of the consequences is important for grasping the limits of his etymologic. See Empson, *The Structure of Complex Words*, 80f.

25. *The Encyclopedia of Philosophy*, ed. Paul Edwards, 8 vols. in 4 (New York and London, 1967), 2:273–75. Citations are to this article.

26. Williams, *Keywords* (London, 1976), 79.

27. Williams, *Marxism and Literature* (Oxford, 1977). Subsequent references in the text cite *ML*.

28. For Eliot's version of culture as religion, see *Notes towards the Definition of Culture*, 28f.

29. For discussion of Voloshinov and Bakhtin, see Tzvetan Todorov, *Mikhail Bakhtin: The Dialogical Principle* (Minneapolis, Minn., 1984), 6–11.

30. On Barfield's semasiology in *Poetic Diction* (London, 1928) see Empson, *The Structure of Complex Words*, 375f. Barfield's classic study is *History in English Words* (London, 1926). See also C. S. Lewis, *Studies in*

Words (Cambridge, Eng., 1960). All participate in what might be called the moment of semasiology, including (but not limited by) Richards and the formation of Cambridge English.

Chapter 4

1. See Murray Cohen, *Sensible Words: Linguistic Practice in England, 1670-1785* (Baltimore, Md., 1977); and Hans Aarsleff, *From Locke to Saussure: Essays on the Study of Language and Intellectual History* (Minneapolis, Minn., 1982).

2. M. H. Abrams, *The Mirror and the Lamp*, 101-3. References in the text cite *Mirror*.

3. Its originality was qualified by Robert Mayo's research in the magazine verse of the period ["The Contemporaneity of the *Lyrical Ballads*," *PMLA* 69 (1954), 486-522.] What was original was not the ballad as lyric, but the successful treatment of it—and, in the second edition, the large poetic claims for it. Mayo turned Coleridge's sense of the project, in the *Biographia*, against a *modern* idea of originality. By Coleridge's own standard, however, the volume was original in the most important ways, and far from denigrating its achievement he was preeminently responsible for promoting it. On the development of the idea of originality in the romantic setting, see Thomas McFarland, *Originality and Imagination* (Baltimore, Md., 1985), 1-30. A detailed argument for the qualitative difference of Wordsworth's ballads from magazine verse is mounted by Mary Jacobus, *Tradition and Experiment in Wordsworth's "Lyrical Ballads" (1798)* (Oxford, 1976), 18-48.

It is perhaps worth noticing, in point of comparison, that *The Waste Land* deliberately drew on familiar models and voices; its originality lay in its heteroglossic mixing of the dramatic monologue and in the rhythmic equivalents which Eliot found for the modern break-up. Here, as in the case of *Lyrical Ballads*, the modern criterion of originality occludes the vital relation to traditional practices. Eliot's sense of originality, familiar from "Tradition and the Individual Talent," reverts to an older conception continued by Coleridge.

4. Bruns, *Modern Poetry and the Idea of Language* (New Haven, Conn., 1974), 45.

5. See Fruman, *Coleridge, the Damaged Archangel* (New York, 1971), 282-88.

6. See McFarland, *Romanticism and the Forms of Ruin*, 56-64. A more positive emphasis on Coleridge's role in their collaboration is proposed by Richard Gravil, "Imagining Wordsworth: 1797—1807—1817," in *Coleridge's Imagination*, ed. Richard Gravil, Lucy Newlyn, and Nicholas Roe (Cambridge, 1985), 129-42.

7. See Aarsleff, "Wordsworth, Language, Romanticism," in *From Locke to Saussure*, 373. For development in detail of Aarsleff's premise as it applies

to Coleridge, see McKusick, *Coleridge's Philosophy of Language*, 111–15.

8. Bialostosky, *Making Tales. The Poetics of Wordsworth's Narrative Experiments* (Chicago, 1984). Subsequent references in the text cite *MT*.

9. For a different but related understanding of Wordsworth's poetics of speech, see Frances Ferguson, *Wordsworth: Language as Counter-Spirit* (New Haven, Conn., 1978), 18f., who puts it that Wordsworth's idea of a poetic language based on rustic speech *cannot* be grasped mimetically. Or, more accurately, that Wordsworth did not think of it this way himself, as the later essays on epitaphs show. The difficulty, as Ferguson recognizes, is that Wordsworth did not conceive of language philosophically. She resorts to phenomenological discourse to render his ideas, but they do not add up to a stable position on the subject. The problem is archaeological: Coleridge himself found Wordsworth's idea hard to draw out (see chapter 4, "Some New Combinations of Language," p. 100), while Bialostosky is driven to Plato for something resembling it. Hence the difficulty of situating Wordsworth on language in intellectual history as Aarsleff does, and as Coleridge seems to have attempted in passing in the analogy to Locke as discussed below on p. 104f. This is the meaning of Wordsworth's primitivism.

Coleridge's address in Chapter XVII to the question of language as raised in the "Preface" shows how attentive he was to this feature of Wordsworth's argument, and especially to the rustic language theorem. See *BL* II, 39f.

10. Hamilton, *Coleridge's Poetics* (Oxford, 1984), 35f. (Subsequent references in the text cite *CP*.) If there is a Condillac connection at all, it must have transpired through Mackintosh, his follower, notes on whose lectures Coleridge records in *CN*, 634. Even so, Coleridge showed impatience: "Makes Idea (of course) mean Image—" Coburn dates this indicative set of responses to Coleridge's attendance at Mackintosh's lectures, 22 January–6 February 1800.

11. Barfield's emphasis [*What Coleridge Thought*, 148–49, 154] on the theological setting of his subject's first assumptions is unique, and uniquely valuable against the background of Richards's claims and those of recent commentators. That Coleridge's intelligence was consciously and pervasively Hebraic ought to be a first premise. How fundamentally such an orientation affects his sense of language Barfield makes clear:

> It must never be forgotten that for him nature and the human soul were not two separate entities. Not only was their creation not two consecutive processes; it was not even two simultaneous ones; it was one and the same—nature being "in" man no less than man is "in" nature. The Word continues active in the word. Thus, what he has to say about, for instance, the genetic function of the verb and the noun in human speech is intended neither as mere philosophy nor as mere psychology. It must be equally relevant to natural history. But behind all that, and as it were underpinning it stands the divine Tri-unity. The *origin* of species cannot fruitfully be considered apart from the origin of *all* "distinctities" in the

proceeding Word. Nor this in turn except in connection with the formula of creation propounded in the opening verse of St. John's Gospel: that the Word was in the beginning, that the Word was "with" God and that the Word was God. (148)

Some poetic consequences are discussed by Anthony John Harding, *Coleridge and the Inspired Word* (Kingston and Montreal, 1985), 7f., 29–57.

12. See L. A. Willoughby, "Coleridge as a Philologist," *Modern Language Review* 31(1936), 176–201. Kathleen Coburn expanded the context of his findings in the introduction to her edition of the *Philosophical Lectures* (London, 1949), 47–51, opening Coleridge's formulation of language to the wider network of his thought. An important revision based in part on new materials has been undertaken by McKusick, *Coleridge's Philosophy of Language*, 53–85.

13. Appleyard, *Coleridge's Philosophy of Literature* (Cambridge, Mass., 1965), 84.

14. Following Richards at a generation's distance, Marks takes Coleridge's linguistic interests as prototypical of modern developments in poetics. See *Coleridge on the Language of Verse*, 27. In a similar vein, see Timothy J. Corrigan, *Coleridge, Language and Criticism* (Athens, Ga., 1982).

15. Cohen, *Sensible Words*, xxiv.

16. *An Essay Concerning Human Understanding*, ed. A. C. Fraser, 2 vols. (Oxford, 1894; rpt. New York, 1959), II, 9 (III, 2:1 in Locke's numeration). Subsequent references cite *Essay* and Locke's numeration.

17. See Charles McCracken, *Malebranche and British Philosophy* (Oxford, 1983), 234.

18. See *PL*, 384 and my introductory discussion, p. 13.

19. Bacon, *Novum Organum* I, 59. I follow the translation of Rev. G. W. Kitchin (Oxford, 1859), 29, with exceptions for emphasis, where the Latin is cited for comparison. *Idola* properly means "phantoms," as Kitchin translates, except in the Church Fathers. It conveys the flavor of Bacon's association of vulgar understanding with superstition. "Idols" conforms to Coleridge's sense of the idolatry of regarding words as images: he translates it this way himself in *PL*, 333 and elsewhere. Subsequent references to Kitchin's translation cite *NO*.

20. Thus Hamilton, who in *Coleridge's Poetics* makes sense of Godwin's role as recipient: "If, as Coleridge thought, a proper understanding of language has important philosophical implications, then the poet's sensitivity to language will be a powerful philosophical weapon. With this poetic enrichment of Godwin's philosophical role Coleridge can now return to a favorable discussion of Godwinian radicalism. Transformed into a philosophy of language through a critical consciousness of its own medium, Godwin's theory of 'moral progressiveness' can appeal to a much wider audience" (105).

21. Tooke, *The Diversions of Purley*, 2 vols., vol. I (London, 1786; 2nd.

ed. 1798); vol. II (London, 1805). Rpt., revised and corrected by Richard Taylor (London, 1857). Subsequent references cite *DP*. For a detailed discussion of Tooke's book in historical context, see Aarsleff, *The Study of Language in England, 1780-1860* (Princeton, 1967), 44-114.

22. *TT*, 70-71. Also, "On the Curious Circumstance, that in the German Language the Sun is Feminine and the Moon Masculine," *CPW* II, 968-69.

23. See Christensen, *Coleridge's Blessed Machine of Language*, 58f. The three volumes of Hartley's *Observations on Man* (1754; rpt. 1791) are in the British Library. Coleridge's notations are of uncertain date, but confirm the direction of the letter to Godwin. Thus, he heckles Hartley's account of the particles with three exclamation points. The offending text runs thus: "Lastly, the particles the, of, to, for, but &c. have neither definitions nor ideas" (I, 279). The tone of Coleridge's notes is railing throughout. The most explicit, inserted at the end of the volume, is clear enough to stand on its own:

> It might be said, I think, that Hartley himself must have *felt* that association was not of itself capable of explaining all the phaenomenon of the human mind—in several parts he (unconsciously perhaps) presupposes a power of abstraction always acting—ex. gr. when he talks of the "stable part of ideas" in his explanation of such words as White, whiteness, sweet &c. The whole of p. 279 presents almost a humorous instance (if in the works of so good & great a man one could permit oneself that sort of feeling) of explaining the obscuriorum per obscurius.—It is singular, that Hartley, a good algebraist, & who so clearly saw the analogy of Language in its effects on the mind to the operations of algebra, did not set himself about explaining by an accurate analysis what those operations are in—"

24. *Observations on Man*, 2 vols. (London: 1749), I, 268. Subsequent references cite *OM*.

25. Including myself, in "Coleridge on Language: A Poetic Paradigm" *Philological Quarterly* 62 (1983), 56 and 63. The phrase is misleading. Context provides what I now believe to be grounds for an improved understanding. The emphasis throughout is on words as instruments of thought and feeling, without reference to objects. In confirmation, see *PL*, 201: "[W]ords are things. They are the great mighty instruments by which thoughts are excited and by which alone they can be expressed in a remembrable form." For a different understanding of the passage, conforming with his view that Coleridge was in pursuit of a natural theory of signs, see McKusick, *Coleridge's Philosophy of Language*, 41f.

26. See *CN* I, 634, where Coleridge's notes on lectures by Mackintosh include the line, "Few words excite ideas." Coleridge finds Mackintosh contradicting himself with this, but it also violates Hartley's portrait of the role of language in the association of ideas. The notes appear to confirm the orientation I am describing.

27. Griggs confirms that the letter is of Coleridge's composition. See his headnote, *CL* II, 664.

28. Altieri, "Wordsworth's 'Preface' as Literary Theory," *Criticism* 18 (1976), 122–46.

29. For the distinction between *Erfahrung* and *Erlebnis*, and what Benjamin makes it bear, see "Über einige Motive bei Baudelaire," *Walter Benjamin Gesammelte Schriften*, 6 vols. (Frankfurt, 1972–79), 1, pt. 2:605–53, esp. 615f. Translated in *Illuminations*, ed. Hannah Arendt (New York, 1968), 157–202, esp. 165f.

30. See Hamilton, *Coleridge's Poetics*, 145: "Coleridge's unfair concentration on the strain of literalism in the 'Preface' is his way of emphasizing the artifice defining poetry—the significant difference of imitation from original, and the aesthetic purpose of the self-advertising features of diction and metre which Wordsworth had pronounced superfluous."

See also Bialostosky, *Making Tales*, 27, on Coleridge's "Neoclassicism"—an inadequate reduction of his position dictated by the delusive analogy to Aristotle.

31. The phrase is that of L. C. Knights, "Introduction" to *Coleridge's Variety*, ed. John Beer (London, 1974), xx.

32. From a letter of 1833 to John Sterling, cited by Alice D. Snyder, *Coleridge on Logic and Learning* (New Haven, Conn., 1929), 10.

33. The clear contrast drawn by Coleridge in Chapter XVII between effective and ineffective voicing in Wordsworth's dramatic poems shows that it was not the procedure per se to which he objected, but certain illusions about low and rustic life, and the consequent debasement of expressive language to unreflective ends. The characters of "Michael" and "The Brothers," among others, were successful because broadly representative; those of "Goody Blake and Harry Gill," "The Idiot Boy," and "The Thorn" unsuccessful because merely instinctive—unrepresentative of ordinary reflectiveness. The latter appears to be the real criterion for Coleridge. Poetry was reflective, either directly or dramatically, or it was not interesting. What was good in "The Thorn" "might as well or still better have proceeded from the poet's own imagination, and have been spoken in his own character" (*BL* II, 36). Expressive language was identified in this way with the voice of the reflective subject.

Jacobus (*Tradition and Experiment*, 248) defends "The Thorn" and its narrator on grounds that "Wordsworth's story-teller lacks the skills of the sophisticated narrator . . . but, like the stormy weather which had transformed the thorn in Wordsworth's original glimpse, his mind 'produces impressive effects out of simple elements'; and it is this that he has in common with the poet himself." By Coleridge's criterion, however, such "effects" do not constitute reflectiveness.

34. The insistence on poetic thinking is available as early as 1796, in the letter to Thelwall on Southey's *Joan of Arc*: Coleridge praises Southey's "natu-

ral, perspicuous, & dignified" language while complaining that "he adjures *thinking* — & lays the whole stress of excellence — on *feeling* — Now (as you say) they must go together" (*CL* I, 293–94). Similarly, he wonders of the opening lines of Southey's "Hymn to the Penates," "have they any *meaning?*" — a very characteristic emphasis, and the ground in his response of an expressive language committed to reflection, not to "beauty" of diction, as he put it there (*CL* I, 291). His sense of the relation of poetic thinking to diction is constituted historically in his discussion of English poetry in the opening of the *Biographia*, where "natural thought" and "natural diction" are out of phase until the end of the century. Wordsworth earns his place in tradition by joining them in his poetic idiom.

35.   Coleridge's note to his citation of Aristotle in Chapter XVII shows him to have been acutely conscious of the normative trap lurking in a mimetic poetics. From *The Friend* on Shakespeare, he argues that it is not the "abstractions" of the typical that he is commending, "for these class-characteristics which constitute the instructiveness of a character, are so modified and particularized in each person of the Shakespearean Drama, that life itself does not excite more distinctly that sense of individuality which belongs to real existence" (*BL* II, 33). In the practice of the master, no conflict of interest rives expression and the canons of representation, for the particular is realized within the typical without loss of distinction. It is such a solution that Coleridge recognizes in "Michael" and elsewhere.

36.   Richards, as cited by Mulhern, *The Moment of "Scrutiny,"* 27.

37.   For corroboration of Coleridge's inclusive idea of the symbol, see J. Robert Barth, *The Symbolic Imagination* (Princeton, N.J., 1977). Against the narrowly idealist sense of Coleridge's position, Barth argues that his symbol is constitutive:

> For Coleridge a symbol is an idea; although by its nature an idea is supersensuous, in symbol it is bodied forth in sense images. A symbol results from the conjoined working of reason and understanding . . . All this is a far cry from the subjectivism of Kant . . . For Coleridge, ideas, and therefore symbols, are not merely regulative but constitutive. Consubstantial as they are with 'the truths of which they are the conductors,' symbols convey the apprehension not only of the self but of reality beyond the self, both supersensuous reality (because it involved the work of reason) and sensible reality (because it also subsumes the work of understanding). At least in a Coleridgean perspective, Romanticism is no mere subjectivism. It is not simply a way of feeling, but a way of knowing. (111–13)

38.   The symbol might be described as the product of the unsatisfactory opposition of image and idea in Coleridge's formulation of the problem; it was to this that he turned late in his career for an alternative to the corpuscular idea. That it represents a development from a more limited notion of the symbol is indicated by *CN* I, 918, as cited. Words, as "arbitrary symbols in

Imagination," had only an indirect relation to objects in reference. As much is true of the constitutive symbol, of course, yet there is little sign of inclusiveness here or again in *CN* I, 1387. His mature formulation of the symbol thus appears to have coincided with his growing understanding of language, the symbolic process par excellence.

39. Johann Gottfried Herder, *Eine Metakritik zur Kritik der reinen Vernunft* (1799); rpt. in *Sprachphilosophische Schriften*, ed. Erich Heintel (Hamburg, 1975), 183–227.

40. A copy of *Kalligone* (1803) with Coleridge's distinctive marginalia is in the British Library. His notes are scanty, but in heckling Herder's attack on the third critique he invokes Kant's discussion. For a resume of the influence of the *Critik der Urtheilskraft* (1790) on the four "aesthetical essays" appended to Shawcross's edition of the *Biographia*, see G. N. G. Orsini, *Coleridge and German Idealism* (Carbondale, Ill., 1969), 167f. The parroted assertion that "all the fine arts are different species of poetry" (*BL* II, 220) is cardinal in this context, indicating in advance the limitations of Kant's aesthetics as applied to poetry properly speaking. For its symbolic constitution distinguishes it essentially from such iconic arts as painting and sculpture. Poetry was a way of thinking: this was the force of Coleridge's conviction from early on (see n. 34). As an imitative art it was of course iconic in its means, and Coleridge recognized the claims of the aesthetic on it: the judgments of the sublime and beautiful had something to do with the pleasures of poetry, as his letter to Allsop on the subject suggests (*BL* II, 309n.). But the judgment of value in poetry was never primarily aesthetic, as his discussion of Wordsworth clearly indicates.

41. See *CN* I, 1675 (and n.) for notes on a German discussion of mountain glory apparently related to Burke. Coburn lists no references to Burke's essay in the notebooks—a reliable index of his reading, or at least of extended participation. There is a dismissive reference in *TT*, 54 (July 12, 1827).

42. On Coleridge's ambivalence toward Schelling, see Thomas Mc-Farland, *Coleridge and the Pantheist Tradition* (Oxford, 1969), 11, 134–35, 147–48. Also, in passing, Hamilton, *Coleridge's Poetics*, 88.

The definitive discussion of secondary imagination as derived from Schelling, and of its poetic implications, is that of McFarland, *Originality and Imagination*, 90–147. His preliminary conclusion is of permanent value for approaching Coleridge's criticism: "Imagination is therefore primarily a connective developed because of Coleridge's commitment to systematic philosophizing. It would not appear to be rewarding, accordingly, to try to make very much critically of its presence in particular poems," though McFarland goes on to observe it at work there (95). He thus recapitulates in a finer tone the partitioning of the *Biographia* into critical theory and critical practice. There is no better demonstration of their peculiar relation in Coleridge's thinking about poetry. For such an idea of imagination *might* indeed be applied to the poetic situation (and Coleridge so applied it), yet what it turns up there is little more than the mechanism that has been posited. Coleridge nevertheless employs the term as a judgment of value, leading his readers to attend to a process interesting in itself but of unresolved status.

Important recent studies confirm the limited value of secondary imagination — and, by implication, of Schelling's aesthetic — for Coleridge's mature understanding. See especially Harding, *Coleridge and the Inspired Word*, who concludes that "in the central statement of his best known theoretical work, he wished to guarantee the distinctively human character of Imagination and could do so only by grounding his definition on the biblical phrase that called back the Jewish prophets and chieftains to the acknowledgment of God's personëity and established Judaic religion as 'the reference of an intelligent responsible Will Finite to an Absolute Will'" (73). More pointedly, Jonathan Wordsworth ["The Infinite I AM: Coleridge and the Ascent of Being," in *Coleridge's Imagination*, 22–52] traces the process by which secondary imagination attained to critical authority, on the way to reconsidering the sources and real orientation of Coleridge on imagination.

43. Wellek, *A History of Modern Criticism, 1750–1950* (London, 1955), 159–61.

Chapter 5

N.B.: All citations to the text of Coleridge's poems refer to *CPW*.

1. William K. Wimsatt, Jr., "The Structure of Romantic Nature Imagery," in *Romanticism and Consciousness: Essays in Criticism*, ed. Harold Bloom (New York, 1970), 88.

2. Ibid., 82.

3. M. H. Abrams, "Structure and Style in the Greater Romantic Lyric," in *From Sensibility to Romanticism*, ed. F. W. Hilles and Harold Bloom (New York, 1965), 550.

4. It is usual in considering this passage to dwell on the grate-film rather than the *stranger* — on the image, that is, rather than the word. Thus, Reeve Parker in his careful reading of the poem in *Coleridge's Meditative Art* (Ithaca, N.Y., 1975), puts it that "the crucial image is 'the stranger,' the film of ash fluttering on the fire grate, which provides an associative link to the poet's recollection of childhood experience" (127). To confine "the stranger" to an image is I believe to confuse the poem with the conventional forms of experience — in the event such an image might indeed lead to recollection: the poem depends on our admitting as much. Yet in its construction (or rehearsal) of the experience the poem follows its own means. Here it is not the sight of the thing, but the sense of the word that matters. The image is not lost in the

transaction, it is included in an associative process which is essentially verbal. Coleridge recognizes this process within the poem both by setting the word off in italics and glossing it in a note: signs of its wordliness. Not an isolated instance, as it might seem — the consequences are conspicuous in the conversation poems which followed, as suggested later and discussed in chapter 6 of this book.

5. McFarland, *Coleridge and the Pantheist Tradition*, 34f.

6. Engell, *The Creative Imagination, Enlightenment to Romanticism* (Cambridge, Mass., 1981), 328–66.

7. The disinclination of most readers to look further than the critically formed definition of imagination accounts for the continuing emphasis on the German sources, even after these have led to recognizable distortions. Following Coleridge's own emphasis, and the lead of influential readers since the time of Shawcross, commentators have defended his idea of imagination on Kant's ground, and on Schelling's, without considering the long native tradition to which it responded in the first place. Fruman's debasement of Coleridge's idea to a shoddy copy is a predictable consequence of this approach. (See *Coleridge, the Damaged Archangel*, 179f.) If Coleridge declined to develop the critical formulation, it was perhaps because his own idea led in other directions.

An important contribution to recovering this original context is to be found in John Beer's study of Erasmus Darwin on delirium and mania and its impact on Coleridge's distinction of imagination and fancy. See *Coleridge's Poetic Intelligence* (London, 1977), 76–94, 152–53. Engell's book, cited in n. 6, provides essential background for a reformed understanding of Coleridge on imagination. Hamilton's account of Coleridge against empiricism, pursued fitfully throughout his book, points in the direction of such an understanding despite his distraction by the critical formulation of imagination and its German informants.

8. For preliminary discussion, see Marks, *Coleridge on the Language of Verse*, 14–15.

9. Cited by C. Day Lewis, *The Poetic Image* (London, 1947), 17, 20.

10. See McFarland, *Originality and Imagination*, 95–96. Cf. my discussion in chapter 4, n. 42.

11. Most influentially perhaps in the Clark Lectures of Humphry House, 1951–52, published under the title *Coleridge* (London, 1952; 2nd impr., 1962). Without putting the case in this way, House emphasized his subject's "reaction against eighteenth-century mechanism, against utilitarianism . . . against the politics which emphasized rights as opposed to duties" (15). He was instrumental in asserting the breadth of Coleridge's response, and of his legacy, against a narrowly "philosophic" understanding of his importance, which consigned him in effect to a footnote in the history of ideas. House's insistence on the importance of the still largely inaccessible notebooks contin-

ued the emphasis of Richards and Empson, while seeking an altogether more comprehensive version of Coleridge's achievement.

12. See McFarland, "The Poetic Working of Secondary Imagination," *Originality and Imagination*, 120-47. In his discussion of related issues, Mc-Farland portrays Coleridge as playing Leibnitz (through Tetens) to Hartley's Locke—an evolved version of his early effort to free himself from Hartleyan automatism through its Lockean foundations (109-11). Coleridge's course was set against Locke and his inheritors by 1801, as the letters to Wedgwood show. His German informants expanded the scope of the argument, providing connective tissue and philosophical terminology, yet they did not, I think, significantly alter the original *intent* of Coleridge's critique of empiricism. McFarland makes a plausible case for Kant as the prime mover in his conversion to this point of view (114, n. 78), but it would perhaps be more apt to describe it as a confirmation of doubts which came to rest on the figure of Locke. This is the decisive context for a developing conception which was not only philosophical, but broadly social in intention.

Coleridge's protracted attention to Locke touches again and again on the question of language, probably because it was here that he found a way through Hartley, as his marginalia would lead us to understand. Kant cannot have motivated such attention, and if Leibnitz made an elementary contribution through his attack on the "idea," the development of the critique still belongs to Coleridge's own effort and occupation. Consider the terms of this note of 1804, which looks back perhaps to the "Preface" and forward to the treatment of common and philosophical language in *The Friend* and elsewhere:

> Common people, and all men in common Life, notice only low & high *degrees*, & frame words accordingly/philosophers notice the *kind* & as it were *element*, & often finding no word to express this are obliged to invent a new word or to give a new sense to an old one/thus what Philosophers since the time of Mr Lock have called association was noticed by all men in certain *strong* instances & was called CUSTOM . . . (*CN* I, 1835)

The note goes on to speculate about the degeneration of language in a general philosophical context, with Locke's discussion evidently in the background. The originality of Coleridge's approach to the empirical tradition is apparent in his long meditation on common language, which hesitates over Locke's reforming impulse before deciding for an essentially continuous vocabulary binding philosophical to ordinary employments.

13. House, *Coleridge*, 82.
14. Ibid., 83.
15. Kermode, *Romantic Image* (London, 1957). Subsequent references cite *RI*.

16. George Whalley, "Coleridge's Poetic Sensibility," in *Coleridge's Variety*, ed. John Beer, 23.

17. James, "Tennyson's Drama," *The Galaxy* (September, 1875); rpt. in *Views and Reviews* (London, 1908), 171; cited by Christopher Ricks, *Tennyson* (New York, 1972), 133.

Chapter 6

N.B.: All citations to the text of Coleridge's poems refer to *CPW*.

1. The type of this position is undoubtedly Goethe, whose equivocal attitude to revolution (as related to Soret, January 4, 1824) culminated in disaffection with the new order and the conviction that he was counted among the survivors of a transitional golden age which the rising democrats had spoiled: "Eigentlich ist es das Jahrhundert für die fähigen Köpfe, für leichtfassende praktische Menschen, die, mit einer gewissen Gewandtheit ausgestattet, ihre Superiorität über die Menge fühlen, wenn sie gleich selbst nicht zum Höchsten begabt sind. Lass uns soviel als möglich an der Gesinnung halten, in der wir herankamen; wir werden, mit vielleicht noch Wenigen, die Letzten seyn einer Epoch, die so bald nicht wiederkehrt." Cited by Walter Benjamin, *Deutsche Menschen*, in *Walter Benjamin: Gesammelte Schriften* 4, pt. 1, 151.

The antidemocratic bias is present in Coleridge nearly from the beginning, in a political context. See for instance his discrimination of three classes of "friends of liberty," in the "Introductory Address" (1795) of *Conciones Ad Populum*: "The majority of Democrats appear to me to have attained that portion of knowledge in politics, which Infidels possess in religion" (*CC* 1:37). His political instincts, dissenting but principled in a way that would lead him back to Burke, characterize his sense of poetry's vocation in changing circumstances. His defense of traditional poetic values against Wordsworth's poetics of prose extended an idea of poetry as vatic utterance even as he addressed himself to a revolutionary situation. The poet-critic as broadly social sage, mediating the opposing forces of tradition and change by recourse to principle, was the role that he laid claim on. Against the vitality which he brought to it, Arnold's dismissiveness about the newer literature (beginning from the romantics, who "did not know enough") and Eliot's dyspathy for the voices of the modern condition appear more than just antidemocratic. Both hew to a standard conjured from the past without Coleridge's effort of mediation, and despite acute social awarenesses. Modern writing is for them simply the absence of adequate precedent, for the most part. The unprecedented circumstances of its production enter into their calculations only after the judgment has been passed.

2. For discussion of the bearing of theoretical reflection on the poetics of the period, see Albert Cook, *Thresholds: Studies in the Romantic Experience*

(Madison, Wis., 1986). Thus, "Coleridge is elusive not only because he carried the possibility of systematizing with him as a constant aspiration, and as a leaven for producing aphorisms. He is elusive in his poems, and for the same reason. Whereas it is easy to weave a consistency, and also to establish a hierarchy, among fancy, imagination, symbol, metaphor, and myth as he uses these terms for prose definition, in his actual poetry Coleridge may shift abruptly from a concentration on *reference* to an assertion of *system*, bypassing the *analogy* . . . " (78). Cook's attention to the equivocal status of reference in Coleridge's practice underlines a symptomatic equivocation about the function of language which the investigation of 1800 and after would attempt to resolve, against the dominant values of the "Preface."

3. For the sense of an ending in modernist self-consciousness, see Roger Meiners, *The Last Alternatives: A Study of Allen Tate* (Denver, Colo., 1963).

4. The public exchange with Richards in *The Use of Poetry and the Use of Criticism* practically defines Eliot's role as poet-critic in relation to the ascendent institution of Cambridge English. In conjunction with Leavis's struggle with his authority, the polemical attack by Yvor Winters and the response to it on the part of Frank Kermode constitute a main line of consideration within Eliot's life time, and even in his prime. See Winters, "T. S. Eliot: The Illusion of Reaction," *Kenyon Review* 3 (1941), 7–30; and Kermode, *Romantic Image*, 138f., esp. 150–61.

5. For preliminary discussion of the "play of Coleridge's Mind," see Parker, *Coleridge's Meditative Art*, 61–78. For discussion of the influence of "Frost at Midnight" on Wordsworth's developing idiom, see Jacobus, *Tradition and Experiment*, 118f.

6. Early reviewers did not consider the conversation poems as a group, nor as distinctive among the "Meditative Poems in Blank Verse"—among which, indeed, "Dejection" was not included. Of the "Nightingale," the poem whose subtitle names the type, it was observed that "we do not perceive it to be more conversational than Cowper's *Task*, which is the best poem of that style that our language possesses." From an unsigned review, *British Critic* (October 1799); rpt. in *Coleridge. The Critical Heritage*, ed. J. R. de J. Jackson (London, 1970), 56. The emphasis on their distinctiveness and originality is modern and reflects a later sense of value. It is their thoughtfulness which distinguishes them from related verse (including Coleridge's own), and their contribution to the formation of Wordsworth's voice which defines their originality. As revisions of Bowles and Cowper, they did not appear notably original to their first readers.

7. The association psychology which informs Coleridge's play of mind as described by Parker (n. 5) has usually been treated as an embarrassment, in reaction to the automatism underlying it. Coleridge spent a career struggling with its implications, yet he never entirely escaped them, as his continuance of Tooke's reductive etymologizing shows. The conversation poems are involved

in an incipient critique of association through their doubts about the pathetic fallacy; they can hardly be considered apart from the Hartleyan formation of Coleridge's early thinking. More might have been made of this as antecedent to developments in modern writing if the case had not been prematurely closed both by the idealists of imagination and by those who reacted against them. The conversation poems do not simply adopt the Hartleyan posture, passively automatic. They enact their own deepest assumptions, taking these to limits which expose and even challenge an assumed validity. Hartley was as much the victim of Coleridge's poetic development as the muse. The trajectory of the conversation poems might be described in terms of the exhaustion of association as a viable premise for an idiom committed to original thinking. For related discussion of Coleridge's struggle with associationism in the period, see K. M. Wheeler, *The Creative Mind in Coleridge's Poetry* (London, 1981), 1-16.

8. See the opening of "Monody on the Death of Chatterton" and, as though in reply, "Religious Musings" and "The Destiny of Nations." All were begun before 1795 and subsequently modified and expanded. For discussion of their reliance on the example of Milton's blank verse, see House, *Coleridge*, 59-67. In the monodic vein I count also some of the "Poems Occasioned by Political Events or Feelings Connected with Them," as indexed later in *Sibylline Leaves*: "Ode to the Departing Year" (1796), "France: An Ode" (originally published as "Recantation: An Ode," 1797), and "Fears in Solitude" (1798). The last has sometimes been considered conversational. It illustrates the real proximity of monody and conversation in Coleridge's practice.

9. For a discussion of the extended family as social ideal in Wordsworth's verse, with implications for Coleridge's abortive aspiration to community in this period, see McFarland, "The Significant Group: Wordsworth's Fears in Solitude," in *Romanticism and the Forms of Ruin*, 137-215.

10. Colmer, *Coleridge: Critic of Society* (Oxford, 1959), 29.

11. Ibid., 49-50.

12. See CC 2:13ln.

13. Kermode, *Romantic Image*, 44f. Kermode's insistence on the moral function of the poetic image (66-67) in the line which runs from Coleridge through to Yeats represents an effort to save romantic writing from the merely iconic reading accorded it under the auspices of Cambridge English.

14. Thus House, *Coleridge*, 77:

> This ending is difficult to accept even in the earlier version before *Sibylline Leaves*; because the vague Neo-Platonist speculation does not seem wholly compatible with the scheme of Christian redemption. It is possible that the sudden *volte face* in that version is to be explained less by a wish to repudiate the doctrine than by an anticipation of the later thought about the possible origin of moral evil "in the streamy nature of association" . . . But what is now evident is that the ending as it stands seems to

involve a rejection of the vital personal experience which was added in 1817: it murders the new-born life.

In *Coleridge the Moralist* (Ithaca, N.Y., 1977), 89, writing with Coleridge's moral commitments in mind, Laurence S. Lockridge sees the capitulation at the end as a sign of "how fragile his faith in the heresy is from the beginning." Faith is perhaps too strong a word: the heuristic attitude of the poem, characteristic of the conversational line at large, precludes I believe so dramatic a sense of the contradiction.

15. For a full treatment, see McFarland, "Coleridge and the Dilemmas of Pantheism," *Coleridge and the Pantheist Tradition*, 107–90, where the ambivalence is the point: "This inability either really to accept or wholeheartedly to reject pantheism is the central truth of Coleridge's philosophical activity" (107).

16. For an extended discussion of the problematic will in the romantic setting, see Michael G. Cooke, *The Romantic Will* (New Haven, 1976), 1–51.

17. Jacobus, in *Tradition and Experiment*, 40n., associates the poem with Thomson's bird chorus in "Spring," lines 547–51, from *The Seasons*. Yet it must be Wordsworth's voice he had in mind here. The rhythmic qualities of the opening of "Tintern Abbey," its "sweet inland murmur" as it were, sound uncannily through the opening despite the earlier point of composition. Other echoes of Wordsworth have been noticed in the text, and the address to the poet and his sister encourage the assumption that Coleridge was projecting a Wordsworthian persona.

18. For a different account of Coleridge between Milton and Wordsworth, see Harold Bloom, *Figures of Capable Imagination* (New York, 1976), 1–17.

19. For a discussion of the modernist suppression of Milton's voice, see Terry Eagleton, *Walter Benjamin, or Towards a Revolutionary Criticism* (London, 1981), 3f.

20. For a detailed discussion, see McFarland, *Romanticism and the Forms of Ruin*, 56–103.

21. Parker, *Coleridge's Meditative Art*, 181.

Chapter 7

1. For a detailed summary of critical reaction to the "Ancient Mariner" at first issue see Thomas Hutchinson, *Lyrical Ballads*, 2nd. ed. (London, 1907), xiii-xxiv. For an account of the course of its reception, with conclusions of interest, see Richard Haven, "The Ancient Mariner in the Nineteenth Century," *Studies in Romanticism* 11 (1972), 360–74. Subsequent references cite *MNC*. Criticism has mostly followed lines of observation laid down by Wordsworth and Lamb, regretting the poem's failures of coherence while de-

fending its symbolic values. These responses are broadly paradigmatic and can be seen to reflect stresses within Coleridge's developing idea of poetry.

2. See Empson's essay in *Coleridge's Verse*, 31. Subsequent reference in the text cites *CV*.

3. See Richards, *Practical Criticism* (London, 1929), 277.

4. Robert Penn Warren, "A Poem of Pure Imagination: An Experiment in Reading," *The Rime of the Ancient Mariner* (New York, 1946), esp. 61–69.

5. McGann, "The Meaning of the Ancient Mariner," *Critical Inquiry* 8 (1981), 35–67. Subsequent references in the text cite *MAM*.

6. There is no antecedent for such a treatment in Percy's *Reliques*. Elizabethan chronicles of exploration by sea appeared in the prose which suited the purpose. If as seems likely "The Wandering Jew" was the ballad Coleridge had in mind, it was a spiritual journey and not an exploration narrative that was his model. The ballad type can hardly be identified as the source of all of the later poem's features, but it does provide a strong generic framework. The persistence of ballad quatrain and meter, of archaic diction, and even of the plaintive appeal of the narrator links the "Ancient Mariner" at every turn to this popular idiom. Coleridge made use of these in his own way and to his own ends, certainly, but McGann's effort to dissociate the poem from this dominant orientation does not make sense.

Wordsworth's version of the poem's genesis (see Hutchinson, *Lyrical Ballads*, xlvii–xlviii) shows, and source study confirms, that Shelvocke's *Voyages* was an important informant for its imagery. Wordsworth asserts at the same time the psychological emphasis in terms different from, but compatible with, *Biographia* XIV and DeQuincey's observation, cited below, of Coleridge's debt to Darwin's hypothesis about delirium. The voyage is little more than a pretext, then, even if it provides the canvas for an exercise in pictorialism. Nor can its reference be considered historically specific on the scant evidence adduced by McGann's curious source, who was only applying the narrative perspectivism of the new criticism out of appropriate context. See *MAM*, 41; and Huntington Brown, "The Gloss to the Ancient Mariner," *Modern Language Quarterly* 6 (1945), 319–24.

7. For a recent discussion of this approach, see McGann's "Introduction: A Point of Reference," in *Historical Studies and Literary Criticism* (Madison, Wis., 1985), 3–21. The grasp of Coleridge's position in this presentation is firm, and consonant with my own sense of the bearing of his quarrel with Wordsworth: "Coleridge's critique of the insistently referential aspects of Wordsworth's poetry—what he calls its 'accidentality' and its 'matter-of-factness'—is merely the critical reflex of his positive position: that 'poetry as poetry is essentially *ideal*, and avoids and excludes all *accident* and apparent individualities.'" He goes on to remark, against the grain of Ricardian understanding, that "Coleridge is himself an impressive historicist critic, as his commentaries on the Biblical tradition show. Nevertheless, his theoretical

ground would eventually be appropriated by those idealist and subjectivist forms of criticism which emerged out of twentieth-century linguistics and semiology" (5). The "renovated historical criticism" which McGann sketches here would appear to have little in common with Coleridge's example, however. His position can be summarized by the claim that "criticism justifies itself in its social praxis"—that it must be projective instead of "recollective." His is then a pragmatic idea, in the line of Richards rather than of Coleridge—or of Raymond Williams, whose engagement is always projective without sacrificing its historical footing.

8. Wordsworth's note to the "Ancient Mariner" in the 1800 edition provides an exceptionally clear view of his subordination of Coleridge's voice. He takes credit for the poem's qualities while imputing its problems to "the Author," from whose effort of suppression he has saved it for the new edition. "The Poem of my Friend has indeed great defects"—four of them—"Yet the Poem contains many delicate touches of passion, and indeed the passion is every where true to nature; a great number of the stanzas present beautiful images, and are expressed with unusual felicity of language . . . " For the full text, see *The Prose Works of William Wordsworth*, ed. Rev. Alexander B. Grosart, 3 vols. (London, 1876), III, 16-17. Lamb rebutted the terms of Wordsworth's criticism while affirming his attention to the imagery: "I dislike all the miraculous part of it; but the feelings of the man under the operation of such scenery, dragged me along like Tom Piper's magic whistle." Cited by Haven, *MNC*, 367.

9. Cited by Hutchinson, *Lyrical Ballads* xxiv.

10. John Livingston Lowes, *The Road to Xanadu* 2nd ed., rev. (London, 1951).

11. Ibid., 94-99. For related discussion see Beer, *Coleridge's Poetic Intelligence*, 50-57.

12. William K. Wimsatt, "The Structure of Romantic Nature Imagery," *The Verbal Icon* (Lexington, Ky., 1954), 103-16.

13. According to Beer, *Coleridge's Poetic Intelligence*, Coleridge held "a view of nature in which the phenomena of life were seen as a threefold process of evolving form, free-playing energy and shaping spirit" (55). On the basis of a passage in *The Friend*, Beer infers that such was the original source of Coleridge's organicism, antedating his German exposure. This is an important case for the argument that Coleridge's intellectual orientation had everything to do with specifically English conditions, however his thinking may have been captured (and diverted) by his later reading.

14. Ibid., 152.

15. Erasmus Darwin, *Botanic Garden, Containing The Economy of Vegetation, A Poem*, Part II (1789), 41 (Interlude). Subsequent references in the text cite *BG* II.

Index